淺談香港仲裁法

HOW TO BE AN ARBITRATOR:
A PERSONAL VIEW

作者 芮安牟

翻譯 陳星楠

SUNNY ANSELMO
CHAN REYES

中文譯本前言

承蒙芮教授（稱呼至今仍然彆扭）所託，譯者以僅有的中文水平，希望盡量把教授多年的經驗和領會翻譯成書。中文版多有不精、不準、不順之處，責任全在於譯者。

也藉此多謝師傅多年來的栽培和教導 —— 法理、為人、處世。

陳星楠

二零一三年一月十五日

序　淺談仲裁

本書的藍圖來自早前筆者承蒙香港海事法協會邀請進行的演講，是淺談系列的第二本著作。透過淺談系列，筆者希望能研究香港的民事法律系統，如何能更有效地回應社會大眾的需要。

淺談系列的內容基於一個假設：現狀並不完美，而我們需要改善現行系統中的不足。具體地，筆者認為現行的民事訴訟的程序過於繁複以及成本太高。若不改善，則即使公義得以伸張，其所收益者亦稀。

淺談系列中的第一本書是《淺談新民事司法訴訟》[1]（內容源於筆者在二零零九年於香港海事法協會的演講）。該書討論了在二零零九年四月民事司法改革生效後，有關的改變如何能實在地提高民事訴訟的效率。有關改革大刀闊斧地嘗試去除舊系統中導致訴訟曠日持久的程序障礙。改革後，法庭希望審訊的時間可縮短（令更多人可使用法庭）、減少審訊前夕突然提出的臨時申請，以及大幅調低休庭次數。

我們仍在等待社會各界對改革的成果作出評價。但像筆者在書中序言所說，[2]但願改革不會弄巧成拙。除非業界（法官、律師和當事人）了解改革能帶來的好處並小心思考，否則，訴訟雙方仍然可以就對是否按新規矩辦事，做出冗長而缺乏實際意義的爭議。如果業界沒有紀律性，我們很可能回到改革前的狀況，浪費時間金錢，為爭拗而爭拗，為改革而改革。

除了民事程序和本書所提到的仲裁結構外，筆者還希望在淺談系列的第三本書中研究法官應該如何在辦案時處理道德矛盾的情況。第四本書則會關注大律師業界的未來。筆者認為大律師職業在未來十年會遇到很大的挑戰，業界必須透過改變來維持競爭力和保存現行的優勢。第五本書會討論香港的法律教育情況。筆者想這可能會包含許多個人的看法。

還是先回到本書。淺談系列的第二部分介紹仲裁是甚麼一回事。

仲裁是按雙方意願所成立的一個獨立評核機構，其作用是審理雙方間的爭議並提供一個經過分析的裁決。評核機構的成員便是仲裁員。

本書的出發點是每個人（如果努力）都可以成為有合理能力的仲裁員。筆者希望此書能提供一套實用知識，為有興趣成為仲裁員的讀者帶來相對全面的仲裁法律基本知識。

但本書不是全面的仲裁法律手冊。市面上已經有不少的著作去剖析仲裁的各個方面，尤其是新的《仲裁條例》（Cap. 609）。這些書籍就仲裁提供全面及學術性的分析，筆者不能奢望與那些書籍的知識和內容相比。

筆者的目的是簡單，但進取的。簡單，是因為筆者只希望就如何成為仲裁員提供最基本所需的知識，故此書中不會有過多的引述案例，亦不會有太多的技術性分析。雖然法律訓練有一定的用處，但仲裁員不一定是律師，而筆者希望閱讀此書的讀者不僅僅限於律師同業。進取，是因為我樂觀認為即使僅靠在此書中能學到的知識，讀者仍然能成為一名相對有能力的仲裁員。前提是在任何情況下讀者都必須維持公平、耐性和開放的態度，以有效率的手法處理每件案件。

當然，不是每一位讀者均能成為偉大和知名的仲裁員。這並不驚訝，生命中每樣東西均有長短。這就好像每個人，若練習均能打網球，而在所有會打網球的人裡只有一個費達拿。但是，就像不是每一場球賽均需要費達拿的參與一樣，不是每一個糾紛均需最好的仲裁員審理。

人類喜歡爭拗，而爭拗的種類層出不窮。有些需要特殊的知識，有些則需要對人性的理解。重點是，如果我們堅持，則很可能找到專門的領域，使我們的服務得到應得的報酬。

讀者不應相信仲裁業界存在著個別「圈子」獨攬所有案件的傳聞。每個行業都有炙手可熱的人，而且不是每個人都能加入圈內。但我們可以競爭，慢慢地建立起幹練、勤勉和具效率的名聲。其過程可能孤獨，會有沮喪，但決非不可能。

「淺談」的內容許多是筆者個人的經驗和意見。筆者主觀的態度少不免有偏頗或失誤，而本書中筆者也強調許多情況需要仲裁員按實際情況去處理。就這些情況所提出的建議是筆者在擔任法官時每日處理類似案件時的總結。

筆者不認為書中的提議會是唯一的辦案方法。讀者能從提議中選取適用的。筆者的目的是希望大家思考如何處理案件，才能達至最有效和符合經濟原則的結果。

這就是筆者希望透過此書而達到的結果。那麼，此書如何切合筆者在本序開首所提到的理想？

筆者認為仲裁能與訴訟爭一日之長短。在時間和成本日益上漲的訴訟文化中，如果市場提供足夠和有能力的仲裁員，那麼仲裁便可與訴訟並立為有效和具成本效益的解決爭議渠道。

市場總會為客戶提供選擇。跟其他市場一樣，法庭只提供其中一種解決爭議的服務，另外兩種方法便是仲裁與調解。當某一種服務過於昂貴的時候，使用者便自然會另行選擇了。自然，法庭的判決永遠是最可靠的，這是因為法庭背後有強大的政府體制支持。藐視法庭命令會導致多種不同的懲罰直至抗命者屈服為止。

正因如此，仲裁比起調解的優勢，是仲裁裁決可按《紐約公約》[3] 在香港以及全球一百四十個公約國家轉換成法庭命令作出執行。此外，仲裁的優點是有高度的彈性。一方面，雙方可選擇心儀的仲裁員（通常在爭議的專業領域中有一定名聲和資歷）去快速處理爭議；另一方面，在取得裁決後，雙方能在本地或其他地方，將裁決按當地法庭命令一樣去執行，不受個別法庭的地域性所局限。

只要司法機構做好完善的把關工作，制定一套合適的程序，確保裁決能在不受太多干擾的情況下快速轉換為法庭命令執行，仲裁便能成為得天獨厚的工具：既享有保密性（仲裁聆訊不會公開進行）又享有政府機構在執行裁決上的完善優勢。

仲裁與法庭存在互補關係。仲裁案件越多，則法庭案件越少，而法庭則更能關注有需要的案件，包括非商業性的申請，如司法覆核和刑事案件等。這些均是仲裁所不能處理的。

為令仲裁行業更具競爭力，業界需要更多的仲裁員。不然，如果只有少數執業者，則當事人選擇無多，只能依賴既有的幾位仲裁員。在仲裁需求日益增多的情況下，業界收費必定水漲船高，導致訟費過高。所以，本書希望吸引更多的人成為仲裁員。

當然，仲裁並不完美。仲裁多有批評者。如訴訟一樣，許多人以為現在的仲裁市場被律師騎劫，導致仲裁過程失去了彈性，變得技術化，使費用變得高昂，耗時更多，比起訴訟更為複雜。[4]

在二零一二年六月舉行的國際商業仲裁會（ICCA），當時新加坡的首席檢察官（the Hon. Sundaresh Menon SC）在致辭時提到我們身處在一個仲裁的黃金年代。[5] 但弦外有音，致辭中檢察官也提到仲裁正面臨嚴峻的情況，他關注到仲裁的時間和成本正日益上升，並未受太多監管。這些不如意處必須改善，否則仲裁的黃金年代不會長久。

就上述問題筆者希望透過本書提出有關的看法。此書分為三個部分：效率、成本和可信度。效率與成本固然與任何一個解決糾紛渠道有關。但可信度？

仲裁的成本問題導致學者們（包括筆者個人的看法）認為調解才是最能控制成本的方法。這也是筆者在第一本書中提出的觀點。但在筆者跟就讀牛津大學的學生進行對話後，筆者改變了看法。筆者仍然認為調解具有相當的效率，並能快速解決糾紛。但是，筆者開始理解調解並不會適用在所有的情況當中。

很多糾紛的當事人並不只在意爭議的結果。他們希望有人能彰顯他們的權利和贊同他們的看法。這也是為何社會認為法庭能彰顯正義的原因，使許多人願意付出大量訟費贏得一個正確的結果。

在純粹經濟的角度看，這想法不合邏輯。如調解能便宜快速地提供合理的經濟回報，為何要費時失事地尋求法庭協助？

可能金錢不是一切。許多人希望告訴對方，不道德的做法是錯的，而個人原則不能被金錢收買；也可能是面子令當事人騎虎難下。無論如何，筆者不認為堅持己見的當事人無理取鬧，而且，筆者明白歸根結底法庭的責任便是就社會發生的事決定對錯責任。

調解不能做出以上的原則性濟助，但仲裁可以。這是因為仲裁受到法庭監管，並可透過法庭執行裁決。這個互動性賦予仲裁高度的可信性。

法庭在仲裁過程的參與度是雙方可以透過協議所控制的。無論如何,仲裁是具彈性的。筆者會在稍後的章節中介紹《仲裁條例》如何給予當事人豐富的選擇。

有趣地,許多人不希望仲裁受到任何法庭干擾。在現行體制下,雙方是可以完全拒絕法庭參與的。但是,筆者認為適當的法庭參與是可以避免許多尷尬的情況,並有助雙方更有效地保障自己的利益。

本書中,筆者會不斷重複《仲裁條例》。每次筆者都從不同角度討論相同的條文,希望這不會太過沉悶,並希望有助讀者了解條文的意義。

第一章描述《仲裁條例》的架構。筆者會總結條例中大部分在仲裁時常用到的條款。之後,會透過列舉三個例子把條文應用在實際情況中。

第二章會仔細地研究整個仲裁過程,此章為本書最重要的部分,並提示仲裁庭應如何管理仲裁案件。

第三章融入在亞太地區常見的五種不同的仲裁機構規則,最後部分會總結五種規則的相同處。

第四章會研究法庭執行裁決的方法。筆者強調法庭有需要做出一套有效的監管和轉換裁決為法庭命令的程序。

本書最後一章會重申本書開首的幾個重點。筆者會比較仲裁和調解兩者的區別,並觀望業界的未來趨勢。

筆者希望本書重複處有助讀者吸收仲裁的基本原則。筆者明白本書敍事並非最有娛樂性。但希望讀者在閱讀過程中能學到一些知識，並能促進思考。筆者時刻強調實際應用，而非關注理論性的東西。

本書中，《仲裁條例》簡稱為條例。

筆者在討論時假設仲裁涉及兩方當事人。但是，討論的內容原則同樣適用於多方面的仲裁。此外，雖然筆者分開調解和仲裁為兩種不同的系統，但筆者並不反對使用調解去協助仲裁，務求協助雙方解決矛盾。

---

1. 英文版本是 *Reflections on Civil Procedure under Civil Justice Reform*（私人出版）；中文版於二零一二年三月由三聯書店出版。

2. 芮安牟著，陳星楠譯《淺談新民事司法訴訟》（香港：三聯書店，二零一二年）。

3. 公約內容在第四章詳述。

4. 參閱 Stone, "Judicial Reflections Arbitration", [2012] *Asian Dispute Review 83*。

5. 會議影像（包括首席監察官的演講）網址 www.arbitration.icca.org。

Introduction

This work (which is based on lectures delivered earlier this year under the auspices of the Hong Kong Maritime Law Association (HKMLA)) is the second of a projected series of 5 books. The series examines how various aspects of the Hong Kong civil (as opposed to criminal) law system can become more responsive to the needs of the public.

The series assumes that we cannot continue as we have been doing and there is need for change. In particular, the series is predicated on the belief that, as a means for resolving disputes, the present civil law system is too expensive and cumbersome. Something has to be done to change that, otherwise there will be justice and the rule of law, but those abstractions will come at a price (both in terms of time and cost) which few can afford.

The first book in the series, *Reflections on Civil Procedure under Civil Justice Reform*[1] (based on lectures sponsored by the HKMLA in 2009), explored the changes in civil procedure which the Judiciary introduced on 2 April 2009. Civil Justice Reform (CJR) (as the changes have come to be known) was a bold attempt to cut through the red-tape of overly technical nicety which had beset litigation in the Court. The hope was that, after CJR, there would be shorter trials, fewer last minute interlocutory applications, and almost no adjournments.

The jury of public opinion has yet to deliver its verdict on whether CJR has been successful. But in a Preface to the Chinese edition[2] of the first book, I warned that CJR was in danger of becoming its own worst enemy. Unless everyone (judges, lawyers and litigants) is vigilant, the Courts are in danger of becoming bogged down in lengthy interlocutory arguments over whether one party or another has adhered to CJR in taking (or omitting to take) some procedural step. Without proper discipline, we will soon find ourselves back where we started, wasting time and money, simply arguing about what we should be arguing about, all in the name of CJR.

The third book in the series will consider how judges deal with moral dilemmas.

The fourth book will deal with the future of the Hong Kong Bar. It will argue that there is a need for change if the Bar is to maintain its vibrancy and pre-eminence in matters of advocacy and dispute resolution in the next decade.

The fifth book will look into the education of a lawyer. It is envisaged that this will be the most personal book of the series.

Let me, however, focus on this second book in the series.

This work reflects on arbitration. Arbitration may be defined as a process whereby disputes are resolved by the reasoned decision of a tribunal consisting of one or more independent persons appointed by the parties to the dispute. The independent persons are referred to as "arbitrators".

It is a premise of this work that anyone can be a reasonably competent arbitrator, provided that the person makes an effort. From this comes the first half of this book's English title: "How to be an arbitrator". It is hoped that this book will serve as a toolkit. In other words, this book is intended to impart the "nuts and bolts"which one needs to know about or, at least be aware of, if one is to set up shop as a competent arbitrator.

The book is not a comprehensive manual. There are already several excellent commentaries on arbitration in general and the new Hong Kong Arbitration Ordinance (Cap.609) in particular. Those commentaries provide detailed scholarly analyses of the arbitration process from beginning to end and beyond. I cannot hope to compete with them in the breadth of their knowledge and utility.

My goal is somewhat more modest in one sense, but a little more ambitious in another.

My goal is modest in that I only seek to introduce the basics of being an arbitrator in Hong Kong, with as little technicality and citation of cases as possible. Although legal training will undoubtedly help, one does not need to be a lawyer to be an arbitrator or to read this book.

My goal is ambitious in my optimism that, even knowing only the basics found here, one can be a reasonably competent arbitrator, provided that one maintains a fair, patient and open mind while proceeding in a brisk "no-nonsense" manner towards the resolution of a dispute.

This, however, does not mean that everyone reading this work will become a great and famous arbitrator. It should not come as a surprise that some will inevitably be better at the task than others. Everyone can learn to become a reasonably competent tennis player, but only one or two can be Roger Federer or Serena Williams. Then again, just as not every tennis competition will justify paying for a Federer or a Williams, not every dispute will justify engaging an expensive top-of-the-line arbitrator.

Human beings are prone to argument. There will be all sorts of disputes wanting resolution. Some disputes will require specialist knowledge, while others will merely call for an understanding of human nature. The point is that, if we persevere at becoming reasonably competent, we each should be able to find some niche, where our services as arbitrator will be appreciated at a fair recompense.

One should not be discouraged from becoming an arbitrator by rumours of a "mafia" or "magic circle" which has supposedly cornered up all the plum cases for itself. One may never become a member of this mythical elite. But at least one can compete with it, slowly and surely, by building a reputation for quiet competence, hard work and steely efficiency. The task will be lonely on occasion and there will be setbacks, but it is not impossible.

The second part of the English title of this work ("A personal view") warns that this text will be opinionated, possibly idiosyncratic. I will be suggesting, sometimes strongly, ways in which a would-be arbitrator might deal with typical problems that can arise in an arbitration.

My suggestions are based on my experience as a judge attempting to deal with the same questions on a nearly daily basis in the Court.

I do not claim that my prescriptions are the only way. The reader may pick and choose from my recommendations as he or she feels appropriate. My purpose is more to provoke reflection on how an arbitrator should manage disputes to ensure their speedy and cost-effective resolution.

So much for one's goals. How does this work fit within the series which I started this Introduction by describing?

I think that greater resort to arbitration is one possible response to the ever increasing costs and time required by conventional civil litigation in the Courts. Thus, for instance, if there is a sizeable pool of competent commercial arbitrators, the latter can compete with the Courts by offering to resolve disputes more affordably within a reasonable time.

One can look at the market for dispute resolution as involving a number of service providers. The Court is only one such service provider. Two other service providers are arbitrators and mediators (of which I shall say more in a moment). Where a service provider is too expensive or unsatisfactory in its performance, the consumer can seek the services of another provider.

Of course, the Court will always, must always, have the edge over other dispute resolution service providers. That is because Court orders may be enforced with the backing of the state. Failure to comply with a Court order can lead to a variety of powerful sanctions being taken against a recalcitrant party to ensure compliance.

It is here that arbitration enjoys a feature which mediation does not share. Arbitration's advantage is that arbitral awards may be converted into Court orders and enforced as such, not just in Hong Kong, but also in the 140 or so states which are signatories to the New York Convention.[3]

Arbitration thus has flexibility. On the one hand, parties can engage an arbitrator of their choice, presumably having knowledge in the subject of their dispute, to resolve their differences quickly. On the other hand, parties can enforce the arbitrator's award both here and abroad in the same way as an official order of the state.

So long as the Judiciary can ensure that appropriate procedures are in place for scrutinising an award and converting it into an order of the Court with a minimum of technicality, then the arbitral process will have the best of all possible worlds: the confidentiality of a tailor-made tribunal for the purpose of determination, and recourse to state machinery for the purpose of enforcement.

The arbitral process is in effect a parallel avenue of dispute resolution. It operates in cooperation with the Court system which enforces its awards. But it also competes with the Court in attracting disputants to try its dispute resolution services in lieu of those of the Court. The more commercial disputes that are tried by arbitrators, the less the pressure there will be on limited judicial resources. Judges will be freed to hear the many other cases which they have to deal with, including public (that is, non-commercial) matters, such as criminal trials and judicial reviews, which arbitration cannot really address.

In order to make arbitration even more competitive, the field needs more, not fewer, practitioners. Otherwise, if only a small number of persons act as arbitrators, parties will have little option but to resort to the available few, no matter how good or bad they may be. The fees charged will be exorbitant in the limited market and the quality of awards produced may not justify the resources spent. This book is accordingly written in the hope of attracting more to become arbitrators.

That is not to say that arbitration is a panacea.

Arbitration has its detractors. Like civil litigation, arbitration stands accused of having lost its way and become more costly, lengthy and technical. Some have gone so far as to say that, having been "hijacked" by the lawyers, the arbitral process may now even be more expensive, time-consuming and complex than normal litigation in the Courts.[4]

At the June 2012 Congress of the International Council for Commercial Arbitration (ICCA), the then Attorney General of Singapore (the Hon. Sundaresh Menon SC) delivered a keynote address which began by lauding the ushering of "a golden age of arbitration" in the present era.[5] But the speech was not a paean. Halfway into it, the Attorney cautioned that there were clouds over the horizon (such as the fact that arbitration had become too costly and too lengthy, while possibly being too free of Court supervision). These threats had to be dealt with, if the benefits of the golden age were not to be undone.

In an attempt to address these concerns, I focus in this work on 3 critical matters. Those are the efficiency, cost and credibility of arbitration as a dispute resolution mechanism. Efficiency and cost are obviously relevant to the effectiveness of any mechanism of dispute resolution. I should explain what I mean by the "credibility" of arbitration.

The perceived problems with arbitration have led many commentators (myself included in the first book in this series) to push mediation as a possible means of resolving disputes at a reasonable price. But since then, as a result (among others) of a discussion with students described here in Chapter 4, I have had second thoughts.

I still believe mediation is a highly effective means of resolving a dispute swiftly and early. It is difficult to argue with its impressive success rate in a wide range of situations, but I have come to realise that mediation will not be an appropriate or adequate solution in all cases for all persons.

Sometimes, individuals will feel a strong desire to be vindicated in a dispute through a pronouncement of right by the Court. That will be the case even where the Court's declaration requires much time and effort to obtain.

On a crude "dollars and cents" reckoning, this innate desire may seem irrational. If mediation offers the prospect of a reasonable (or more than reasonable) monetary or other settlement at an early stage, why hold out for a declaration of right by the Court?

Perhaps in a majority of cases, it would be foolish to turn down a "good deal" reached through mediation. However, in some cases, a person might understandably prefer a Court pronouncement over a "good deal". An obvious example is where a person wishes to show an unscrupulous adversary that not everyone's compliance can be bought for a price. Money or money's worth will not then be the sole issue.

There may of course be a large element of pride or "face" involved. But, as a matter of first impression, there are situations where I do not think that one can fairly criticise a person as irrational for insisting on a pronouncement of right by the Court. That is, after all, what the Courts are supposed to do: namely, to declare and protect the rights of members of the public.

Mediation will not cater for this innate desire which I have posited, but arbitration can. That is because arbitration proceedings and the enforcement of awards are ultimately subject to the supervision of the Court. It is this backing by the Court which (I suggest) gives arbitration its credibility.

The appropriate degree of Court supervision may be a matter of debate. In any event, arbitration is versatile. As we shall see, the parties can agree among themselves whether the Court is to have a maximum or minimal degree of supervision in their case.

Ironically, some would limit the degree of interference which the Court may exercise over an arbitration to almost nil. In this book, I side with those who argue the contrary. I suggest that, exercised with moderation, the Court's ability to scrutinise the arbitral process and awards should be held up as an advantage, and not an embarrassment.

The method of this book is to examine the arbitral process over and over, albeit from different perspectives each time. I hope that such repetition will not be found too tedious.

Chapter 1 sketches the framework provided by the Arbitration Ordinance. The chapter summarises the salient provisions of the statute. It concludes by giving a "feel" of how the Ordinance works by answering 3 sample questions about the arbitral process.

Chapter 2 revisits the arbitral process in much greater detail. It is the heart of this work and concentrates on the case management of an arbitration.

Chapter 3 goes over the ground already covered in the previous 2 chapters. But this time it does so from the standpoint of 5 bodies of rules which parties commonly adopt for arbitrations in the Asia-Pacific region. The 5 sets of rules have common features which are identified at the end of the chapter.

Chapter 4 looks at the enforcement of awards by the Court. It stresses the need for efficient procedures for the scrutiny of awards and their enforcement as orders of the Court. The argument which I have started in this Introduction is fleshed out here.

The final chapter recapitulates the themes of this Introduction. It compares arbitration and mediation and ends with reflections on the future of arbitration as a means of resolving disputes.

I hope that this reiterative process will help the reader to absorb, bit by bit, the basics of arbitration. I accept that the plan may not be the most riveting way into the subject of arbitration, but I hope that the journey will still be rewarding or at least provocative. Throughout I attempt to stress what is practical, in preference to the overly theoretical.

In the remainder of this book, I will normally use "Ordinance" to mean the "Arbitration Ordinance". I shall use the expression "tribunal" to mean a panel of arbitrators. The panel may consist of one or more arbitrators. By similar token, when I refer to "arbitrator", I do not necessarily just mean a sole arbitrator. Depending on context, I may be using that word interchangeably with "tribunal".

I discuss arbitration on the basis of a 2-party paradigm, a claimant against a respondent. But the discussion is equally valid for arbitrations involving more than 2 parties. Further, although I contrast arbitration and mediation, I should not be taken as excluding the possibility of using mediation in aid of arbitration.

1. Privately published in 2 printings of 1,000 copies each.

2. Reyes (trans. Sunny Chan), 《淺談新民事司法訴訟》 (Hong Kong, 2012).

3. The Convention is discussed in detail in Chapter 4.

4. See, for instance, Stone, "Judicial Reflections on Arbitration", [2012] *Asian Dispute Review* 83.

5. Film footage of ICCA's XXIst Congress (including the Attorney's keynote address) may be accessed at www.arbitration-icca.org.

目錄 Contents

淺談香港仲裁法

第一章　香港仲裁法結構

《仲裁條例》（Cap. 609）為香港仲裁的主要法律架構。本章會首先宏觀地描述《仲裁條例》所涉及的範疇，並介紹條例中最為重要的條款。然後，筆者把條例應用在數個仲裁中常見的情況。本章的目的是透過簡單和基本的例子，讓讀者對仲裁的實際過程取得基本認識，並協助讀者去了解本章之後較深入的單元討論。

第一部分　《仲裁條例》

新的《仲裁條例》在二零一零年十一月十一日通過，二零一一年六月一日實施。除了數項針對已經組成的仲裁庭和已展開仲裁的過渡措施外，新條例現已全面取締舊有的《仲裁條例》。

I. 仲裁基要

無論仲裁的性質是本地或具有國際性，所有在香港進行的仲裁均受《仲裁條例》所約束。

《仲裁條例》採納了在二零零六年七月七日修訂的《貿法委示範法》（UNCITRAL Model Law，後簡稱《示範法》），透過本地立法賦予《示範法》法律效力。

商業仲裁是國際潮流。聯合國國際貿易法委員會（貿法委）早在一九八五年十二月便推行了針對商業仲裁的《示範法》，目的是希望就不同地方進行的商業仲裁提供一套具統一性的法規。至今，《示範法》的條款已被很多國家以不同形式採納為國內仲裁的基本模式。《示範法》不單就在本地進行的仲裁提供一套程序守則，還包含了如何在本國執行外地裁決的條款。

不同國家在立法時會在《示範法》中篩選適合的條款，再按國情需要修改為本土法例。故此每個國家的《仲裁條例》都不盡相同。但實際上，如各國均以《示範法》內容作為立法基礎，儘管條文細節不盡相同，在架構上各國的《仲裁法》均會無可避免地有很大程度的相似。

統一的法律架構有助國際貿易。在不同地區經商和投資的人最討厭因地方法律相異而對其經濟利益帶來不便。他們最不願意看到仲裁裁決因地域法律所限而在執行上遇到困難。從國際貿易的角度看，發生越少意外的地方往往是投資者最樂意投資的地方。

新條例實施前，香港的《仲裁條款》帶有「本地仲裁」和「國際仲裁」兩種不同的規則。新條例實施後，除了數項過渡性措施外，本地和國際仲裁的概念已不再適用。在香港進行的所有仲裁都將受到新條例所採納的《示範法》規管。統一法規是新條例的主要改革。

在往下的篇幅除了另行指出外，所有條款均為《仲裁條例》內的編號。

第三條指出新《仲裁條例》的目的「是促進在省卻非必要開支的情況下，藉仲裁而公平及迅速地解決爭議。」

要達到條例所定的目標，仲裁員和法庭須謹記兩項原則。第一是「除須奉行為公眾利益而屬必要的保障措施外，爭議各方應有協議應該如何解決爭議的自由」；第二是「法院應只在本條例明文規定的情況下，才干預爭議的仲裁」。

第一原則是要尊重仲裁雙方的意願，按仲裁（而非訴訟）程序去解決爭議。在此原則下，只有在事態干擾雙方協議的情況下，法庭才應該介入，給予讓雙方按原本定案實行仲裁協議的必要援助。就此，法庭不會就實體糾紛作任何判決。

第二原則與第一原則相輔相成。當實行仲裁協議遇到障礙時，法庭需介入協助執行雙方之間的協議。在這情況下，法庭會採取保守的政策，盡量避免介入雙方的糾紛。即使介入，法庭亦會嚴格遵守《示範法》所定明的規則。法庭會盡力避免干預仲裁機構就糾紛的裁決權。

第五條（《示範法》第一條〈條例適用的仲裁〉）指出條例適用於所有在香港進行的仲裁。仲裁協議簽注的實際地點並不對條例的約束力有任何影響。

針對在香港境外進行的仲裁，則有局部條例適用。適用於海外仲裁的條例包括第二十條〈違反仲裁協議在本港法庭展開的訴訟〉；第二十一、四十五、六十條〈有關仲裁的臨時濟助〉；第六十一條以及條例第十部分就海外裁決的承認和執行等。這些均是促進香港國際貿易，讓法庭協助當事人在本港執行外地裁決的方便措施。

第六條指出條例適用於政府及中央人民政府在香港特別行政區設立的機構。筆者會在本書第六章詳細討論這方面的細節和產生的法律問題。在華天龍號（No.2）[1] 一案中，法庭指出中央政府所成立的機構在本港享有跟《普通法》中，英國殖民政府一樣享有的訴訟豁免權。這個分析對商業糾紛的解決影響可能深遠，故此筆者會在第六章探討這豁免權的定義。

II. 一般條例

第八條採納了《示範法》第二條〈定義及解釋規則〉，列出了《仲裁條例》內的用詞定義及解釋規則。

更重要的是第九條。透過採納《示範法》第二A和第九條，《仲裁條例》訂出了重要的條例解讀原則。解讀原則補充了《仲裁條例》第八條的釋義。

按第九條，在解讀《仲裁條例》時，法庭應考慮《仲裁條例》的「國際淵源」、「統一施行原則」和其「遵循誠信」的立法宗旨。在這基礎上，在《仲裁法》所管轄的範圍內，如法例在某方面未有明確定義，法庭和仲裁庭應按照以上提到的立法原則推譯條例內文。

第十條採納《示範法》第三條〈收到書面通訊〉。條例列明以書面進行的通訊，一經投遞便被視為收到。至於即時通訊〈如電郵或傳真等〉，第十（二）和（三）條修改了《示範法》的規定，定明相關通訊能有記錄證明通訊已被有效傳達，通訊即被視為在即日收到。

第十一條採納《示範法》第四條〈放棄提出異議的權利〉。如果當事人在知道對方違反《示範法》規定,則應及時提出反對。如當事人沒有及時提出反對,並仍然參與仲裁,其沉默會被視為放棄就對方違規提出異議。當然,不是每項違規都是需要對方反對的,違規的後果必須視乎其性質和參照條例的規定。

第十二條採納《示範法》第五條〈法院干預的限度〉,列明除《仲裁法》明文規定外,法院不能干預由《仲裁法》所規管的事項。

第十三條定明法院和香港國際仲裁中心(HKIAC)為本港協助和監察仲裁的機構。香港國際仲裁中心是一所擔保有限責任公司,專責提供有關仲裁的資源和服務。

按第十四條,《時效條例》的應用範圍包括仲裁糾紛。

時限的計算不會被雙方的協議影響。即使仲裁協議訂明雙方在仲裁有結果前不能進行訴訟,時限不會因雙方之間正進行仲裁而押後至裁決結果後起計。根據《仲裁條例》第十四(三)條,時限同樣從訴訟因由產生的日子計算。強制仲裁的條款叫做 Scott v Avery 條款,名字來自十九世紀同名案例中的合約條文。按原則,合約條款可有效阻止當事人在仲裁前沿訴訟途徑控告對方違約,但並不影響時限的計算。

第十四(四)條規定,如裁決最終被擱置,那麼從仲裁開始到裁決被擱置之間的時間則不在時限計算內。

第十六條指出在法院進行涉及仲裁的聆訊時，聆訊均以非公開形式進行。法庭有權在有需要的情況下安排公開聆訊。當事人亦有權向法庭申請聆訊以公開形式進行。

為確保仲裁的保密宗旨，除第十六條外，第十七條禁止任何對非公開聆訊的內容作任何的公開披露。第十八條則禁止任何人在沒有當事人應允下披露仲裁的任何過程及裁決。

當然，在處理有關仲裁事宜時，法庭希望能透過書面判詞去建立一套針對仲裁的法律原則和法庭程序。當公開有關判詞時，法庭通常會刪除判詞中涉及仲裁內容的細節（包括當事人的名字），令公開的內容純粹針對相關的法律原則。

III. 仲裁協議

仲裁協議的定義十分廣泛，包括的糾紛種類也十分多樣化，不一定純粹限於源自合約條文的商業訴訟。第十九條採納了《示範法》第七條的備選案文一〈仲裁協議的定義和形式〉。備選案文一就何謂仲裁協議作出定義。按例，有效的仲裁協議只需要雙方同意，把某個法律關係中所產生的爭議，交由仲裁解決即可。爭議的起端需源自雙方之間既定的法律關係。這關係可以是契約性（附帶合約）或非契約性（例如疏忽）。備選案文並指出仲裁協議可以是雙方合約的一部分，也可以被理解成單獨於合約其他條文的一份獨立合約。[2]

第七條規定有效的仲裁條文必須是書面的。書面的定義十分廣泛。書面協議包括經電子、磁化、光學或其他相似的方法傳送的資訊。

第十九（一）條把《示範法》第七條就書面所作出的定義伸展。十九（一）指出有效的書面協議不一定需要當事人雙方簽注。有效的協議只需在雙方授權的情況下被記錄在案，即使沒有雙方簽注或是經第三者準備，有關文件都構成有法律效力的仲裁協議。

第二十條採納《示範法》第八條〈仲裁協議和向法院提出的實體性申訴〉。本條文針對如當事人違反仲裁協議，直接向法院提出實體性訴訟時法庭的處理方法。按條文，如當事人違反仲裁協議向法院提出需經仲裁解決的實體訴訟，只要被告人按時向法院提出反對，在大部分情況下法庭都必須擱置訴訟，把爭議交由仲裁庭作先行處理。例外的情況是當法院裁決雙方的仲裁協議為無效，不能實行或不能履行。被告人需要在向法庭作第一次申述之前提出擱置訴訟申請。一旦被告向法庭作實體申述，申述本身便可被視為被告同意訴訟和放棄仲裁的證據。

即使仲裁協議具法律效力，如果爭議涉及勞工糾紛便能被勞資審裁處所處理，法庭可以酌情考慮是否應擱置訴訟或把糾紛交予審裁處處理。

有關船務的案件，法庭可考慮在仲裁前有條件擱置訴訟。法庭可命令被告向法庭存入保證金。被告存入的保證金可被用作支付仲裁裁決的命令。

法庭因仲裁而擱置訴訟的責任不是絕對的。第十九（三）條指出法庭在處理擱置申請時需考慮《管制免責條款條例》（Cap 71）（CECO）第十五條。

CECO 第十五條保障消費者。如果申索人以消費者的身份從被告處購入貨品，而買賣過程中雙方定下了仲裁協議，那麼法庭只有在兩種情況下才會實行仲裁協議。第一就是仲裁協議是雙方在糾紛發生後達成的。這說明消費者在簽注的仲裁協議時，同意把糾紛交付仲裁，並不影響消費者的訴訟權利。第二種情況是消費者曾透過仲裁解決同一項買賣的其他糾紛。

法庭按《示範法》第八條而擱置訴訟的命令是不能上訴的。相反，當事人可以就法庭拒絕擱置訴訟而提出上訴。這重申了法庭應尊重雙方仲裁協議，盡量避免介入仲裁過程的原則。

第二十一條指出當時人可在仲裁前和仲裁過程中向法庭提出臨時濟助申請。

IV. 仲裁庭的組成

第二十三條採納《示範法》第十（一）條〈仲裁員人數〉。當事人能自由設定仲裁員的人數。如果雙方不能決定仲裁員的人數，香港國際仲裁中心會按需要編制一或三名仲裁員組成的仲裁庭。

第二十四條採納《示範法》第十一條〈仲裁員的指定〉。本例明文指定委任仲裁員的程序，尤其是當雙方不能就指定程序達成共識或單方面不遵守既定程序。

第二十五條採納《示範法》第十二條〈迴避的理由〉。在被授權為仲裁員時，仲裁員必須主動透露任何「可能引起對其公正性或獨立性產生正當懷疑」的情況。如當事人對仲裁員的公正性或獨立性存有合理懷疑，當事人可以就任命提出反對。另外，如果仲裁員不符合雙方在仲裁協議中訂明的資格，仲裁員的任命可被撤回。如果當事人在任命生效後對其公正或獨立性產生合理懷疑，或發現仲裁員不合資格，當時人可以引用在任命生效後所獲悉的新情況要求仲裁員迴避。

第二十六條採納《示範法》第十三條〈申請迴避的程序〉。此條文解釋如何挑戰仲裁人的任命，並在提出挑戰任命後的程序。

第三十和三十一條容許由雙數仲裁員組成的仲裁庭任命一位公斷人。當事人或仲裁庭成員（在雙方不能同意的情況下）有權決定公斷人所扮演的角色。第三十一條指出公斷人能在仲裁庭不能就某爭議達成一致裁決時，取締仲裁庭並自行作出有效裁決。

第三十二和三十三條處理協助仲裁的調解安排。條例容許仲裁員在展開仲裁前扮演調解員的角色。雙重任命可以是仲裁協議所指定，也可以是當事人在調解展開後經書面同意而進行。若調解失敗，再展開仲裁前，曾參與調解的仲裁員必須向雙方透露任何他在調解過程中所得悉的資料，並認為對仲裁有關鍵性影響的資料。

調解在《仲裁條例》中的定義包括調停（conciliation）。

V. 仲裁庭的管轄權

第三十四條採納《示範法》第十六條〈仲裁庭對其管轄權作出裁定的權力〉。仲裁庭能對其管轄權作出自行裁決。就管轄權作出的爭議必須在抗辯人呈交抗辯書之前提出。即使雙方已經任命仲裁員，當事人仍然可以就仲裁庭的管轄權提出挑戰。

《示範法》第十六條背後的思維十分重要。

仲裁協議可以是獨立合約，或是當事人之間合約條文的其中一款。

如果仲裁協議是雙方合同的一部分，在法律上，《仲裁條例》會被視為「並立及可分割」的條款。這代表即使整體合約因某些原因作廢（例如因欺詐、失實陳述或錯誤等），仲裁協議可以不跟隨合約主體一同作廢，並繼續擁有法律效力。

由於仲裁協議在法律上具獨立性，所以仲裁庭能在不影響自身管轄權的情況下裁決合約主體是否作廢。否則，假設仲裁協議是合約的一部分，而仲裁庭裁決該合約在法律上作廢，那麼仲裁庭在裁定合約失效的同時，亦會自相矛盾地否定了仲裁庭本身按合約所衍生的管轄權，導致裁決因合約失效而失去約束力。為避免這個問題，仲裁協議在法律上必須是獨立並可從合約主體分割的。

仲裁庭本身亦有權裁定自己是否符合仲裁協議就仲裁員所定下的要求。《示範法》第十六條賦予仲裁庭「自我裁決」的權利，令仲裁庭可按仲裁協議的內容對仲裁庭的自身權利及管轄權作自行裁決。

但是，按《仲裁條例》，仲裁庭針對管轄權的自我裁決並非最終定案。就有關問題，法院有最終決定權，以防止仲裁庭的自我裁決失當。在仲裁庭就自身權利或管轄權作出裁定後，不滿裁決的當事人可以就裁決向法院上訴。而原訟庭就上訴作出的判決則是最終判決。

相反，如果仲裁庭裁定自己沒有管轄權，裁決將不能被上訴。法庭在這情況下需要透過聆訊就爭議本身進行實質判決。

VI. 臨時措施和初步命令

《仲裁條例》第三十五條採納《示範法》第十七條，使仲裁庭能在裁決前採取臨時措施去維持雙方現狀，以防止可能損害雙方利益的舉動。例如保存雙方資產，確保敗訴人可以支付裁決賠償。仲裁庭同時亦可命令，容許當事人從另一方手上取得對案情十分重要的證據。

第三十五（二）條的措辭十分隱晦：「《貿法委示範法》第十七條所提述的臨時措施，須解釋為包括強制令，但不包括第五十六條所指的命令。」

第五十六條列出了仲裁庭可行使的一般權力。仲裁庭就支配仲裁程序有相當大的權力，例如仲裁庭可以要求當事人提供保證金、取證、提供證據或經宣誓的證供，或查驗與保存資產等。

頒布臨時措施（強制令）的權力與仲裁程序的指令多有互相重疊處。故《示範法》第五十六與十七條在字面上看起來似乎十分相似，那為甚麼要分開兩條不同的條文？筆者在第二章會仔細陳述有關答案。暫時，筆者只希望提出兩者的意義是頗有不同的。

第三十六條採納《示範法》第十七Ａ條〈准予採取臨時措施的條件〉。條文訂明仲裁庭在考慮是否作出臨時措施時需要考慮的因素。仲裁庭需要平衡相關措施對雙方所帶來的利益和損害。若果利益多於損害，則相對給予濟助。自然，任何臨時措施的必要條件，一定是仲裁庭認為申請人的案情最終有合理勝訴的可能，否則不必浪費時間命令任何臨時措施。

第三十七條容許當事人單方面向仲裁庭提出臨時措施申請，申請的首次聆訊不會有抗辯方參與（抗辯人甚至沒有知情權）。

第三十九至四十二條定出仲裁庭可給予申請人的臨時措施。其中包括要求當事人就申索提出保證金和要求一方支付對方訟費或就訟費作出特定分配等。

第四十五條容許香港法庭就在香港或海外進行的仲裁提供支援。在香港境內進行的仲裁，法庭有與仲裁庭一致的平行管轄權，可以與訴訟程序一樣給予申請人臨時濟助。如果仲裁在海外進行，法庭則需確認有關的仲裁可產生能在香港執行的裁決（無論是最終或暫時性裁決）。同時，所申請的臨時濟助必須符合香港法庭一般可依法頒布的命令。

第三十五（六）條列明，在海外進行的仲裁即使不能在香港進行訴訟，法庭亦可給予臨時濟助。

VII. 仲裁程序

《仲裁條例》第四十六條要求仲裁庭公平對待雙方的當事人。

仲裁庭必須獨立、持平和中立，並必須給予雙方合理機會就其案情和論據作陳詞。仲裁庭需要採取最適合案件性質的程序和手法審理案件，並避免不必要的拖延或資源的浪費，致使爭議能公平地解決。

第四十七條採納《示範法》第十九條〈程序規則的確定〉。雙方能協定仲裁的程序規則，如雙方不能同意，仲裁庭則可自行按合適的方法行事。

必須謹記仲裁庭不是法庭的代替品。故仲裁庭毋須受制於法庭的舉證規則,仲裁的優點是富有彈性。所以,適當地彈性處理舉證規則很多時能提高效率並減低仲裁成本。

第四十九至六十三條就仲裁規則定出一套指引。法庭可在必要的時候協助仲裁庭作出具約束力的命令。條例訂明的指引包括:第五十條〈涉及仲裁語言〉、第五十二條〈涉及口述陳詞〉。如果一方當事人違反仲裁庭命令,仲裁庭可以作出強制性命令,並採取懲罰性措施。按第五十三條,仲裁庭可委派專家就某專業領域提供意見。

第五十六條容許仲裁庭提供臨時濟助,如提供保證金等。要注意的是仲裁庭不應單因為當事人為海外居民(或公司)便要求有關當事人提供保證金。

第五十六(八)條容許仲裁庭為證人監誓,並要求某證人出庭作供。

第五十七條容許仲裁庭就雙方可取回的訟費定出上限。

仲裁庭可按第五十八條寬限當事人展開仲裁的時限,或寬限其他展開仲裁前雙方必須完成的條件(如首先進行調解等)。

如當事人不合理地拖延申索,仲裁庭有權按第五十九條直接剔除有關申索。筆者在第二章會解釋甚麼是不合理的拖延。

仲裁庭可按第六十條容許當事人查驗證據，或命令當事人保存證據。這與法庭的權力相似，但法庭有更廣的權力就非在本港進行的仲裁頒令。

按第六十一條，經法庭許可後仲裁庭的臨時命令可以轉化成法庭命令。

按第六十三條，仲裁中代表雙方當事人的法律代表不受香港法律執業者條例規管。故任何人都可以在仲裁中代表當事人。理由是仲裁的認受性源自當事人雙方的私人協議，他們有權要求任何人作為代表。

VIII. 裁決及終止仲裁

第六十四條採納《示範法》第二十八條〈適用於爭議實體的規則〉。仲裁庭需要按照雙方所選擇的法律判案。如有爭議，協議中就「適用法律」所定的條文由香港法庭按香港法律解讀條文。法庭在解讀有關「適用法律」的條文時將參照有關法律的實質部分，並略過其中的程序性規則，以避免產生香港法和適用法互相參照的情況（renvoi）。例如有關的情況可能是香港法要求法庭參考的外國法判決，而有關的外國法則定明在相應情況下該國法庭應按香港法判決，出現互相循環的法律僵局。

第六十四條定明在雙方同意的情況下，仲裁庭可按照公平正義原則裁決（*ex aequo et bono*），而毋須參照任何法律條文。

第六十五條採納《示範法》第二十九條〈仲裁庭作出的決定〉，定明仲裁庭的實質裁決必須經大比數贊成，但有關程序的問題則可由單位仲裁員決定。

第六十七條按《示範法》第三十一條〈裁決的形式和內容〉，定明裁決必須以書面作出，並具有多數仲裁員簽名。除非雙方同意，否則裁決必須陳述理由。

按《示範法》第三十一（四）的要求，裁決需要送交雙方當事人。但按《仲裁條例》第七十七條，雙方必須在取得裁決前支付仲裁庭的所有費用和有關支出。一般來說，在雙方付款前仲裁庭可以扣起裁決。

第六十九條採納《示範法》第三十三條〈裁決的更正和解釋；補充裁決〉。條例容許當事人要求仲裁員糾正裁決中的書寫錯誤。如雙方同意，仲裁庭會解釋裁決中任何雙方認為不清楚的部分。

條文並容許仲裁庭覆核和修改訟費分配。如果仲裁庭在安排訟費時沒有考慮與訟費相關的資料，譬如是雙方在有關安排作出時為保密的和解協議，仲裁庭則可在收到有關資料後更改之前的訟費安排。

訟費通常由敗訴方支付。但如果勝訴方曾不合理地拒絕對方的和解協議（例如比裁決更優厚的提議），那從拒絕有關提議往後的訟費可以說是浪費的。這是因為繼續仲裁並沒有為勝訴人帶來任何好處，在這情況下，仲裁庭可頒令在和解協議被拒絕的日期起，敗訴方毋須支付任何訟費。

第七十條賦予仲裁庭與法庭同等的濟助頒授權，仲裁庭在大部分的情況下可頒布於法庭一樣的濟助。但仲裁庭不能在涉及土地的協議上要求當事人強制執行涉及產權的合約。

第七十一條容許仲裁庭在仲裁不同階段就爭議的不同部分作個別裁決。

第七十四條容許仲裁庭彈性處理訟費的分配。

按第七十八條，雙方當事人就支付仲裁庭費用有共同和不分割責任。

第七十九條容許仲裁庭在裁決上加上利息。

IX. 不滿裁決的程序

第八十一條採納《示範法》第三十四條〈申請撤銷，作為不服仲裁裁決的唯一追訴〉。條文列出《仲裁條例》結構下僅有的數個可以擱置裁決的理由。

《仲裁條例》下擱置裁決的理由包括：（1）當事人在定下仲裁協議時欠缺行為能力；（2）協議按「適用法律」被定為無效；

（3）當事人就仲裁過程不知情，或沒有被給予合理陳述機會；
（4）裁決結果超越雙方所要求的濟助；（5）仲裁庭的委任不
當；（6）按香港法律雙方的爭議不能透過仲裁解決；以及（7）
裁決有違公共政策。

當事人可在獲得裁決後三個月內而提出反對。

X. 裁決的認受性和執行

第八十四條規定裁決可在經法庭容許後，當成是法庭判決一樣
執行。《仲裁條例》第十部分提供一套簡易程序，容許當事人
申請將裁決轉化成判決。

第八十五條規定，除內地或其他地方按《紐約公約》所作出的
裁決外，申請執行裁決時必須呈交裁決以及仲裁協議的正本。
注意：香港仲裁不受益於《紐約公約》，也亦非國內裁決。故
此，在申請執行香港裁決時申請人需要提供合約和裁決正本。

《紐約公約》在一九五八年於聯合國國際商業仲裁會議中通
過。公約促進國際間互相承認並協助執行在公約國中所進行的
仲裁裁決。

如沒有公約，在跨境執行裁決時當事人會遇上相當多的程序阻
礙。國家 A 的裁決如果想在國家 B 執行，則需在 B 國提出申請
和經過繁複的法律程序方可取得該地的法庭許可。整個過程可

能十分費時失事。

相反，透過《紐約公約》，公約國間就裁決的相互認受和協助執行程序變得簡單很多。仲裁在國際間的認受性是其勝過訴訟的一大原因。

中國（包括香港），是眾多公約國之一。

但是，透過香港仲裁所產生的裁決自然不能算是國外裁決。另外，由於香港是中國的一部分，故國內的裁決亦不能算是國外裁決。在此基礎下，《仲裁條例》在執行上分開三種類別：公約裁決、國內裁決及非公約裁決。

按《仲裁條例》第二條的定義，國內裁決必須是透過受認可的國內仲裁機構，按中華人民共和國仲裁法規定所作出的。所謂「受認可的仲裁機構」是香港律政司長所認可並公布的名單所陳列的機構。

第八十六條規定法庭在處理執行申請時有權拒絕。容許法庭拒絕執行裁決的原因與擱置裁決的原因相若。

按第八十六（二）（c）條，如法庭認為公正，則可以拒絕執行裁決。

第八十七條容許裁決按第八十四條所定的程序，或直接向法庭申請執行。同時，不管裁決是否被執行，任何公約裁決對仲裁雙方均具有約束力，裁決可在任何法律程序中被用作抗辯理由或用作抵消債務。

公約裁決在大部分情況下可以在香港被強制執行。只有在數個特定的情況下法庭才會拒絕，這些情況陳列在《仲裁條例》第八十一條。

留意，第八十六（二）（c）條不適用於公約裁決，所以法庭不能因第八十一條以外的其他原因拒絕執行裁決。

第九十二條容許國內裁決按第八十四條透過法庭程序執行。國內裁決一旦作出對仲裁雙方均有約束性。

第九十三條定明如果裁決在國內已經被申請執行，則不能在香港作平行申請。但如在國內的執行程序未能完全滿足裁決金額，則可在香港執行裁決餘下的部分。

第九十五條列出拒絕執行國內裁決的理由。這些與拒絕執行公約裁決的理由大致相同。唯一分別是第八十六（二）（c）容許法庭以公正原因拒絕執行。

XI. 雙方可明文採納以及自動生效的條文

按第九十九條，雙方可明文採納《仲裁條例》附件二內的條文。如果雙方在協議中指明雙方的仲裁為「本地仲裁」，則附件二內的條文在指定時間內（最多六年）自動生效。

第一零一條針對建築合約中的仲裁條款。第一零一條的立法原意是針對在比較舊的建築合約內有本地和國際仲裁之分。兩者在舊的《仲裁條例》架構下有許多分別，故第一零一條澄清了有關問題，以免業界憂慮新的《仲裁條例》未有簡化以往的舊程序。

按第九十九條，當事人可考慮採納以下的附件二條款：-

1. 附件二第二條：仲裁的合併處理；

2. 附件二第三條：容許原訟庭就初步法律問題作先行判決；

3. 附件二第四條：以嚴重不當事件為理由質疑裁決；

4. 附件二第五條：就法律問題而針對裁決提出上訴；

5. 附件二第六條：就法律問題針對裁決上訴的上訴許可申請。

這些可選擇的條文強化了仲裁的彈性，當事人可針對其需要選擇合適的條文並採納在仲裁協議中，按雙方的糾紛性質度身訂做合適的仲裁方案。筆者在第六章將解釋選擇條文的優點。

XII. 其他

按第一零四條仲裁以及調解員只會在不誠實作業的情況下才需
為其行為負上法律責任。按條文，調解員是按第三十二條所委
任的調解員。

第二部分　《仲裁條例》在數個常見情況下的應用

隨著《示範法》在國際間漸趨廣泛，有關《示範法》的國際案
例也越是變得豐富（包括香港）。豐富的案例有助國際間互相
借鑒，尤其是實行《普通法》的國家。了解國際案例有益於
仲裁員了解仲裁的趨勢，並協助業界更能有效地提高辦案的
質素。

仲裁員、律師和法官們尤其需要留意有關《示範法》的國際案
例，確保在辦案時盡可能保證《示範法》的國際一致性。

若非如此，如仲裁員只按照本土法規以及本土仲裁機構的規矩
狹隘地解讀《示範法》，則無可避免會導致國際標準不一致。
《示範法》的原意是達致國際間仲裁基準的一致性以促進國際
經貿，故業界必須協力在應用《示範法》時盡量保持一致。

不過，法律必須考慮實際情況。故本土情況必然會影響裁決爭
議的結果，而這些情況也必然在適當情況下影響仲裁庭或法庭
對《示範法》的解讀。在熟悉本土情況的基礎下，了解其他國
家的案例，有助判案機關考慮哪些案例有參考價值。

在本部分筆者會分析三個在仲裁中常見的問題。這些情況不只適用於香港，並在國際間均常會遇見。這三個情況在《仲裁》期刊二零一一年第七十七期找到。

這些問題為：

　　I. 當事人是否能剔除《示範法》為不適用於其仲裁？

　　II. 當事人是否可以因裁決存在嚴重錯誤而擱置裁決？

　　III. 當事人是否可以因裁決理由不足而擱置裁決？

本書希望從務實的角度出發令讀者對《仲裁條例》有實際的理解。故此，筆者不會在以下章節就有關題目的案例進行太多的引述和研究。筆者希望提出的只是按《仲裁條例》和國際案例，香港法庭在遇到以下問題是應該如何處理。筆者希望這樣能讓讀者對《示範法》有更深入的了解。

I. 當事人能否不選用《示範法》

第四十七條採納《示範法》第十九條〈程序規則的確定〉。條例規定雙方能在仲裁中自由同意適用的程序。但是，這方面的自由不是絕對的，《示範法》第十九條列明，選擇的前提是要按《示範法》的相關條款而定的。

就字面，《仲裁條例》第四十七條產生出以下兩個後果。

首先，在很多情況下，《示範法》條文本身會指出當事人可自行選擇與《示範法》不同的程序。[3]

第二，如果《示範法》條文指出該條文是強制性的，則無論雙方是否有明文定名，《示範法》均會強制適用。

簡而言之，在香港現存的仲裁制度下雙方不能完全抽離《示範法》的架構。

故此，在《示範法》沒有設定強制措施的範圍內，雙方可執行指定適用的程序架構，而《示範法》的作用則是填補雙方協議中留白的部分。至於《示範法》提出強制措施的範疇，則無論協議條文如何草擬雙方均不可更改。[4]

II. 裁決是否可因嚴重錯誤而擱置？

條例列出四個可能的情況。

第一，如雙方沒有採用《仲裁條例》附件二內的選擇性條款，則唯一能擱置裁決的條文為第八十一條（《示範法》第三十四條）。

不滿裁決的一方必須證明仲裁庭的嚴重錯誤產生了《示範法》第三十四（二）。除非第三十四（二）條適用，否則《仲裁條例》第八十一（三）條定明法院沒有權力擱置裁決。

在《示範法》第三十四條所定的有限情況下，嚴重錯誤在兩個情況下適用。第一是三十四（一）（a）（iii）定下的裁決內容超越雙方協議；第二是三十四（二）（b）（ii）所定的裁決有違公共政策。

但依上述兩項條文所作的擱置申請均不容易成功。要明白仲裁歸根結底是雙方的協議，按雙方共同制定的程序和安排進行。在委任仲裁庭的同時，雙方亦接受了仲裁庭可能犯下法律錯誤的風險。所以，即使裁決有嚴重錯誤（無論是法律上或是事實上），當事人很難提出，仲裁庭犯下的錯誤導致裁決超越雙方仲裁協議所定（協定並不保證某一個特定的裁決）。相反，在大部分的情況下，錯誤是雙方所同意接受的風險之一。

至於公共政策，有關第三十四（二）（b）（ii）的案例為按裁決違反公共政策而提出的擱置申請造成了許多障礙。

在筆者所審理的案件 *A v. R HCCT No. 54/2008*（30 April 2009）中，筆者在判決中強調公共政策只有在特殊的情況下才會擱置裁決。筆者在做出有關決定時參考了英國、新加坡和香港的有關案例。所有案例均指出，只有在仲裁構成「不道德或應受譴責」的活動，又或者裁決結果有違客觀道德標準，或明顯傷害公眾利益的情況下法庭才會考慮擱置裁決。

換而言之，按違反公共政策提出的擱置裁決申請中，申請人必須證明裁決完全違反了一位理性，並對案情有充分了解的旁觀者的價值觀，或裁決違反了法庭最基本的道德正義觀。

所以，法庭不能輕易單單因為裁決有嚴重錯誤而總結整個裁決有違公共政策。錯誤往往不一定就違反社會的基本價值觀。引述 *A v. R* 的判詞，法庭必須小心防止當事人利用公共政策作為重開爭議的藉口，間接削弱了仲裁的約束力。這樣有違筆者在第一部分所總結的兩個《示範法》的大原則。

所以，在第一個情況中，在雙方沒有選擇《仲裁條例》附件二的基礎上，裁決的嚴重錯誤不會導致裁決被擱置。

第二個情況是雙方的仲裁協議選用了《仲裁條例》附件二第五條〈容許就裁決中的法律問題上訴〉。在這個情況下，雙方可以就法律問題向法庭申請擱置裁決。但嚴重錯誤並不足夠，申請人必須證明裁決在法律層面上有商榷餘地（不一定是非常明顯的法律錯誤）。如果裁決純粹就案情有錯誤了解，則不足以構成擱置理由。

第三個情況是當事人選擇《仲裁條例》附件二第五和第六條。附件第六條需要申請人就法律問題在裁決提出上訴前，首先向法庭取得許可。

按第六條提出的上述許可申請必須符合數項條件，他們是：

1. 有關問題的決定，會對一方或多於一方的權利造成重大影響；

2. 有關問題是仲裁庭被要求決定的問題；及

3. 基於裁決中對事實的判斷：

i. 仲裁庭對該問題的決定，是明顯地錯誤的；或

ii. 該問題有廣泛的重要性，而仲裁庭的決定最起碼令人有重大疑問。

上述的法定考慮因素在 *Swire Properties v Secretary For Justice* [5] 一案中所用的一致。該案是在舊的《仲裁條例》框架下判決的，故筆者相信在有關上訴許可方面的有關案例而言，舊的案例依舊適用。

這並不代表所有的錯誤都會容許當事人就裁決提出上訴，只有在錯誤嚴重影響雙方的利益時法庭才會給予許可。

在其他地區，法庭曾把「嚴重錯誤」（Manifest Error）的概念與「明顯錯誤」的概念分開。就字面了解，第六條的措辭似乎與明顯錯誤比較相似，所以有人認為《仲裁條例》附件二第六條提出了與嚴重錯誤不一樣的標準。

但在實際操作下，法庭很難就「嚴重」、「明顯」和「顯然」這些形容詞作微細的斟酌。在這方面咬文嚼字對解決問題沒有幫助。所以筆者認為香港法庭會採取務實的態度，在處理上訴許可申請時會幹練地考慮裁決的錯誤有否嚴重影響雙方的利益，不會聽取冗長和咬文嚼字式的陳詞。

第四個情況是雙方採納了《仲裁條例》附件二第四條。這容許

當事人以「嚴重不當事件」為理由而質疑仲裁裁決。

嚴重不當事件指原訟法庭認為已對或將會對申請人造成嚴重不公平，屬以下一類或多於一類的不當事件：

1. 仲裁庭沒有遵守第四十六條；

2. 仲裁庭以超越其管轄權以外的方式，超越權力；

3. 仲裁庭沒有按照各方議定的程序進行仲裁程序；

4. 仲裁庭沒有處理向它提出的所有爭論點；

5. 獲各方就仲裁程序或裁決而賦予權力的任何仲裁或其他機構或人士，超越其權力；

6. 仲裁庭沒有根據第六十九條，就效力不能確定或含糊的裁決作出解釋；

7. 該裁決是以詐騙手段獲得的，或該裁決或獲取該裁決的方法違反公共政策；

8. 作出裁決的形式，不符合規定；或

9. 仲裁庭或獲各方就仲裁程序或裁決而賦予權力的任何仲裁或其他機構或人士，承認在進行該仲裁程序中或在該裁決中有任何不當事件。

第四條的條文並不包括嚴重錯誤。錯誤可能嚴重，但並不一定構成第四條所定義的程序不當。

在第四條所提出的理由中，第四（b）、（c）、（d）、（g）和（h）對於嚴重錯誤最有關聯，但沒有一項直接提供上訴權。

按第四（b）條，即使仲裁庭犯錯，也不一定代表錯誤導致仲裁僭越了仲裁協議所賦予的權力。越權與錯誤嚴重與否沒有直接關係。這是因為協議沒有保證仲裁庭是完全正確的，錯誤是雙方必須承擔的風險之一。

按第四（c）條，即使仲裁庭的裁決有錯，也不一定代表仲裁的過程出錯。仲裁庭的裁決原則上是按照雙方所同意的程序所產生的。

按第四（d）條，所指稱的嚴重錯誤應該是仲裁庭所曾處理的。

按第四（g）條，如上所述，嚴重錯誤與詐騙或違反公共政策通常不是同一回事。

按第四（h）條，嚴重錯誤與裁決的形式規定不一定相關。

故此，筆者認為《仲裁條例》附件二第四條不能協助當事人按裁決犯下嚴重錯誤為理由而擱置裁決。

總括而言，除非當事人在仲裁協議中採納附表二第五條，否則在新的《仲裁條例》下裁決將很難因仲裁庭犯下明顯錯誤而被擱置。香港的做法符合其他採用《示範法》的地方。

III. 裁決是否會因理由不足而被擱置？

按《仲裁條例》第六十七條（採納了《示範法》第三十一條），除非當事人同意省去裁決理由，否則仲裁庭必須在裁決內表明裁決的原因。

衍生的問題是：（1）甚麼是足夠的原因和（2）法庭會如何處理理據不足的裁決？

第一個問題的答案可在澳洲案例 *Thoroughvision Pty Ltd v. Sky Channel Pty Ltd and Tabcorp Holdings Ltd* 中找到指引。案中，Croft J 強調裁決原因應符合比例，判詞第五十五段指出：

「裁決理由僅需顯示仲裁庭明白當事人雙方所提出的理據。裁決理由需宏觀地透露仲裁庭如何達致裁決結果。裁決須讓讀者明白結果的原因，但不需冗長或細緻分析。仲裁庭需要注意所有按仲裁協議提出的事項，但這並不代表仲裁庭不能按仲裁的宏觀因素，如爭議的複雜性、事項在爭議整體的重要性，以及仲裁協議中所訂明的金錢或其他原因來決定裁決理由如何表達。」

Croft J 法官在案中引用了 *Gordian Runoff* 一案。該案中，Allsop 法官指出仲裁與訴訟存在本質性的分別，故當事人若選擇仲裁，則不能要求裁決具備像法庭判詞一般嚴謹的理據分析。Allsop 法官在判詞二一六段指出：

「法庭是政府的一環；法庭帶有公認的權威性，並受普通法和當事人上訴權利的監管。相反，仲裁是當事人之間按協議進行的解決爭議辦法，它省卻了訴訟的成本，技術和複雜性（這與仲裁結構的正確性無關）。」

筆者認為香港法庭會按 Croft 和 Allsop 法官的分析去判別裁決是否給予足夠理由。兩位法官的邏輯和實際性毋庸置疑。

法庭可按《示範法》第三十四（二）(b)(ii) 條，以公共政策為由擱置沒有充分理據的裁決。由於仲裁法的目標是確保仲裁過程的整體公平性，法庭不能支持沒有足夠理據支持的裁決。

純粹從公平的角度出發，敗訴方有權知悉敗訴的原因。如裁決沒有充分的理據，敗訴方當然會就仲裁庭的公平性產生合理的懷疑。這樣，如法庭不採取糾正措施，則有違基本的公平原則了。自然，沒有理據支持的裁決並不普遍，故大眾不應過分質疑仲裁庭會否專業地處理案件。

但是，法庭未必一定因裁決理由不足而擱置裁決。按《示範法》第三十四（四）條，法庭可以暫停法庭程序，讓仲裁庭有機會更正或補充裁決的不足。法庭在獲當事人要求和接到當事人要求時，通常會運用暫停程序的權利。

這符合《仲裁條例》第六十九條（《示範法》第三十三條）所訂立的規則。《示範法》第三十三條規定，在頒布裁決三十天（或在當事人預先訂下的日期）內仲裁庭可按當事人要求，就裁決內容作解釋。

故此，如法庭認為擱置整個裁決是過分激烈，法庭會邀請勝訴方同意把裁決發還仲裁庭，讓其釐清相關有欠清晰的理據。留意《示範法》第三十三條，就當事人要求仲裁庭釐清理據定下了時限，第三十四（四）條有關法庭發還裁決而釐清理據則沒有相關的時限。

第三部分　總結

本章總結新《仲裁條列》所建立的仲裁結構。以下列出結構的幾個大重點。

1. 仲裁條例的目的是造就公平快捷的仲裁結構，讓當事人在具成本效益的環境下透過仲裁解決糾紛；

2. 法律盡可能容許當事人自行決定爭議如何解決；

3. 法庭應盡量避免介入雙方的仲裁協議，即使法庭介入，其程度亦不得超過《仲裁條例》所容許的尺度；

4. 《仲裁條例》只適用於書面仲裁協議；按例，書面的定義十分廣泛；

5. 仲裁協議在法律上是獨立協議，故此，即使雙方合約因某些原因被告無效，仲裁協議依然繼續；

6. 按自裁管轄原則，仲裁庭有權自行裁定是否就爭議具管轄權；

7. 但是，在仲裁庭自行裁定具管轄權時，法庭有權推翻有關裁定；

8. 仲裁員在審案時必須獨立、公正和保持中立；

9. 仲裁庭並不需要完全遵從法定的舉證程序；

10. 裁決必須說明理由；

11. 裁決的上訴空間甚少；

12. 仲裁裁決可以被轉換成法庭命令執行；

13. 當事人不能完全豁免《示範法》；

14. 在現行機制下當事人很難以嚴重錯誤推翻仲裁裁決；

15. 裁決可因理據不足而被法庭擱置。同時，法庭亦有權把案件發還仲裁庭釐清理由；

16. 在解讀《示範法》時，仲裁員應留意其他使用《示範法》地區的案例。

1. [2010] 3 HKLRD 611 (Stone J).

2. 「第二選擇」不包括這句子。這是「第一選擇」跟「第二選擇」的唯一分別。

3. 參照與比較條文三（一）、十（一）、十一（一）和（二）、十三（一）〔取決於十三（三）〕、十七B（一）、二十（一）、二十一至二十六、二十八（三）、三十三（一）。

4. 《示範法》中不容許偏離的條文有：第四條〈《示範法》有法律地位〉；第七條〈仲裁協議的定義與格式〉；第十六條〈仲裁庭就自身權利的自裁權〉；第二十八條〈適用於實質糾紛的規則〉和第三十一條〈裁決的內容與格式〉。

5. [2003] 2 HKLRD 986 (CFA).

第二章　仲裁過程細節

承上一章就仲裁程序所作的概觀，本章會從委任仲裁庭起，以至頒布裁決的每一步作深入討論。討論會針對仲裁員在仲裁過程中應注意的事項，並列舉在仲裁期間仲裁員會經常遇到的問題，並就問題提出解決方案以供參考。

此章共分五個部分。第一部分解釋仲裁如何展開；第二部分列出仲裁庭作出臨時措施的權力；第三部分列出仲裁庭應如何管理案件；第四部分解釋審訊的過程；最後的一部分解釋裁決要注意的事項。

第一部分　展開仲裁

I. 仲裁要求

仲裁隨著申索人就爭議向抗辯人遞送仲裁要求而展開。時間從抗辯人收到請求書的日期起計。

《仲裁條例》第四十九條定明有關請求必須以書面提出。

如何算是收到請求書的細節在條例第十條內詳列。基本上，請求在送出當天被視作收到。

在雙方未有另行協議的情況下，「作出通知」按條例定義為把請求遞送到抗辯人的營業地點、住所或慣性通訊地址。如果以上地址在申索方經過合理查詢後為不詳，則應遞送到抗辯人最後所為人知的營業地點、住所或慣性通訊地點。遞送應以掛號信或任何其他能被記錄的途徑。按此，遞送日期依法被視作收到日期。

條例第十條容許仲裁請求由即時通訊遞送，如電郵、傳真等能記錄送出的方法。電子遞送的收到日期為電子通訊送達接受方的記錄日期。

II. 委任仲裁庭成員

仲裁展開後，雙方應著手委任仲裁庭成員。雙方能同意仲裁庭的人數（一、三或更多）以及委任成員的程序方法。一般來說仲裁庭的人數應保持為單數，以避免在出現意見糾紛時仲裁庭出現裁決僵局。

通常的委任方法是雙方各自委派一位仲裁員，再由雙方的仲裁員共同委派第三位仲裁員為首席或裁判。

第三位仲裁員的作用取決於雙方訂立的協議或在少數情況下按另外兩位的仲裁員制訂。[1] 舉例，第三位仲裁員的角色可能與其餘兩位相同，或只在另外兩位仲裁員持相反意見時方投下關鍵票。

三人仲裁庭的問題是成本相當高昂。同時雙方必須調配三位仲裁員以及本身法律代表的時間表，這過程往往會導致長時間的延誤。

因此，並非所有的糾紛都必須由三位仲裁員共同處理。雙方應仔細考慮是否值得投下三人仲裁庭的昂貴資源和犧牲調動人力上的靈活性。

雙方的仲裁協議很可能已經包含委任仲裁庭的方法，在這情況下雙方則只需按照既定協議行事即可。

但是，很多時雙方的仲裁協議僅說明雙方之間的糾紛透過仲裁解決，協議本身不會定出委任仲裁庭的程序。同時，在矛盾產生後雙方往往不能就任何事情達成協議，包括委任仲裁庭事宜。即使雙方就委任事宜達成共識，所同意的程序亦可能因外在因素變成不可能（譬如仲裁機構倒閉等）。

在上述情況下，按《仲裁條例》第二十四條雙方可要求香港國際仲裁協會或法庭指派仲裁庭的成員，[2] 在處理有關申請時，有關機構需要注意爭議的性質並委任具資格能力的仲裁員處理案件。同時有關機構必須致力委任能獨立公正處理案件的仲裁庭。

III. 就委任仲裁員提出反對

在最初獲當事人或其法律代表接洽被委任為仲裁員時，仲裁員應就仲裁爭議的性質作初步了解，並索取雙方的仲裁協議。按上述兩項資料，仲裁員應能足夠評估自己是否有足夠的專業知識，以及仲裁庭是否有管轄權（起碼按仲裁協議中的條文有具爭議性的管轄權）。

被接洽的仲裁員在接受委任前，應確定沒有任何可能令人懷疑自己獨立秉公審理案件的情況。[3]

在香港，法庭在評估某人是否獨立公正時會應用 *Porter v Magill* [4] 一案內所定下的原則，來評核某情況是否存在表面不公（apparent bias）。法律原則是從一位清楚案情，並取態不偏不倚的旁觀者的角度出發，考慮仲裁員是否確切地有可能偏私。如果案情讓法庭覺得仲裁員的確有可能偏幫某一方，則很可能以「對仲裁員的獨立公正性有正當懷疑」為理由推翻有關仲裁員的委任。

故此，如果仲裁員在爭議中有任何利益衝突，則不應接受委任。至少，他應該把利益衝突的細節通知雙方當事人，以免日後產生糾紛。

一旦仲裁庭的委任落實，雙方的當事人有十五天時間申請推翻有關委任。[5] 申請一般會以仲裁員存有實際或表面偏私的理由提出。仲裁庭本身會先行處理有關申請，在作出有關裁決後，雙方有三十天時間向法庭或香港國際仲裁協會就委任的裁決上訴。上訴期間仲裁庭有權繼續處理爭議，包括作臨時或最終裁決。

IV. 仲裁員委任細節

在接受委任時，仲裁員需要與委任人商議委任的具體細節，例如薪酬結構等。

仲裁員收費可按小時計算，按時收費的機構可加上最高薪酬限制，同時也可按爭議金額收取某個百分比。仲裁員需考慮是否收取訂金，訂金是否可以退回和薪酬是否一次性支付，或按仲裁進度分期支付等。另外，雙方可能需要與仲裁員定明薪酬是否包括涉及仲裁的相關開支等。

額外需要商討的事項包括：如雙方不在合理時間內展開仲裁的後果、因某些原因法庭擱置裁決把爭議發還仲裁庭重審、仲裁員是否額外收費、又或者如仲裁員在仲裁過程中因病無法繼續的後續安排等。

注意，《仲裁條例》第六十二條定明在法庭推翻仲裁員委任或仲裁員無法繼續仲裁的情況下，法庭有權扣減或剝奪仲裁員的收費。

某些仲裁員有相當詳細的委任合約。但經驗尚淺的仲裁員應考慮作出比較簡單的條件。仲裁員的委任條件越複雜（不具退款的訂金或複雜的定期付款機制），則越容易失去競爭力。筆者提議新晉的仲裁員考慮採取簡單的委任條件，譬如是在設最高收費的基礎下按小時計算薪酬，以及收取合理的委任費等。

V. 仲裁地點

在決定開始仲裁時，雙方應考慮仲裁在何處進行。仲裁地點直接影響仲裁的整體過程。舉例說，如雙方選擇香港為仲裁地點，仲裁則會受到香港《仲裁條例》監管，而仲裁也必須符合《示範法》的規定。

不同地方有不同的仲裁法律，故在不同地方進行的仲裁，程序上也不盡相同。從當事人的角度出發，雙方應比較和考慮不同的仲裁規則會否為雙方帶來不便或好處，例如相關的時限規定和收費監管等。

不過，無論雙方選擇的仲裁地點是哪個地方，仲裁庭均可以在任何方便雙方的地點進行實際審案，不必規限於某個既定的地方。[6]

VI. 初步指示

獲委任後，仲裁庭在雙方沒有指定的情況下需自行決定審案時仲裁庭所採用的語言。[7]取決於有關決定，仲裁庭可能需指示雙方翻譯某些文件。

一般來說，新被委任的仲裁庭會盡快就仲裁的進程與雙方定下藍圖。第一輪的程序指示可透過電話或簡短的會議作出，為了簡便，雙方可考慮向仲裁庭各自呈交書面陳詞，並容許仲裁庭在閱讀雙方提議後書面作程序指示。

第一項指示應是甚麼？

筆者至今沒有花費太多篇幅解釋有關狀書的細節。[8]在仲裁庭成立之際，雙方很可能已經交換狀書。如是者，仲裁庭應仔細閱讀有關文件，以便對雙方糾紛作深入及充分的了解，使其思考如何從最有效的方法化解和處理爭議。[9]

但是，很多時在仲裁庭成立之際，雙方只不過是簡單交換各自對爭議的取態。在雙方未有詳盡交代爭議的因由時，仲裁庭便應指令雙方呈交和互換包含更詳盡內容的狀書。申索人應把申訴的具體案情詳盡列出，而抗辯人亦應逐一回應申訴指控。雙方在呈交狀書時應附上所有相關的文件證據。

在上述情況下，第一指令便應是就交換詳盡狀書制定時間表。

第一指示的第一段可要求申索人在約二十八天內，呈交仲裁庭，以及送遞予抗辯方申索要點，並把所有文件證據一併附檔。

指示第二段可要求抗辯方在收到申索重點後二十八天內，呈交仲裁庭並送遞給申索方抗辯要點或作出反申索，並把所有文件證據一併附檔。

指示第三段可指示在有需要的情況下，申索方在收到抗辯書後十四天內就抗辯書或反申索的內容作回應，並把有關回應書在時限內呈交仲裁庭和送遞給抗辯方。

指示第四段可指示抗辯人在有需要的情況下，在十四天內就申索人的回應作否認或進一步解釋，或容許申索方對反申索所提出的抗辯作回應。所有有關的文件應一併呈上。

一般而言，在第四段的狀書交換完成後，整個交換案情的過程便告終結。所以，指示第五段可以明確指出在狀書交換完成後，雙方需與仲裁庭安排會議，為下一步的程序作安排。

第一指示的目的是容許雙方和仲裁員，在既定的時間表內盡快找到雙方分歧的重點，在找到準確的爭議點後容許雙方和仲裁庭把焦點放在有關的重點上。

狀書的交換容許各方清楚雙方所同意的案情和具爭議性的事實。雙方陳列的證據則容許雙方評核各項指控和論據的強弱。

從閱讀雙方的狀書開始，仲裁庭在一、兩個月內即可知道應如何制定最有效的程序來處理案件。[10] 按狀書的內容，仲裁庭可決定是否純粹以書面形式處理，或安排開庭聽取證人口供、雙方是否需要呈交進一步的證據、是否需要聽取專家意見，如要開庭的話，需時多少天及應在何時進行。

仲裁庭可在制定程序時聽取雙方意見，並把有關決定以第二指示的形式書面傳達雙方。

第二指示應該包括甚麼？

第一段可以指示雙方在二十八日內呈交和交換雙方的證人證供，書面證供可在審訊時被證人採納為主問供詞內容，以便節省時間和避免內容重複。

同時，仲裁庭應考慮是否需要安排證人被盤問，或仲裁庭是否可以在單憑未經盤問的供詞上作出裁決。

第二段可在有需要的情況下就專家證人的作供作安排。

指示可提議雙方在收到第二指示後十四天內同意專家證人的專業範疇（會計、外地法律、測量師、工程師等）並規定雙方的專家人數。一般而言雙方應只需要一位專家證人。

雙方應在指定時間內同意並呈交一系列需要專家意見的事項表。事項表的內容應以「是」或「否」，或以選擇題的形式（給予專家數個可能的答案，包括「以上均否」供其選擇）作出。

就專家意見內容作指示可大大幫助仲裁庭辦案。很多時候，雙方在委任專家證人時會沒有協調性地給予專家空泛的指示。結果是雙方的專家報告各自陳述不相關的事項，專家報告內容之間毫無關聯性。在這情況下仲裁庭根本不能受惠於專家的專業知識，並只能盡力理解供詞內哪些內容於案情有關。

在規定雙方需要專家意見的題目達成一致共識後，仲裁庭的工作便方便很多。如專家報告的內容是一連串「是」、「否」或選擇題答案，仲裁庭在書寫裁決時便只需採納專家的答案和理由，而毋須對專家報告的內容妄自猜測了。

仲裁庭可要求雙方在交換事實證人供詞後約二十八日內交換不具約束力的專家報告。之後，雙方專家要在約十四天內進行會面並就報告內容達成共識，和指出雙方在意見上的分歧。

在專家會面約七天後，雙方專家需呈上一份共同專家報告，報告內需明確指出雙方專家同意以及分歧的地方。

在共同報告呈交約七天後，雙方的專家可各自呈交不具約束力的最終專家報告。報告內應陳述雙方不能達成一致意見的地方，並說明為何自己的意見更為中肯準確。

指示第三段可就證據披露作指引。

在實行《普通法》的國家（例如香港）的訴訟中，訴訟雙方有各自披露證據的責任。訴訟雙方需要透露自己擁有、控制和管有，並與訴訟有關的證據。有關的證據包括任何有助於對方，或損害自己案情的證據。同時，與案情有關的證據，包括任何在披露後可引起對自己有利或不利質詢的證據。

比起《普通法》，仲裁的搜證過程較相似於施行民法的國家。民法國家大部分不設自動披露程序，搜證往往針對指定的證據。故此，雙方會把所有依賴的證據附列在狀書中，如某方認為對方藏有未披露的證據，則可向仲裁庭申請針對該文件作特殊披露。

仲裁庭在考慮是否命令特定披露時，會按上述的原則考慮證據是否與案件有關、披露是否符合公義，以及披露是否可以為仲裁節省時間金錢。

另外，在閱覽狀書時雙方可能就某些指控要求更詳盡陳述，在有需要的情況下，仲裁庭可在第二指令加上第四段，指示有關方面在既定時間內提供更詳盡陳述。

第五段可就開庭審訊的時間地點作指引。這是一個具爭議性的做法，許多仲裁員不願意過早定下審訊日期，但按經驗，設下期限是引導雙方及時準備案件的好方法。

仲裁員需要作明確清晰的指引。如仲裁庭明確指定審訊日期，並清晰依照指令，那雙方則只有按命令及時地準備案件，這對雙方當事人均有益處。除非情況十分特殊，否則仲裁庭不應輕易擱置審訊日期。

指引第五段可同時規定仲裁庭是否需要文件檔，和有關文件應如何分類和存檔等。

仲裁庭亦應考慮是否指示雙方呈交開案陳詞或呈交陳詞大綱。

所有文件應盡早交予仲裁庭以容許仲裁庭充分準備案情。仲裁庭越清楚案情，則越容易有效地審理和裁決案件。

第一與第二指示應能就開庭作充分的準備。當然，雙方可以在過程中向仲裁庭申請更多的指示，但如仲裁員採納第一和第二指示的建議，筆者認為能有效減低個別申請的需要。

第二部分　仲裁中的臨時濟助

I. 就仲裁庭頒布臨時濟助權的擔憂

第一章中提到仲裁庭能按《仲裁條例》第三十五[11]和五十六條頒布禁止令等的臨時濟助。筆者提出第三十五條賦予的權力比五十六條為廣泛。

第三十五條是《仲裁條例》所新設的條款。由於業界以往作出臨時濟助時一直依賴第五十六條，故在闡析第三十五條時多有擔憂新的權力容易被濫用。有關的擔憂甚至成為報章的頭條新聞。[12]

按報道，有法官和律師認為第三十五條賦予過多權力予仲裁庭，尤其是當許多仲裁員的背景為非法律界人士。業界所擔心的是仲裁庭似乎不應有頒布資產凍結令或查察令等滋擾性高的濟助。

資產凍結令（Mareva Injunction）（下稱「凍結令」）的作用是在仲裁裁決前封存一方的資產，命令通常針對當事人的銀行戶口或樓房資產，令其不能在仲裁進行期間轉移或變賣命令所針對的財產，以確保勝訴方能得到裁決所賦予的賠償金額。

容許查察令（Anton Piller Order）（下稱「查察令」）是容許申索人進入某人的私有產業進行取證。

凍結令和查察令通常是申請人單方面向仲裁庭提出的，單方面申請的原因是若對方知道有關申請時，便會迅速轉移或銷毀有關的證物。

估計到凍結令和查察令對受管人所帶來的嚴重滋擾，一般情況下法庭只有在申請人能證明對方確實有轉移資產，或有消滅證據的風險時，法庭才會頒布有關的禁令。

報章所恐懼的風險是一旦頒布禁令的權力落入法庭以外的機構，則任何人均可以仲裁員的身份任意頒布以上的命令。

如上述情況屬實，則固然令人擔憂。但筆者不認為《仲裁條例》

第三十五條會帶來以上所說的情況。

筆者曾經在演講時表示過就《仲裁條例》給予經驗尚淺的仲裁員權力作出禁制和查察令而擔憂。但同時筆者亦指出只要仔細分析，便會發覺大眾的憂慮很可能誇張了實際情況。

在解釋第三十五條的優點前，筆者強調給予仲裁庭發出臨時濟助的權力能推動仲裁成為最有效處理商業糾紛的模式。新的條例不應帶來恐慌；相反，有關條例是為業界帶來了喜訊。

筆者認為如要充分利用新《仲裁條例》，業界需要調整既有的「仲裁與法庭為獨立個體」式思維。法庭、仲裁庭和當事人雙方在新的《仲裁條例》結構下應該是各有其職，互有關聯的系統。故此，如三方互相合作，各司其職，則可把仲裁變成有效而不昂貴的解決爭議方法。

筆者會在第五章提到有關業界思維的改變，現繼續在這裡解釋仲裁庭頒布臨時濟助的事宜。

按新《仲裁條例》第三十五條，[13] 仲裁庭可命令仲裁的一方遵從以下的命令：

1. 在爭議獲裁定前維持現狀或恢復原狀；

2. 採取行動防止目前或即將對仲裁程序發生的危害或損害，或不採取可能造成這種危害或損害的行動；

3. 提供一種保全資產以執行後繼裁決的手段；或

4. 保全對解決爭議可能具有相關性和重要性的證據。

就第三十五（一）條有四點需要留意。

第一點是條例所賦予的權力受雙方仲裁協議影響。

第二點是臨時濟助可以裁決書或其他形式作出（例如是命令 A 作出某行為）。但按第三十五（三）條，如當事人向仲裁庭提出要求，仲裁庭可就臨時措施作出同等效力的裁決。[14]

命令與裁決在實際上分別可能不大。但在程序上可能會產生不同的後果。

舉例，《仲裁條例》第六十七條（《示範法》第三十一條）就裁決的格式定出了監管。按例，除非雙方另行同意，否則裁決必須解釋原因。如果臨時濟助的形式是以命令作出，仲裁庭則毋須書面交代頒布命令的理由。

臨時措施的作用是在仲裁進行期間，令雙方之間的平衡和狀況盡量維持現狀。故仲裁庭不會在開庭審案前考察證據，並做出任何事實性的裁決。決定採取臨時措施時，仲裁庭只會按雙方案情的表面證據就雙方狀態作基本的平衡。

若然當事人需要就臨時措施向法庭提出上訴，則應要求仲裁庭頒布書面裁決。

縱使仲裁庭毋須在非裁決的命令中陳述理由，作為負責任的仲裁庭在作出臨時措施時，即使不作書面命令，最起碼都應該就有關決定，口頭交代理由。

第三點是所有就第三十五（一）條作出的臨時措施都是要求仲裁的一方做出或禁止其作出一些行為。措施的強制性源於雙方之間仲裁協議的承諾，僅此而已。

假設仲裁庭作出一項臨時禁制令。命令禁止 B 從某銀行戶口中提出或存放資金，以保存 B 的資產方便用作日後執行裁決。

得到有關命令後，原則上 A 是不能手持仲裁庭的命令到銀行，並要求銀行即時凍結 B 的戶口。這是因為銀行並不是仲裁協議的一方，並不受制於雙方之間的仲裁協議。[15] 銀行並不會因不遵從命令而被控藐視法庭。

如果 B 從戶口裡提款，B 則會違反仲裁協議。違約的後果可容許仲裁庭在日後的仲裁過程中對 B 作出懲罰性的命令。但是，除非仲裁庭的禁制令在執行前經法庭批准並轉化成法庭命令，否則 A 能做的便只是在法庭控告 B 違反合約。

第四點是第三十五（二）條中引述第五十六條的分別：「藉第一款而具有效力的《貿法委示範法》第十七條所提出的臨時措施，須解釋為包括強制令，但不包括第五十六條所指的命令。」其意義為何？

第五十六條賦予仲裁庭一系列的權利，這些權利可經雙方協議更改。按第五十六（一）條，仲裁庭能够：

1. 要求申索人就仲裁費用提供保證；

2. 指示透露文件或交付質詢書；

3. 指示以誓章提出證據；

4. 就任何有關財產，指示由仲裁庭、仲裁程序的一方或專家檢查、拍攝、保存、保管、扣留或出售該有關財產；或

5. 指示從該有關財產檢走樣本，或對該有關財產進行觀察或試驗。

第五十六（八）條給予仲裁庭監誓、訊問證人，以及指示證人出庭作供和展現證據的權力。

相比第三十五條，第五十六條的權力明顯地比較程序性，舉例說，第五十六條並不容許仲裁庭作出禁制令。

按上述的分析，如果仲裁庭的權力限於協議的雙方，那麼仲裁庭如何要求不受協議所限的證人出庭作供？的確，仲裁庭所作的證人邀請不具法庭強制令般帶有懲罰性。除非仲裁庭的邀請預先被法庭批准轉化成強制令，否則仲裁庭不能合法地強迫證人出庭。

但三十五與五十六條之間明顯地有很多重複處。例如，三十五

條就保存證據的命令，並於五十六條下的要求仲裁方保存財產的條文重疊。

仲裁員應該如何理解條例間的重疊？

除了禁制令外，筆者提議仲裁員應把三十五和五十六條看成是獨立分開的條款。舉例，如仲裁庭按第五十六條作出資產保存令，其令不應被視作是按三十五條作出的臨時措施。

但在發出禁制令時，情況則有所不同。按三十五（二）條，禁制令可按三十五或五十六條作出兩者之間的作用重疊。這是因為禁制令的性質是禁止受制方進行某項舉措（非強迫地做出某項舉措），而五十六條中所賦予仲裁庭的程序性措施很可能需要借用到三十五條的禁制性權利，故三十五條特別指出並容許仲裁庭借用三十五條的禁制權利作五十六條的程序措施。

為甚麼條例會作出如此複雜的安排？

筆者在思考這個問題時謹記第三十五條描述仲裁庭頒布臨時措施，以確保雙方利益平衡為目的；而五十六條的權力則是為了讓仲裁庭能有效管理案件進度的程序性權力。按這個基準，筆者認為三十五與五十六條的互動能有效容許仲裁庭靈活處理不同種類的案件。

仲裁有許多類別。有些倚重仲裁庭的法律知識，另一些則毋須法律分析，純粹要求仲裁員在某個專業領域內的經驗和知識去解決某個技術性問題。在後者中，仲裁庭實在沒有頒布禁制令的必要。

其他仲裁處理的可能是僱員或家庭糾紛。處理這些糾紛時仲裁庭可能需要使用第五十六條所有條文作程序指引，並使用某些三十五條內賦予仲裁庭的臨時濟助措施。

如仲裁純粹是商業糾紛，仲裁庭則通常需要三十五和五十六條內所有就程序和臨時措施賦予的權力。

由此可見，三十五和五十六條的互動性容許仲裁庭處理不同種類的爭議。

在當事人能自由決定仲裁庭權力的前提下，《仲裁條例》容許當事人自行揀選最適用於爭議的條文，自行決定仲裁庭的角色。有些人可能只選擇第五十六條內的程序設定權力。有些人可能認為三十五條內的臨時措施更能有效保障雙方間的利益而不就條例適用性作任何更改。

有些人可能會在三十五和五十六條中各自選取某些適用的條款。在自行設定仲裁庭權力時，雙方及其法律代表必須仔細分析，去制定一套全面和足夠的系統讓仲裁庭能有效管理案件之餘，並能頒布足夠但不過分的臨時措施。

《仲裁條例》的其中一個創新處是容許當事人自行設定希望給予仲裁庭的權力。要善用條例為當事人帶來的彈性，雙方必須在仲裁開始前，按爭議的性質決定需要仲裁庭扮演一個甚麼樣的角色。雙方必須平衡和保障本身資產周轉靈活的需求，和互相確保對方在仲裁完成後有足夠資產去賠償爭議損失的需要。

靈活性是《仲裁條例》的一大優點，雙方應善用條例以便制定最適合雙方的仲裁系統。

剩下的問題是仲裁庭就三十五條和五十六條所頒布的臨時措施是否能約束第三者。顯然，有關命令如要施行在第三者身上必須得到法庭協助。

法庭的協助大致可分兩種。如筆者在第一章中指出，按《仲裁條例》第三（二）（b）條，法庭只能在條例容許的情況下參與仲裁事務。第十二條重申了這個原則。

按條例，法庭能將仲裁庭頒布的裁決轉化成法庭命令，同時法庭亦能自行頒布協助仲裁的臨時濟助。

當事人能獨立向法庭申請臨時濟助。《仲裁條例》第二十一條指明：

在仲裁程序開始前或進行期間，一方當事人請求法院採取臨時保全措施和法院准予採取這種措施，並不與仲裁協議相抵觸。

按《仲裁條例》第四十五（四）條（豁免《示範法》第十七（j）條的適用性），法庭有權在申請人已經在仲裁庭就相同的臨時濟助提出申請時，若覺得仲裁庭比法庭更適宜考慮有關申請，則應拒絕申請人的呈請。

但是，就字面上理解，條例並不防止當事人不經過仲裁庭而直接向法庭提出臨時濟助申請。因為如當事人直接向法庭提出申請，法庭則不能以申請已被仲裁庭處理為理由而拒絕，而《仲裁條例》第四十五（四）條亦不適用於這個情況。

同樣地，第六十（四）條容許法庭，在仲裁庭正在處理，當事人保存資產的申請時，拒絕自行頒布同樣的臨時濟助。

但如果當事人直接向法庭提出臨時濟助申請，第六十（五）條則不適用。法庭可直接處理有關申請，在適當情況下，法庭可在命令中指出仲裁庭有權擱置法庭的命令。

這代表除非法庭小心處理，否則雙方可能在臨時措施的申請上拉開兩條戰線：一為法庭的訴訟；二是仲裁庭的審議。這是筆者不願意見到的，在臨時措施中花費如此多的資源得不償失。

我們比較一下兩個可能發生的情況：

第一個情況：

A 在沒有知會仲裁庭的情況下，直接單獨向法庭提出禁制令申請。法庭是否應該以仲裁庭更為適合處理有關申請為理由而拒絕處理案件？

假設法庭認為應該給予禁制令阻止 B 轉移財產，在舊的《仲裁條例》體制下，法庭便會在單方面申請作出禁制令後，指示雙方準備證據並安排一次雙方聆訊，以決定是否在仲裁裁決前繼續禁止 B 取用財產。

以上程序是否依然適用？如果法庭安排雙方準備證據進行聆訊，那麼仲裁的進展會否受到拖延？一定會，因為雙方必然集中火力準備禁制令的雙方聆訊，而法庭的安排也很可能會影響到仲裁的進展。

進一步假設，為報復 A 的禁制令申請，B 要求仲裁庭按第三十五條頒令制止 A 執行法庭的禁制令，或強制要求 A 向法庭申請注銷有關的禁制令。如上述的情況發生，則雙方將耗費時間金錢作戰略性的姿態，利用法庭和仲裁庭的管轄權互相鉗制。過程會產生高昂的訟費，並對解決雙方實際糾紛毫無幫助。

第二個情況：

在第二個情況中，A 按《仲裁條例》第三十五條向仲裁庭提出禁制令申請，仲裁庭經聽取雙方陳詞後決定以裁決命令方式頒布禁制令。然後，A 向法庭申請把裁決轉化成法庭命令。法庭應如何處理？

按《仲裁條例》第十部分的條文，仲裁庭的裁決可在法庭批准後按法庭命令執行。按以往的規則，申請人會單方面向法庭作純文件性的申請，法庭在審閱有關的裁決和文件後會按裁決內容作出臨時命令。由於法庭只閱讀了申請人的文件，故臨時命令內通常會註明除非抗辯人在二十八天內反對申請，否則命令馬上生效。如果抗辯人在二十八天內提出反對，命令則在法庭處理抗辯人反對申請前暫時擱置。

假設上述程序仍然適用。如果 B 申請擱置仲裁庭的命令，法庭會指示 B 準備誓章和定下處理 B 的擱置申請的確實日期。

在聆訊前，仲裁庭的禁制令還是否能夠執行？原則上仲裁庭的命令按雙方的仲裁庭協議是繼續生效的。原因是法庭就裁決的處理不影響雙方之間的協議。但仲裁庭的禁制令則不會對第三者，例如是銀行，有任何法律約束力。因此，申請人應提醒法庭在處理 B 的擱置申請時，在命令中寫明在申請處理期間，B 不得轉移銀行內的存款。

不管如何，上述程序的最大問題，是當事人仍然需要在兩個不同的法律體系，就一項臨時命令作出兩個昂貴的平行申請。

新的《仲裁條例》給予申請人一個相對簡單直接的裁決執行方法。A 可依《仲裁條例》第六十一條向法庭申請直接將仲裁庭的臨時措施換成法庭命令。這是新《仲裁條例》的另一項革新，故現行階段法庭仍然未就有關申請作出明確指引。當然，如法庭不留意平行申請所浪費的時間和費用，則不能利用六十一條提供更直接的轉換方法。

上述的問題不是必然發生的，而當事人亦可透過仔細分析來避免平行申請所產生的浪費。即使按傳統程序行事，如仲裁庭在作出裁決時已經聽取雙方陳詞和審核有關證據，法庭有權以一案不能兩審拒絕，安排擱置聆訊直接把裁決轉換成法庭命令。[16]

當然，最理想的解決方法是法庭盡早制訂一套清晰明確的程序，去處理就仲裁庭臨時措施轉化為法庭命令的申請。有關的實務指引能有效協助業界和當事人。

在這之前，我們只能希望仲裁庭能就與法庭之間的權力重疊有專業的理解，並謹慎處理案件，避免在作出臨時措施階段，即產生不能控制的法庭程序，導致仲裁進度遭到延誤。

第三部分　案件管理

仲裁從開始到審訊需要大量準備工作，筆者將這過程稱為仲裁的案件管理階段。

即使在最簡單的案件中，正式審訊前仲裁庭均會與當事人雙方進行數次會面。會面可按當事人要求，或是仲裁庭按需要自行安排。會面的目的是要就以下事項作出安排：[17]

I. 考慮仲裁庭是否有管轄權處理案件；

II. 在審訊前要求某一方的當事人提供保證金；

III. 就釐清雙方案情重點，要求雙方提供更詳盡的案情細節或證據（或專家證人）；

IV. 剔除雙方案情中惡意中傷、瑣碎無聊，或無理纏繞的部分；

V. 取得在對方或第三者手中對案情有關的證據。

在本章節中，筆者會解釋仲裁庭在處理以上五種事項時應作出何種指示，並會提出一些案件管理的宏觀考慮。

I. 第一種類：就是否有管轄權作定案

就仲裁庭管轄權的反對，應該在委任仲裁庭後馬上提出。原因是如果當事人不及時提出反對，並參與仲裁的其它程序時，沉默很可能被當成默認了仲裁庭的管轄權，並放棄質疑管轄權的權力。

當然，如果當事人不反對某過程（即使他有權反對），並積極參與該過程，自然不能在大家花費相當的精神時間後，貿然提出自己不受過程的結果影響，這只是常識而已。

法律不容許當事人按自身利益提出矛盾的說法。當事人不能採取觀望的態度、等待仲裁進度，在過程不符合自己心意時才提出仲裁庭沒有處理爭議的權力。這個做法對另一方極不公平，並會浪費所有人的時間資源。

反對管轄權的申請大約有二：第一是質疑仲裁庭成員的公正獨立性；第二是就仲裁協議是否適用於爭議而提出爭議。

仲裁庭的公平獨立性在上面已經提過，不再重複。

就仲裁協議的適用性，筆者認為仲裁庭就管轄權有自我審裁權（*competence-competence*），故仲裁庭可自行裁定是否有足夠的法律基礎去審理案件。但仲裁庭的自我裁定不是最終的決定，法庭有最終裁決權。

假設申請人嘗試就爭議向法庭入稟訴訟，而抗辯人回應向法庭提出擱置申請，讓雙方先行進行仲裁。

在上述情況中法庭可以就雙方的仲裁協議是否適用於爭議作定案，根據結果決定是否擱置訴訟，留待仲裁結果。

但如果根據案情，雙方的仲裁協議未必有法律效力，例如協議有欠確定性或有錯誤，那麼應該由誰去決定仲裁協議是否失效？

實際中，法庭會保守地考慮，仲裁協議的有效性是否存在起碼的爭議性（或具辯論餘地）。若有，法庭則通常會擱置法庭程序，讓仲裁庭自行決定仲裁協議是否有效。保守的做法與法庭對仲裁的不干預政策一致。

仲裁庭可決定仲裁協議是否有效；當然，在得到仲裁庭的有關裁決後，不滿裁決的當事人可向法庭提出爭議。

筆者覺得以上的處理方法未必適用於所有有關管轄權的反對，並且不認為應該將有關程序公式化，法庭應該彈性處理有關申請。

彈性取決於如何處理申請，對雙方解決爭議最為有效。例如，如果雙方的爭議純粹是「按（無爭議的）協議條文，某問題是否應就仲裁解決？」那麼法庭為甚麼不能直接提供有關條文的法律解釋，並決定該爭議是否受條文限制？這樣做可以省卻許多程序、時間和資源。

相反，如果雙方爭議仲裁協議本身是否有效，法庭則可能要傳召證人並仔細考慮證據，去決定雙方當時所同意的事項。在這情況下，由於爭議涉及仲裁協議本身，法庭則應該暫緩處理申請，讓仲裁庭先行就仲裁協議所賦予的管轄權作出裁定，如果當事人在裁決後仍然感到不滿則可上訴有關裁決。

上述的情況可能造成以下麻煩。

假設申請人未能說服仲裁庭沒有管轄權處理糾紛，並就仲裁庭的裁決入稟法院上訴。上訴的其中一個理由，很可能是仲裁庭根本沒有權力裁決管轄權申請背後的事實，故即使仲裁庭有自裁權，整個申請根本超越仲裁協議的範圍，而法庭亦不受制於任何仲裁庭就事實所作出的裁決。

現行法例沒有訂明，在處理仲裁裁決上訴時，法庭是否必須自行就案情事實作出裁定。如需要，法庭則會需要重複仲裁庭的工作。

筆者認為法庭應該採取實際務實態度。如果證據中有仲裁庭處理管轄權申請的謄本或雙方同意的案情簡錄，法庭則毋須另行聽取事實證人和索取證據。整個過程可以當作是像上訴庭處理原訟庭上訴的一樣，只就法律論點作裁決的上訴。

上訴時，法庭會重新聽取雙方的陳詞並重新考慮案件的證據。但是，由於是重審，上訴庭只會考慮在初審時已經呈堂的證據（包括證人口供和初審的謄本）。在一般情況下法庭不會容許新的證據，並會單從文件上配合雙方律師的陳詞來進行判決。

但是，並不是所有的仲裁都會記錄開庭經過；故此，在沒有選擇下法庭可能在處理反對管轄權申請時需要聽取證供。

就管轄權經常發生的爭議，在建築糾紛中時有發生。在建築計劃中僱主通常把工程給予承包商。承包商在接到工程後再把工程的不同部分分拆，再判給若干分包商。這個過程中，這些分包商的合約很多都是按主承包商與僱主的合約草擬。在發生爭議時，分包商通常會爭議合約中《仲裁條款》就「僱主」與「承包商」的定義是否代表「主承包商」與「分包商」。

建築與工程法的一本權威書籍 Hudson's Building and Engineering Contracts[18] 中段落十八至三十二提到：

「訴訟雙方通常會引述合約中一些不符合雙方合約關係的條文或文件。這些條文本應在雙方簽訂合約時作出調整，以切合雙方的商業關係。若雙方沒有更改有關條款，則很可能失去法律約束力。例如是如果承辦商與分包商合約採用與僱主一樣的條款，合約中的仲裁條款很可能需要按承辦商與分包商的關係作一定的修改，否則條款可能被定為無效。

就這方面，海運法的法律分析有很大的參考性。在航運中買賣方的提單中很可能引述和包含託運人與船主的合約。鑒於類似案件繁多，普通法就合約中引述另外條款是否有效，有相當豐富的案例。一般而言，除非合約的仲裁條款符合買賣雙方的合約關係，或在提單中就仲裁條款作出適當更改以符合買賣方的約定，否則即使提單引述和包括託運方與船主的合約，不符合提單雙方關係的仲裁條款會被視作無效。

雖然航運法的案例具參考性，但本書作者認為基於建築業與航運業的性質不同，故建築法庭不應採納航運法中就引用他方合約中仲裁條款的保守取態。但作者的看法未有影響英國上訴庭在 *Aughton Ltd.*（formerly *Aughton Group Ltd.*）*v. M. F. Kent Services Ltd.*（1991）57 BLR 1）一案中的判決。」

較近期的 *Hudson* 二零零四年補充版（頁二九九至三零零）提到英國的建築法庭放鬆了仲裁協議必須嚴謹符合雙方合約內容的要求，法庭認為考慮有關問題時，最緊要是透過審閱所有有關文件去考慮雙方是否共同有仲裁的意願。按文：-

「大部分國家的司法機構，均否決了對建築合約中引述他方合約的仲裁協議時，要求雙方就該仲裁協議作出特別更改。原因是分包商合約的商業考慮與承包商與僱主的合約的商業背景大有不同，而在建築行業中業界對草擬合約的技巧未有像航運業中，因要顧及保險條文變得仔細和顧及法庭案例。故法庭應採取務實態度考慮雙方的意願，而非單純考慮條文字面。」

筆者個人認為 Hudson 是正確的，法庭在考慮合約中引用條款是否有效時，應考慮所有因素而不應作單純的字面解讀。但筆者個人的看法是，在原則上，航運與建築案件是沒有分別的。

在解讀合約時，法庭必須按雙方在簽約時的共同意向，就合約作客觀持平的詮釋。基於合約背景的不同，法庭處理每件案件時都會作相應的考慮，而法律能做的只是定下解讀合約時法庭應注意的大原則。筆者認為這與 Hudson 的看法是一致的，因在書的第三至四十九段中提到「雙方必須互相同意引用他方合約的條款，而雙方合約中的引用條款必須清楚反映雙方的共同意向」。

筆者認為如果承包商與分包商之間的合約只是「搬字過紙」地重複僱主與承包商的合約內容，那麼在條款沒有被修改，或沒有其他證據支持的情況下，筆者認為承包商與僱主合約中的仲裁條款不能代表承包商與分包商的共同意向。如果仲裁協議的條文是把僱主與承包商的糾紛交予仲裁，筆者不認為能客觀地說該條款應該籠統地包括承包商與分包商之間的意願。

另一個就仲裁管轄權提出的反對是雙方爭議的性質超越仲裁協議所限。故此，仲裁庭應暫停處理超越仲裁管轄權的爭議，容許雙方就該糾紛提出訴訟。

如果雙方在單一交易中產生多項糾紛，而這些糾紛不能全部透過仲裁處理（糾紛某部分超越仲裁協議），這情況在法律程序上會產生相當多的麻煩。例如，由於數項糾紛均源自同一宗交易，理論上糾紛的事實基礎應該一致。但是，如果糾紛在不同渠道審訊，仲裁庭與法庭之間可能會作出不一致的事實裁決（這不符合邏輯）。同時，雙方亦可能因解決糾紛的渠道不同而失去提出反申索，或雙方損失抵銷等抗辯理由。

假設以下的複雜情況：

一個大型的建築工程。分包商與承包商之間有多份合約關係。分包商違反與承包商訂立的合約 A。合約 A 不包含仲裁條款，故承包商在法院就分包商違約提出訴訟。分包商就訴訟提出抗辯。抗辯理由是承包商與分包商之間還存在合約 B。按合約 B，承包商應定期支付分包商款項。承包商逾期未有付款，故承包商違反了合約 B。因此，雙方各自違約所產生的損失應互相抵銷。債務的互相抵銷在適當的情況下為合法抗辯理由。

問題是，合約 B 包含有效的仲裁條款。

這產生了複雜的程序問題。首先是媒介不同所產生的問題。如果分包商可以就債務抵銷提出抗辯，那分包商可否要求法庭擱置訴訟等待仲裁結果？法庭應該怎樣處理涉及仲裁元素的案件？

如果法庭拒絕處理反申索（或債務互現抵銷申請），分包商則失去合法的抗辯理由。如果法庭容許債務抵銷為抗辯理由，繼續處理案件，則可能面對仲裁庭有裁定分包商敗訴，產生與法庭不一致的判決。

有關債務互相抵銷的問題，二零零一年版的 *Mustill & Boyd on*

Commercial Arbitration（商業仲裁的權威書籍）頁一四二提出了筆者認為相當混亂的答案：

「有關債務抵銷的現行趨勢是把抵銷分為：『同一交易抵銷』（包括《普通法》和《衡平法》的定義）和『獨立抵銷』兩個種類。法庭一般認為就同一交易所產生的債務抵銷能提供抗辯人真正的抗辯理由，而獨立抵銷則不然。在獨立抵銷的情況中，如果產生債務的兩項獨立交易不能在同一渠道審理（例如是申索A在法庭進行，而法庭必須擱置申索B留待仲裁裁決），抗辯人則沒有合法的抗辯理由。原因是根據有關的債務抵銷法例，抗辯人不能以法庭不能處理的債務作為自己的抗辯理由。所謂法庭不能處理的原因是因為抗辯人所指稱的債務，按《仲裁條例》法庭必須擱置等待仲裁庭的裁決。

就同一交易產生的抵銷，法律立場則不甚明確。有案例說明在抗辯原因不需被擱置的情況下，法庭有權直接審理抗辯所依賴的債務是否有法律效力（*Gilbert-Ash [Northern] Ltd v. Modern Engineering [Bristol] Ltd.* [1974] AC 689）。但是，按《紐約公約》，法庭依例應該擱置整個訴訟，留待仲裁結果。相關案例請參閱 *Aetna Refining and Marketing Inc. v. Exmar NV* [1994] 1 WLR 1634 and *Glencore Grain ltd v. Argos Trading Co. Ltd.* [1999] 2 Lloyds Rep 410」。

本書不是仔細研究有關問題的好地方。無論如何，筆者不認為以上的問題有簡單穩妥的答案。不過，筆者認為預防勝於治療。也就是說在草擬合約時，當事人以及草擬合約的法律人員應前瞻性地，按整個商業關係的性質，盡量估計可能會發生的問題。可惜在現實中很少人願意在發生麻煩前花耗精神去為後果作準備。

在矛盾發生以後，雙方便很難互相合作，反而會透過戰略考慮向對方施以最大程度的麻煩和不便。仲裁庭和法庭應該注意抵銷申請所能引發的程序性問題，盡量採取最實際並有效解決問題的做法。

另一個問題是，如果抗辯人在訴訟中顯然沒有抗辯理由，法庭是否仍然應該擱置訴訟？

一般來說，如抗辯人申請擱置訴訟，留待仲裁裁決，申索人會馬上提出簡易判決申請。原因是抗辯人就訴訟顯然沒有抗辯理由。法庭根本不必處理抗辯，可以馬上判決。同時，申索人會提出如果抗辯人根本沒有抗辯，則沒有爭議可供仲裁解決。如沒有爭議，則仲裁協議本身便不能執行，法庭不必理會仲裁協議。

在處理有關申請時，法庭應採取務實態度。

除非抗辯人無條件地承認自己沒有抗辯，否則雙方就是否有抗辯理由已經產生爭議。基於雙方已經同意把所有爭議交由仲裁解決，法庭應該擱置申索，由仲裁庭決定抗辯人是否有抗辯理由。

故此，除非抗辯人承認責任，否則法庭應該避免就爭議作任何形式的判決，應把案件交由仲裁庭處理。

II. 第二種類：保證金和其他臨時措施

這個欄目下的申請有三種。第一是向仲裁庭申請資產凍結令；第二是向仲裁庭申請保證金；第三是向仲裁庭申請禁制令制止（或要求）當事人作出相應的行為。

筆者在第二部分已經解釋過有關凍結令的申請。有關的申請通常是單方面作出的。[19] 也就是說申請人不會知會對方，以防止對方在仲裁庭發出凍結令前馬上轉移財產。

由於申請是單方面作出，申請人就申請的相關案情有責任作坦誠和全面的披露。[20] 申請人需要知會仲裁庭所有與申請有關的事宜，包括任何不應該頒布凍結令的事項，並解釋為何仲裁庭不應被相關的不利事項影響。

仲裁庭在申請滿足以下兩個條件後可以（而不是必須）頒布禁制令。[21] 這兩個條件其實是一個平衡的考慮。

條件一是就申請人的表面證據看，申請人有合理機會勝訴。

條件二為：「如仲裁庭不頒令的話，金錢賠償無法彌補申請人可能承受的損失，而該損失比起抗辯人所可能失去的嚴重得多。」

在作出單方面的凍結令申請時，仲裁庭可就申請是否符合以上兩點做裁決。如決定頒令，仲裁庭可擇日進行雙方聆訊，令抗辯人有機會就凍結令陳詞。仲裁庭並可命令，從即日直到雙方聆訊日止，抗辯人不可從任何途徑轉移在申請中列明的資產。

臨時命令作出後，仲裁庭必須就發出的命令通知抗辯人，[22] 並應盡早安排雙方的聆訊，以容許抗辯人回應申請人的理據。

除非仲裁庭正式作出臨時措施，否則臨時命令在發出起二十天內失效。仲裁庭必須在二十天內給予抗辯人機會就凍結令申請作陳詞。陳詞時抗辯方可選擇正式就凍結令提出反對。

如在給予抗辯人合理回應的機會後，抗辯人不反對凍結令或不採取任何回應，仲裁庭則應自行考慮是否有足夠證據和是否應該頒布凍結令。

實際上，除了申請人必須有合理勝訴機會外，仲裁庭必須認為抗辯人有很大機會轉移財產才會頒布禁制令。故很多時凍結令申請均不成功，原因在於申請人不能證實抗辯人有實質機會去轉移資產。

第二，禁制令是《衡平法》的濟助。按《衡平法》原則，法律不濟助予延時不報者。所以，如果仲裁庭認為申請人未有及時提出申請，或在申請時有拖延，仲裁庭均有權拒絕給予濟助。

申請人很多時會以抗辯人正變賣房產為理由申請凍結令。如果變賣房產是支持申請的唯一理由，仲裁庭則應小心留意申請。

不是很多人能隨時提出大量現金支付訴訟或仲裁所需的費用。一般人不會為應付訴訟特別儲蓄。故當爭議發生時，當事人很可能需要變賣房產用以支付訟費和繼續訴訟或仲裁。

如果仲裁庭單單因為抗辯人變賣房產便認為抗辯人有轉移資產的重大風險，繼而凍結其資產，仲裁庭很可能變相協助了申索人達成戰略性優勢。原因是申請人透過微薄的證據便換來能對抗辯人的資金周轉作出極大干擾的凍結令。由於凍結令的嚴重後果，仲裁庭必須避免可能造成的不公。

申請人可能沒有抗辯人會轉移資產的證據。在該情況下，申請人可能會採取煽動政策，向仲裁庭提出抗辯人欠還債務或沒有完成其法律責任。仲裁庭可從此發現抗辯人毫無商業責任感，以此作為申請凍結令的依據。

同樣地，仲裁庭應該小心分析類似的論點。很多時申請人所指的「缺乏商業責任感」只不過是重申申請人進行了不如其意的交易，而並沒有就轉移資產提供任何實質證據。

在大部分的情況下，抗辯人不支付「債務」的原因往往就是爭議的主題。抗辯人的論據正正解釋了為何不需支付申索的事項。仲裁庭很難在未有考慮所有證據或進行審訊前便就抗辯人是否盡了商業責任下定案。

再者，如法庭認為申請人未有及時作出凍結令申請，則會拒絕頒布凍結令。仲裁庭會跟隨同樣的原則。

凍結令背後的理由是申請人認為除非法庭頒令，否則抗辯人會轉移有關資產。如果申請人未有及時提出有關申請,有相關企圖的抗辯人則已經會把有關資產轉走,而凍結令亦無補於事。而如果抗辯人在申請人延遲申請的情況下仍然未有轉移財產,則代表他沒有轉移資產的意圖,而毋須法庭頒令。

實際上,法庭在延誤的問題上有兩種取態。第一,如果凍結令針對屬抗辯人的資產,延誤會因上述的理由而導致申請遭拒。但是,如有關資產雖為抗辯人名下持有,但證據顯示申請人才是資產的實益擁有者,法庭則不會僅因延誤而拒絕凍結令,理由是該資產有合理機會屬申請人,而資產擁有人不應因延誤而失去取回屬自己資產的機會。

總而言之,禁制令申請通常只會在抗辯人涉嫌欺詐或不誠實的情況下方會成功。申請人必須就詐騙的指控提供可信的表面證據。在一般的商業案件中並不常見。

第二種常見的申請是抗辯人要求申索人就訟費提供保證金。通常如果申索人是海外居民(機構),或表面證據指出申索人沒有足夠財產在敗訴時支付訟費時,仲裁庭一般都會要求申索人提交保證金。原因是海外申索人在仲裁地點沒有資產,一旦敗訴抗辯人便不能執行裁決取回抗辯費用,故需要仲裁庭的保障。

但抗辯人很可能誇大訟費,而致申索人因不能提供保證金而不能繼續案件。仲裁庭需要仔細審查有關的訟費評估,並考慮評估是否反映抗辯人實際需要的金額。

一般來說申索人不能向抗辯人要求保證金，原因是抗辯人無論資產厚薄，均應該有無條件的抗辯權。

唯一的例外是抗辯人所提出的論據明顯沒有事實支持或邏輯成疑，導致如繼續審理案件很可能導致仲裁庭浪費時間。如果仲裁庭認為抗辯理由不足，但沒有信心馬上剔除抗辯理由，則可能要求抗辯人交出保證金以換取案件續審了。

另一個仲裁庭應該小心的情況，是當申索和反申索依賴同一理據。例如是當申索人控告抗辯人違約而需要賠償Ｘ，而抗辯人反告申索人違約而需賠償Ｙ。

在這情況當中，雙方是否提供保證金對仲裁進度毫無意義。原因是不提供保證金的後果是違命方不能繼續申索。但如果申索和反申索的案情相同，則無論一方是否提供保證金，仲裁庭均需就案情作出判決，

第三種申請是要求仲裁就維持雙方現狀作出相應命令。

通常如申請涉及禁制令，申請人會要求仲裁庭禁止抗辯人做出某項行為。

在某些情況下，申索人可能要求仲裁庭命令抗辯人作出某行為。由於命令通常要求抗辯花費時間、金錢，一般的申請均會被拒，除非仲裁庭認為申訴方有相當大的勝訴機會。

仲裁庭會在平衡雙方利益後（採取上述類似凍結令的考慮）決

定是否頒布命令。

如果申請人認為在知會對方後抗辯人會破壞命令所保障的利益，申請人可單方面向仲裁庭作出申請。在處理有關的單方面臨時命令申請時，仲裁庭應作出類似上述的安排，在頒布命令後盡快安排聽取抗辯方的理據。

III. 第三種類：澄清案情重點

通常的申請是要求對方就案情提供更詳盡的細節。此類申請一般都被允許，使得雙方能更清晰地了解對方案情。

有時候，申請涉及要求對方回答大量狀書中的細節問題，這一般是戰略性申請，原因是希望浪費對方時間，拖慢案情進度和耗費對方金錢。

有些細節性問題不能協助雙方釐清案情重點（狀書的交代可能並無不清晰處），但提出要求的一方可能是想透過發問無人能夠解答的問題去抹黑對方。仲裁庭在處理有關申請時應該留意發問的方法，確定問題有助雙方解決爭議時才批准。

另一種申請是 A 向 B 發出質問書。質問書的內容要求回應方作誓回答。質問書容許發問人準備正審事項。

同樣，仲裁庭必須小心防止質詢書變成壓迫性工具。質詢書內容越長，則越影響回答人準備正審的時間。質詢書的問題必須是雙方了解對方理據所必要發問的。不能純粹是為 A 帶來優勢。即使問題與案情有關，仲裁庭要考慮發問方會否在審訊時重複問題，如會，問題則必不在審訊前回應，而應留待盤問證人時處理。

筆者在第一部分解釋了有關專家證人的安排。需要專家意見的範疇應經雙方同意並被明確指出，以確保雙方專家能就指定問題提供有關聯、互相呼應的意見。

當事人可能提出仲裁庭就問題 X 作先行審訊。理由是 X 是雙方爭議的前提，如果 X 的答案符合申請人的陳詞，則毋須就案件其他問題進行審理，並可省去時間和金錢。只有在前提爭議結果不符合申請人陳詞的情況下雙方才需要繼續仲裁。仲裁庭就 X 的裁決是最終性的。

仲裁庭應爭取在同一審訊中處理所有爭議。但有時候分開審理的確能節省金錢和時間。如真的就前提爭議作先行審訊，仲裁庭需確保前提問題的確能解決所有爭議，前提問題的措辭必須準確，並能簡單解答。最佳的形式是「是」或「否」題，或是雙方共同提出數個可能的答案以供仲裁庭選擇。

當然，最重要的是仲裁庭需確保前提題的確可以免除審訊的需要。最難堪的局面是在仲裁庭就申請人提出的（或是雙方共同提出的）前提爭議進行裁決後，才發覺仍然有其他問題需要處理，這樣便浪費時間了。

IV. 第四種類：剔除申請

在一般的剔除申請中，被告會在兩方面要求仲裁庭剔出申訴人全部或部分的申索。

第一種是就按無理申索要求剔除。一般而言，被告的論點是申索人的要求根本沒有合理基礎。在處理這類申請時，仲裁庭不應考慮任何證據，並應作以下假設：如果申索人在仲裁申請書中的事實描述全部真確，被告是否需賠償於申索人？如要，則應拒絕剔除申請；如否，則應接納剔除申請。

第二種剔除申請是按申索為惡意中傷、瑣屑無聊或無理纏繞為由所提出。被告只有在申索明顯地欠缺事實基礎或法理的情況下方可成功。

原則上，除非剔出申請能用簡明的陳詞處理，否則當事人應留待正審才處理對方立論的不足。這是因為如果剔除申請涉及複雜理由而不能被快速處理，則會延遲仲裁的整體進度，尤其當仲裁庭拒絕剔除，這令當事人花耗更多的資源和時間。

仲裁庭應留意避免單從文件上判別雙方理據的對錯。當雙方就某事實作激烈的爭議，仲裁庭應安排證人作供並接受盤問，以容許仲裁庭判別事實的真偽。

當申索人認為被告缺乏辯護理由，則可以申索欠缺辯解為由向仲裁庭申請簡易判決。

申索是否成立取決於案情事實是否真切。一般而言，仲裁庭必須透過審訊和盤問證人來評定事實的真偽。由於簡易判決申請，要求仲裁庭在沒有審訊的情況下頒布判決，故申索人必須證明在雙方沒有爭議的案情基礎上，或在無可否定的證據下，被告不可能就申索有合法的辯解。

在大部分情況下，即使被告的辯解十分薄弱，被告仍然有權就其辯解透過審訊，提出證據以供仲裁庭考慮。同時，被告亦有權在審訊中透過盤問，考證申索人案情的真切性。因此，除非在極為清晰的案件中，仲裁庭都不應輕易頒布簡易判決，以避免對被告造成不公。

但這並不代表被告可就其辯解作隱晦曲折的陳述。被告必須在辯護書中清楚指出辯護所依賴的事實，以及事實如何提供合法辯解。仲裁庭不可容許被告含糊其辭，讓其就辯護理由作朝令夕改的說法。

雖然剔出和簡易判決申請必須小心處理，它們卻能就釐清案情重點起莫大作用。假如仲裁庭在閱覽陳述書後認為雙方立論欠缺根據，則應在正審前剔出案中多餘事項。

有些時候當事人會向法庭申請剔除證人陳述書的部分內容，理由是證人陳述的內容涉及惡意中傷以及對案情無關緊要，其目的只是為令對方尷尬。更甚者若申請人需就證人的多餘陳述草擬回應，便會拖延仲裁的進度，故剔出陳述內容是為最合適的處理方法。

在處理剔除證人陳述的申請時，仲裁員需小心處理，以免用過多時間在審訊前評核剔除申請的內容是否與案情有關。如果有關的考慮需要太多，則應把證人證供全部保留，以留待正審一併處理。

從善用資源及案件管理的角度，仲裁庭不應在審訊前花太多時間考慮某證供是否有相關的舉證價值，仲裁庭完全可以等待審訊開始，對雙方的理據有更深入理解後，才決定是否容許證供呈堂。

實際上，仲裁庭在處理剔除申請時，未必對案情關鍵有足夠的了解。故此，要在有效管理案件與過分激進之間取得平衡，仲裁庭可邀請當事人，從書面解釋被申請剔除的事項如何與案情有關。當然，此舉會加重訟費，但卻避免仲裁庭魯莽剔除具價值證據的風險。

V. 第五種類：搜證申請

一般的搜證申請有三：（一）就特定證據作出的搜證申請（Specific Discovery）；（二）就當事人管有的證據作妥善保管的申請；以及（三）要求仲裁以外的人士提供證供或文件證據。

筆者已解釋與搜證有關的法律原則。簡單而言，申請人須證明（一）有關人士的確管有相關的證物，並證明（二）所申請的證物是公正審訊所必須，並能有效減低審訊所需的時間和成本。

申請人必須解釋所搜證據如何與案情有關。仲裁庭不能容許當事人透過進行龐大的搜證活動，從中取巧，取得一堆無關緊要的文件後，以求從中找到一兩份有助案情的證物。

除非仲裁庭嚴格管理搜證過程，否則搜證工作很容易會被濫用。在二十一世紀，即使是小型公司的個人電腦中也保存著大量的電郵資料，如當事人在沒有明確目標的情況下要進行地毯式的搜證，不難想像過程可產生的高昂成本。

自然，複雜的商業糾紛必會涉及大量及繁雜的文件證據，處理這些證據必然產生大量費用。縱然如此，仲裁庭亦應與雙方共同探討如何合理地進行搜證，以確保合理安排資源。雙方應盡可能將焦點維持在對案件有必要性的證據，而非堅持透露所有僅對案情相關的非緊要證據上。

仲裁庭更可考慮提出修改「有關證據」的定義。例如就文件透露的要求，定位任何有助或不利己方的證據。這將現行法律的定義縮窄了，當事人不必透露任何可能「引起質詢」的材料。收窄後的定義把文件透露保持在與案情直接有關的證據，有助控制搜證的質和量。

如仲裁庭被邀請作搜證命令，其命令則應針對特定文件，而非概括地形容某一類的證據。仲裁庭應審慎考慮當事人，就某一類的文件所提出的搜證申請，在實際上是否會涉及大量與案情無直接關聯的證據。

舉例，當事人所提出的申請可能是：「所有能證明 X 的文件」。仲裁庭不能批准或作有關頒令，原因是有關的申請內容過於空泛。當事人如何決定某文件是否能證實 X？只有仲裁庭才具資格裁定某文件是否證明 X。故此，在頒布有關搜證令時，仲裁庭應明確指出特定的文件，如「在二零一二年四月一日發出的航運提單」或「在二零一一年十二月二十五日的董事會議記錄」。

仲裁庭有權要求當事人妥善保管某證據，或就某證據進行具舉證價值的試驗。例如查察令（Anton Pillar Order）容許申請人進入對方物業範圍內進行取證。有關的權利對當事人的權利具一定的侵犯性，故在考慮行使有關權力時，仲裁庭需交代具說服性的理由，並需要充分的證據。

仲裁庭並有要求證人出庭陳述或呈交證據的權力。此權力同樣具有侵犯性，故仲裁庭必須小心並留意所有相關情況，並盡量避免過分打擾證人的生活。

仲裁庭需給予相關證人充裕的時間，容許證人安排時間出庭。如需要證人帶同文件出席，仲裁庭則需明確指出何種文件。仲裁庭必須避免要求證人攜帶大量非必要的文件，避免盤問變成投機取巧的工具。

VI. 一般原則

上述是數個一般情況下仲裁庭會遇到的申請，例子並不包括所有可作出的申請，但透過上述例子筆者希望能帶出有效管理案件的重要性，並強調在處理有關申請時，仲裁庭應該留意的重點考慮。

除特定例子，在一般情況下仲裁庭對申請應如何取態？

按《示範法》，仲裁庭需要沿用適合案情的程序處理案件，達至公平的審訊，避免不必要的延誤和耗費不必要的的資源。[23]基於這個原則，仲裁庭必須有效率地著手管理案件，不能容許仲裁庭被連串的審訊前申請拖延處理案件的時間。

管理案件不是一門科學，與生活中其他手藝一樣，經驗和天賦對案件管理同等重要。但是，筆者認為以下的原則對所有仲裁員皆為適用。

首先，仲裁員在任何情況下必須保公持平。仲裁體制容許有心人透過玩弄程序爭取戰略優勢。作為仲裁員必須保障自己的命令不會導致給予任何一方過多或過少的權利。

第二，有效的案件管理需要仲裁庭關注時間以及資源的分配。

仲裁員需要堅持雙方在確定的時間表下達成指定的進度。在處理非審訊申請時，仲裁員在需要時，必須禮貌但強硬地質詢雙方，就某申請耗費的時間是否與解決問題的利益成正比。如當事人不能妥善解答這個問題，仲裁庭則應命令一套省時有效的案件管理指示，並解釋有關指示如何能協助案件的解決。

案件管理以及其他程序性的會議次數不應過多。每次會議應要有會議章程，而章程內容亦應在時間表定下的時間內解決。當事人應盡量透過單一會議處理多項申請，不應就每個申請舉行獨立會議，浪費金錢時間。

會議日期（包括審訊）一旦制定，則只有在特殊情況下方可更改。當事人必須明確解釋為何不能在指定日期參與會議。當事人或其法律代表不能在會議前夕以發現新法律理據推搪仲裁程序。

延誤有違公平原則。但很多當事人認為如果金錢能夠補償拖延對勝訴方造成的影響，則即使不按時行事亦無傷大雅。

但延誤並非僅是從經濟上補償對方的損失或利益。訴訟（和仲裁）會為當事人帶來情緒上的壓力。當事人須調動大量資金以支持持久的法律博弈，這些非在仲裁完結後，所得到的經濟利益所能彌補的。

延誤的結果，是拖慢受害人的補償和延長無辜被告的壓力。

為鼓勵當事人遵守時間表，仲裁庭可採用附帶條件命令。附帶條件命令說明違反命令條款的後果。附帶懲罰的命令相信能更有效協助仲裁庭在指定時間內處理糾紛。

當然，違令的後果必須清晰。舉例，命令的條款可以是：除非 X 在 T 日子和 D 時間內完成 X 事項，否則情況 C 將自動生效。

不過，附帶懲罰性與違令的性質應合乎比例，性質亦必須合乎邏輯。舉例說，如果當事人就狀書中的段落未能提供具體陳述，懲罰條件則可能為自動剔除有關段落。剔除的結果是當事人不能在審訊中依賴狀書中的有關空泛指控。不符比例的條件可能是把整個狀書或其他沒有問題的段落剔除。

在搜證上，如果當事人未能按令提交某文件，懲罰則可能是容許仲裁庭就文件內容作不利相關方面的推斷。

如果當事人沒有及時傳召事實和專家證人，懲罰則可能是拒絕考慮有關證人的逾時陳述。

如當事人屢次未能按令上繳保證金，仲裁庭則可考慮就違令剔除違令者部分或所有的案情，直接進行裁決。

如果當事人無理並嚴重拖延案件進度，仲裁庭應判令剔除有關方面的案情並命令有關方面不可繼續就案件進行仲裁程序。

《仲裁法例》第五十九條容許仲裁庭因不合理拖延而剔除申請。第五十九條要求申請人及時提出申請。有關條例將「不合理」定義為任何有機會對當事人作成不公平，或會損害當事人利益的延誤。

第三，仲裁庭應在仲裁中扮演主導角色。仲裁庭應堅持雙方盡早同意落實審訊需處理的主要爭議點。雙方在準備相關爭議點的過程中，可在仲裁庭協助下修改各爭議點的有關內容。

當然，仲裁庭的指引需雙方配合，從而影響仲裁進度。所以在採取主導的同時，仲裁庭需留意指引是否會干擾仲裁的整體進度。

仲裁庭應避免在不必要的情況下干擾雙方的準備工作。沒有人比當事人和其法律代表更清楚案情細節，故仲裁庭應尊重當事人所呈的案件方案，不應擅自偏離雙方同意的流程表。

良好的主導角色依賴仲裁員對案件有完善的準備。要準備充足，仲裁員需在每次處理申請前審閱有關文件，並仔細思考雙方的立論。仲裁庭不能在毫無準備的情況下，單單倚賴雙方的陳詞和引導去理解案件和進行裁決。

充足的準備能大大節省時間。如仲裁庭毋須雙方就案情背景陳詞，大家便可順暢並迅速地處理申請的重點。如某當事人的陳詞離題或難以明白，仲裁庭亦可即時點出要害或準確垂詢相關的重點。同時，在仲裁庭理解案情後，即可誘導雙方就確實存在爭議的事項辯論，毋須在無關緊要的案情上長篇大論。

第四，仲裁員的取態應強硬和實際，不應過分強調技術性，這代表仲裁時仲裁庭不應過分拘泥於法庭式的舉證規則。

仲裁的優勝在於程序上的靈活性。如仲裁庭過分拘泥程序恰當，則會大大減低仲裁的效率。如仲裁庭容許雙方肆意作技術性申請，仲裁則會變得比在高等法院商務案件更複雜。如此，仲裁便會失去競爭性。

第四部分　聆訊

I. 簡介

仲裁庭可單憑文件證據（包括證人供詞），以及雙方的陳詞就裁決下定案。但是，在大多數包含事實糾紛的案件中，仲裁庭應安排聆訊，讓雙方可盤問證人；讓仲裁庭定奪證人證供的真偽。

故此，整個仲裁審訊的證據應分兩大類：一是文件證據（包括專家報告）；以及口述證供（包括專家證人口供）。

文件證據通常會編列在文件夾中呈交各仲裁員。仲裁庭通常會在審訊前給予充分的時間就呈交文件作指引。

指引的內容應依案情需要採取相應的編列方法，例如按文件的時序、種類、題材等。仲裁庭曾經頒布的命令和指引通常應單獨陳列在另一個文件夾中。如仲裁陳述書中附帶文件證據，是否安排附件副本在相應位置一併陳列或分開陳列。如分開陳列，是否要求雙方在陳述書中指明陳列位置等。

雙方應積極減低陳列文件的數量，雙方只需提供支援案情所必須的文件。在訴訟中，很多文件是不需要的。例如如果當事人所依賴的只是某份文件的數個段落，則毋須呈上整份文件。同樣地，當事人只需把有關的收據、賬簿和其他會計記錄呈堂，而毋須提供所有記錄。理想的方法是把有關的會計記錄透過列表形式歸納在數頁紙上，並提供數個有關文件的樣本供仲裁庭參考。

有些人習慣把所有透露的材料都陳列在文件夾中。這是十分懶惰並欠缺建設性的做法。由於仲裁庭需要在審訊前閱讀有關文件，文件夾中越多雜亂無關的資料，仲裁庭需耗費的時間也越多。這是很費時失事的做法。當事人應盡量選擇與案情相關的文件陳列。

現時的大趨勢是將仲裁電子化。電子仲裁下當事人只需將狀書以及文件證據經數碼掃描存入硬盤或網上儲存庫，在審訊時透過電腦取閱即可。

電子仲裁的確能節省有限的紙張資源，卻不能省卻閱讀文件所需的時間。故即使仲裁他日能電子化，仲裁員依然要留意就呈堂文件給予適當的指示，以避免雙方把所有的文件上載。

一般的審訊有四個環節。首先，控辯方會先後呈交開案陳詞；第二，互相盤問證人；第三，輪流盤問雙方專家證人；第四，由辯方帶頭雙方開始結案陳詞。

II. 開案陳詞

開案陳詞可以口述、書面或書面陳詞口述補充的形式呈交仲裁庭。

無論用何種形式作出，開案陳詞均應明確指出案中主要的爭議點。陳詞的結構可以無爭議的事實背景為開首，然後列出雙方所爭議的事項，再陳述當事人就各爭議事項的立場和理據。在表明我方立場的同時，當事人亦可簡單表明對方立論的弱點。

為節省時間，筆者建議仲裁庭可考慮免卻口述開案，並鼓勵（或指令）雙方在開審前兩星期呈交書面開案陳詞。雙方的陳詞可幫助仲裁庭，進一步了解雙方將在審訊中重點依賴的證據，成為仲裁員了解各個文件夾的導讀文件。

有些仲裁員在時間緊迫下會就開案陳詞的篇幅加上諸多的限制，比如是指定陳詞的最高頁數，或是限制版面的闊窄等。限制的原因是仲裁庭擔心雙方呈上的文件會加長閱讀時間，在仲裁庭緊絀的時間表上百上加斤。

筆者個人不提倡仲裁庭就開案陳詞的格式長短作過多的規限。雙方應自由決定陳詞的篇幅形式。

審訊中書面及口述的部分應有相應的比例。如果仲裁庭免卻口述陳詞，則應容許雙方盡情透過書面向仲裁庭作完整的陳述。反之，如果仲裁庭規限書面陳詞只是列出案情重點，則應容許雙方充裕時間作口頭陳述以圓滿解釋雙方的理論邏輯。

原則上，如果仲裁庭限制雙方的口頭陳述，則不應阻止雙方透過書面作完整陳詞。

III. 證人

雙方的證人會被傳召到仲裁庭就其供詞接受盤問。申索人的證人會首先作供。證人會首先被傳召方作主問，然後接受對方的盤問，作供以證人接受傳召方的補充提問作結。

仲裁的證人同樣是在宣誓情況下作供，故第五十六條給予仲裁員見證宣誓的權利（雙方有權就宣誓另作安排）。

一般而言，主問方不可作誘導性提問。誘導性問題是在問題本身提供答案，比如是：「你曾經作過某事情，是嗎？」又或是「你做某事情的原因是你想達到某目的，對嗎？」

只有在盤問對方證人的時候才可提誘導性問題。

筆者提議雙方採納證人的書面供詞作為作供的主要內容。這代表除了少量就澄清供詞內容所作出的補充性問題外，主問的時間不應超過數分鐘。這也代表多數證人作供時會馬上接受盤問。

盤問過程可能耗時甚久。當事人或其法律代表很多時會向證人提出無聊、重複、空泛或與案情無關的問題。故在證人作供時仲裁庭應仔細留意發問方的問題，如果在數個提問後仲裁庭對問題與案情的關切性不明所以，便應詢問發問方澄清問題與案情的相關性。如發問方不能解釋問題的關切性，仲裁庭則應引導發問方就另項爭議重點進行盤問。

以公平計，被控方必須有機會就針對他的指控作回應。盤問者應向證人指出所有涉及，或針對該證人作出的指控，讓證人有機會就指控直接回應。法律上，舉證規則中有著名的 *Brown v Dunn* 一案。[24] 該案列明，任何作出指控的一方必須將指控的重點事實透過盤問向與該指控事實有關的證人指出。

舉例說，若果申訴人認為某證人的證供不實，則應向其指出不實處，讓證人澄清及就指控作辯護。

如當事人未有按 *Brown v Dunn* 向證人明確指出指控，則不能在結案時質疑有關證人的可信性。

在訴訟中，古板的盤問方法為嚴謹遵守 *Brown v Dunn* 舉證原則，律師通常會在盤問末段提出一連串「你是否同意指控？」的問題。通常這些問題在盤問時證人經已回答（通常的答案是「不同意」）。就 *Brown v Dunn* 所作出，不假思索的盤問會浪費法庭很多時間。

相反，仲裁庭可在公平情況下彈性處理舉證規則，務求在辦案時保持公平，並在時間上保持效率。在公平原則下，仲裁庭可就證人作供提出以下安排：[25]

1. 證人的供詞明顯地就某指控作了表態，盤問者則毋須重複詢問證人是否同意某指控；

2. 就算盤問者未有明確地向證人提出指控，只要盤問整體已經給予證人合理的機會就某指控提出合理解釋的機會，盤問者即可在結案陳詞中就證人的可信性提出懷疑。

在盤問後，主問方可向證人作補充提問，但內容必須是澄清盤問內容。

補充提問的一方不能作誘導性的發問。慣性的技巧是在提問一開始便向證人指出，他在盤問時就某問題作出的回應，然後向他指出與其回應不一致的證據。在證人研究有關證據後，提問方便可不設誘導性的提問證人，是否需要澄清或補充剛才接受盤問時的回答。

當然，上述整個過程只不過是想解釋證人作供上的不如意，並透過證據向證人提醒正確答案，證人所作的補充往往只是讀出文件證據的內容。

在合理範圍內「補充」應獲仲裁庭所容許。但如果補充提問變成當事人透過證人讀出文件夾內的每個文件，則證供的可信性便存疑。仲裁庭應加以管制沒有可信性的作供。

IV. 專家證人

在很多商業糾紛中，專家證人一般會在事實證人完成供詞後作供。這容許專家能就聽取事實作供後更全面地作供。

專家作供的程序與其他證人無異。但仲裁庭可考慮把在某範疇內的雙方專家證人安排一起作供，這有兩個方法：

第一是安排同一範疇的抗辯方專家證人在申訴方作供後作供以及回應。

第二個辦法是澳洲常用的「溫泉式」專家作供。在這個安排下仲裁庭會與某範疇的雙方專家進行會議。會議中雙方當事人、仲裁庭與專家會共同就專門爭議作討論，並謀取有關的共識。如雙方不能達至共識，仲裁庭則會按會議內容就該爭議進行裁決。

「溫泉式」的會議作供在一開始時遇到很多爭議。但在很多地方已被接納成常見和有效的專家作供模式（特別在澳洲新南威爾士）。當然，會議需要仲裁庭就專家事項有充分的準備和主持會議的技巧。

V. 結案陳詞

傳統的做法是自完成證人作供後由抗辯方作口述結案。

但仲裁庭可休庭數日，容許雙方在書面陳詞，在復庭前一到兩天呈交仲裁庭。

第二個做法的優點是仲裁庭可按雙方的書面陳詞更準確的知道雙方的案情重點，更容易在裁決時總結。另外，在閱讀書面陳詞後，仲裁庭可在復庭時向雙方提出任何額外的問題。

若雙方能自由決定書面結案的格式和內容，仲裁庭可指示雙方在復庭只就陳詞內容作補充，以及就對方陳詞內容中的新內容作回應。

結案的內容應呼應開案陳詞。雙方應回答在開案時所提出的案件爭議重點。雙方應考慮爭議重點是否隨著審訊過程變得更為清晰或重要。然後雙方逐一指出對方就每個爭議所提出的論據，並逐一指出雙方立論的錯誤。最後，雙方應強調期望仲裁庭給予的濟助。

雙方就釐清爭議重點的努力能幫助及為仲裁庭提供裁決理由的框架，使仲裁庭更能清晰地分析和審理案件。

第五部分　裁決

仲裁庭在任何適當的時候都能作出裁決，[26] 並能同時就不同時間就爭議不同的部分作裁決。[27] 書面裁決的格式並沒有一定的規格，但是按書寫判詞的原則，書面裁決大概應包含兩個部分。

第一部分是就仲裁過程作程序性記錄。裁決道出雙方間的仲裁協議和雙方的爭議。之後裁決敘述性地指出仲裁庭的委任和開庭審案的過程。敘述記錄雙方曾呈交仲裁庭的狀書和仲裁庭曾發過的指令，並指出仲裁庭正式審理案件的時間。

裁決首部分的末段應明確指出：仲裁庭在聽取及考慮雙方提供的證據和相關的仲裁狀書及陳詞後，現作出以下裁決命令。有關命令的詳細原因在裁決第二部分詳述，裁決的原因是整個裁決的一部分。

筆者提議仲裁庭在書寫裁決原因時可跟隨與以下相若的結構：[28]

1. 簡介部分：應歸納雙方同意讓仲裁庭裁決的爭議問題；

2. 背景部分：歸納雙方不爭議的案情，並簡述要解決相關問題所必須考慮的適用法律，有關法律的解釋只需足夠讓讀者明白仲裁庭的裁決即可；

3. 討論部分：將簡介內指出的問題逐一作仔細解答和解釋裁決理由。在解釋原因時，仲裁庭應把該問題的「敗訴方」論據列出，並解釋該論點為何不被接納；

4. 總結部分：仲裁庭列出裁決的決定，並仔細地列出命令和濟助的細節。

分開兩部分書寫裁決的原因是方便在需要把裁決轉化成法庭判決時，法庭能即時採納裁決第一部分（裁決的流程和命令的總結）成公開的判決。涉及雙方私隱細節的第二部分則不被公開。

按《仲裁條例》第六十一條，裁決必須以書面作出，並要有仲裁員簽署。裁決必須附有日期，並指明仲裁地點。裁決必須附上理由。仲裁過程以「最終裁決」作結。[29] 故仲裁庭需留意相關仲裁規則的時間條款，避免一不留意讓裁決失效。[30]

仲裁庭的權力在仲裁完結後即告失效。法律上，這代表仲裁庭失去司法管轄權就爭議的任何部分作任何裁決。唯一的例外是雙方按第六十九條申請仲裁庭更正或解釋已作出的裁決。[31]

裁決頒布後可能會有其他事項需要仲裁庭處理，通常的事項包括仲裁費用的審核和分配，或就某初步裁決作跟進。

由於有善後需要，仲裁庭在審訊後所頒布的裁決通常叫做「最終裁決首部分」或其他類似字眼，以突顯仲裁庭的管核權尚未完結。

仲裁庭頒布濟助的權力與法庭的民事法庭對等。[32] 故除非雙方另行協議，否則仲裁庭可強制要求當事人作特定行為，如履行合約等。要注意的是，無論雙方是否另有協議，仲裁庭均無權強行執行土地協議或任何給予任何涉及土地的濟助。

仲裁庭可要求雙方支付仲裁全部或部分的訟費。[33] 在考慮訟費時仲裁庭需考慮雙方間曾作出的和解協議。

實際上，仲裁庭在裁決前並不知悉雙方的和解過程，以避免仲裁庭被協議影響。因此，仲裁庭可在裁決中就訟費作初步分配，並在得悉和解過程的細節後，才按協議條件或於裁決後才調整訟費決定。

另一個辦法是雙方能向仲裁庭呈上藏有和解提議的保密信。仲裁庭承諾只有在裁決頒布後，考慮訟費時方會參考信件內容。

除非雙方協議訟費由法庭審核，否則仲裁庭必須決定仲裁訟費數目。[34]

仲裁庭需送遞裁決給予雙方。[35] 但若仲裁庭未被完全支付其費用時，仲裁庭則有權扣留裁決直至收到費用為止。[36] 如果雙方認為仲裁費用太高，當事人可向法庭申請調整仲裁庭收費。[37]

第六部分　總結

此章詳細道出從委任仲裁庭起到頒布裁決的過程，並嘗試列舉過程中仲裁庭通常會遇到的問題和提議可行的解決方法。讀者可在此章找到仲裁庭常會遇到的申請和處理的辦法。仲裁員可在此章找到在辦理案件時應注意的事項。

第二章的重點為：

1. 申索人向抗辯人發出仲裁要求書展開仲裁；

2. 仲裁庭應以單數成員組成，以避免裁決發生僵局情況。仲裁庭成員越多，所涉及的費用也越高。同時，即使是三人的仲裁庭也通常會出現仲裁員時間調配的困難。故此，當事人應認真考慮是否真正需要多於一人組成仲裁庭；

3. 在接受委任時，仲裁員應確定自己有足夠能力和時間處理爭議。同時，仲裁員需確保自己與案件不會有表面或實際的利益衝突。仲裁員應分析雙方的仲裁協議，確保協議起碼具爭議性（arguable）地給予仲裁庭管轄權去處理目前的爭議。

4. 開庭前，仲裁庭應就狀書（包括就狀書內容索取詳情）、事實證人、專家證人，針對性證據披露以及審訊日期等作安排和指引；

5. 按《仲裁條例》第三十五和五十六條，仲裁庭有權頒布臨時濟助。第三十五和五十六條有重複處。但就禁制令而言，第五十六條主要容許仲裁庭就促進仲裁審訊發出命令；

6. 仲裁庭需留意自己會否頒布或重複法庭已經頒布的命令。除非仲裁庭與當事人謹慎留意，否則雙方很容易浪費時間、資源，徘徊於法庭與仲裁庭之間衍生重複性的臨時性申請；

7. 在準備審訊時，仲裁庭可能要處理：質疑其管轄權的申請、要求仲裁庭命令保證金、釐清爭議事項、剔出狀書內容以及進一步取證的申請等。仲裁庭要主動而公平地處理有關申請。仲裁員應分析有關申請對解決爭議的相關利弊，並應確保雙方按時遵守仲裁庭所頒布的命令；

8. 仲裁庭在開庭審訊時亦應留意程序是否公平，有關考慮應包含時間和訟費的考慮；

9. 審訊後，仲裁庭需頒布書面裁決。裁決需要包括理由和能排解爭議的命令。在頒布最終命令後，仲裁庭的管轄權亦同時告終；

10. 仲裁庭有責任把裁決交予雙方當事人，但當事人在取得裁決前必須繳付所有仲裁庭的費用；

11. 在整個仲裁過程中，仲裁庭應務求釐清以及針對指出雙方爭議間的真正重點。

---

1. 第三十一條。

2. 第二十四條（《示範法》第十一條）。

3. 第二十五條（《示範法》第十二條）。

4. [2002] AC 358 (HL).

5. 第二十六條（《示範法》第十三條）。

6. 第四十八條（《示範法》第二十條）。

7. 第五十條（《示範法》第二十二條）。

8. 第五十一條（《示範法》第二十三條），針對狀書的一般規定。

9. 在這情況下，仲裁庭第一指引的內容則會與下列的指引二相同。

10. 第五十二條（《示範法》第二十四條）。

11. 《示範法》第十七條。《仲裁條例》第五十六條並未參照任何《示範法》條文。

12. 詳看二零一二年三月十九日《南華早報》標題 "Rise in Arbitrators' Powers Queried" 的報導。

13. 《示範法》第十七條。

14. 在仲裁庭處理當事人單方面提出（如禁制令等）的臨時濟助申請時，仲裁庭可在聽取受制方理據前頒布初步命令（第三十七條，《示範法》第十七B條（1））。初步命令的定義為防止受制方「阻撓所請求的臨時措施的目的」。初步命令的有效期為二十天。仲裁庭有權在聽取受制方陳詞後繼續或更改有關命令。第三十八條（《示範法》第十七C（五）條）定明雙方當事人均受仲裁庭命令所限制，但法庭並不會自動協助執行有關命令。初步命令並非裁決的一部分。不過，仲裁庭有權在當事人要求的情況下，以裁決的方式頒布臨時命令（非初步命令），一旦作出裁決，當事人便可按《仲裁條例》第十部分把有關裁決轉化成法庭命令。

15. 根據普通法中「合同相對性」（privity）原則，只有契約雙方才受契約限制。

16. 原則為：某爭議一旦經過合格的途徑被處理，法庭則不會容許同一糾紛透過訴訟從新進行審理。

17. 這些原則與筆者在《淺談新民事司法訴訟》第二章陳述的五個申請臨時濟助的原則相同。

18. London: 1995 (11th ed.).

19. 第三十七條（《示範法》第十七B條）。

20. 第四十一條（《示範法》第十七F條）。

21. 第三十六條（《示範法》第十七A條）。

22. 第三十八條（《示範法》第十七C條）。

23. 第四十六條（《示範法》第十八條）。

24. [1894] 6 R 67.

25. 陳志海資深大律師曾把就 *Brown v. Dunn* 的修飾演繹稱為 "the deem put"（譯者按：隱性質詢）。

26. 第七十二條。

27. 第七十一條。

28. 筆者同意並引述 James Raymond 教授就何謂好判詞所提出的觀點。

29. 第六十八條（《示範法》第三十二條）。

30. 法律用語。源於拉丁文動詞 "fungi"。詞語的字面意思為：「已完成〔自身的任務〕」。

31. 《示範法》第三十三條。

32. 《仲裁條例》第七十條。

33. 第七十四條。

34. 第七十四（五）至（九）條。在評估仲裁費用時，仲裁員必須考慮案件所有有關情況，並作出合理的評估。除非雙方另行同意，否則仲裁員有權評估在仲裁展開前當時人在準備仲裁期間所花耗的費用。

35. 第六十七（四）條。

36. 第七十七條。

37. 參閱第七十七（二）至（四）條。在當事人與仲裁庭之間就費用存有合約的情況下，仲裁庭的費用不能按此程序更改。

第三章　仲裁規則縱觀

《示範法》容許仲裁雙方隨意採納任何仲裁機構訂立的規則。
被採納的規則將在《示範法》的框架內。

本章歸納了五種在亞洲仲裁中比較常用的規則，分別為：香
港國際仲裁中心機構仲裁規則、新加坡國際仲裁中心仲裁規
則（SIAC）、倫敦海事仲裁員協會條款（LMAA）、國際商
會仲裁規則（ICC）及中國國際經濟貿易仲裁委員會仲裁規則
（CIETAC）。

第一部分　香港國際仲裁中心機構仲裁規則

此規則的生效日期為二零零八年九月一日。

I. 常規條款

雙方能在爭議發生前透過合約，或是在爭議發生後透過仲裁協議採用仲裁為解決糾紛的方法。

在應用上，雙方可以純粹採納規則為仲裁程序（不涉及香港國際仲裁中心），或者是採用香港仲裁中心按規則監管仲裁的進行。[1]當雙方採用後者，仲裁中心便會介入仲裁，在需要時協助雙方委任仲裁員和確保仲裁按規矩所訂立的模式和進度進行。

規則第二條規管通知和時間的計算。在適當情況下，仲裁中心秘書處可以順延期限。

誰擁有規則的釋譯權？按規則第三條，仲裁庭能就「涉及仲裁員權力和義務的『條文』內容」進行釋譯。就其他事項，由香港仲裁中心理事會保留釋譯權。

II. 展開仲裁

仲裁由仲裁中心接到申訴人的仲裁通知日期展開。如果通知是以書面遞交，申訴人須準備足夠副本提供給所有參與仲裁的各方，包括香港仲裁中心。

仲裁通知書[2]的內容應包括：要求將爭議透過仲裁解決、仲裁各方以及其法律代表的姓名、地址和聯絡方式、雙方間的仲裁協議、涉及爭議的合同或相關的法律文件、對爭議的簡單描述、要求的金額或其他濟助，以及仲裁庭的人數。

遞交通知時申訴人需按香港仲裁中心訂立的「仲裁收費和費用表」繳付受理費。

受理仲裁後，仲裁中心秘書處會將通知轉交答辯方，並要求答辯方在三十日內就通知書的內容作出答覆。答覆內容應包括：是否質疑仲裁庭的管轄權、就通知內容的意見、是否接受申訴人提出的金額或其他要求、是否接受仲裁庭人數的安排。

仲裁中心會把回覆轉交申訴人，並會向仲裁庭提交通知和回覆的副本。

在仲裁的所有過程中，仲裁雙方都能透過代表進行，但不一定要委任律師代表。[3]

III. 委任仲裁員與仲裁庭

如果仲裁雙方不同意仲裁庭的人數，仲裁中心理事會將代為決定。理事會的決定將考慮爭議涉及的金額、複雜性、當事人的國籍、行業慣例、合適仲裁員的人數，以及爭議本身的急切性等等。仲裁雙方在理事會決定前將被邀請，就仲裁庭的委任向理事會提供意見。

如果最後仲裁庭由一位仲裁員組成，正式的委任會在三十天內完成。如果仲裁需要三位仲裁員聯合處理，委任程序則需按規則第八條處理。大致上，仲裁雙方可自行按喜好委任各一位仲裁員，然後經委任的仲裁員共同委任第三位仲裁員。如果第三位仲裁員遲遲不能定案，那理事會則會代為委任第三位仲裁員。

在需要理事會決定仲裁庭人數的情況下，理事會需要諮詢至少三位香港國際仲裁中心的委任諮詢委員會成員。委員會的意見為保密並不具約束力。所有委任（無論是一位或是三位仲裁員）事前都需經理事會確認。

規則第十一點一條要求仲裁員時刻保持「公正和獨立於當事人」。獲委任的仲裁員必須透露任何可能影響其公正和獨立性的情況。如果對仲裁員的合適性有質疑，可在仲裁員獲委任後的十五天內，或在獲悉或理應獲悉質疑理由後的十五天內作出。

規則第十一點二定明，除非雙方同意，否則在仲裁雙方為不同國籍的情況下，仲裁的單一或首席仲裁員應委任第三國籍的仲裁員擔任。

對仲裁員合適性的質疑由仲裁中心理事會處理。如果質疑成立，仲裁員將被取締。除非雙方另行安排，否則新的仲裁員被委任後，仲裁將在上一任仲裁員離去前的階段繼續。

IV. 仲裁 [4]

規則條文十四點一定明仲裁庭必須「採用適當的程序仲裁，以避免不必要的延誤和費用」。但這責任是有條件的，所採用的程序「須保證平等對待各方，並使各方均有合理機會陳述其主張」。

條文十四點七道出，仲裁雙方協助仲裁過程公平順暢的相應的責任：「當事各方應為所需為，以確保仲裁公平而又有效率」。

故此，雙方不應在仲裁時鉅細無遺地就每一個論點（不論好壞大小）作大篇幅的陳述，以拖延仲裁的進度並花耗雙方的資源。應謹記雙方和其代表有責任協助仲裁庭達至公平並有效率的裁決。

承上所述，仲裁庭應在仲裁展開後盡早制定一份基本時間表，並予仲裁各方商討，[5]並把時間表的副本遞交仲裁中心存檔。

雙方不能單方面與仲裁員通訊。規則條文十四點四要求所有與仲裁員的通訊均需複印送予仲裁各方。

仲裁庭在需要的情況下，可和在雙方商議後委任一位秘書協助處理仲裁事務。[6]

如獲仲裁當事人要求，仲裁庭可以追加一或多名未涉及仲裁的第三者作為仲裁當事人。[7]此舉必須獲申請方和第三方的書面同意。

按規則條文十五，除非雙方另行同意，否則仲裁應在香港進行。可是，按案件的實際情況，仲裁庭可在其認為適當的任何地方進行會面，聽取證人口供或口頭辯述。即使仲裁涉及海外元素，規則條文十五點四都將裁決視為在仲裁地點作出。

如果在仲裁庭組成前，雙方尚未互通申請和答覆書，仲裁庭可就仲裁文件交換給予指示。仲裁庭一般會安排雙方交換申請書（列明仲裁雙方的身份、描述案情、案情引發的關鍵爭議點和申索的賠償），有助證明申請書內容的相關文件應附案送交仲裁各方。收到申請書後回應方需草擬答辯書。答辯書的內容應回應申請書的內容，並包括任何反申訴，或就爭議仲裁庭的管轄權提出事實或法律理據。

仲裁文件的內容可以在仲裁庭容許的情況下更改。仲裁庭會在考慮有關更改會否為仲裁帶來延誤和對雙方的影響後決定是否容許更改申請。即使容許，更改都有可能影響仲裁的費用分配。

規則條文二十就仲裁庭管轄權作定義。

條文二十點一保留了《普通法》中的自裁管轄原則（competence-competence）。按義，仲裁庭有權定奪自身針對某爭議點的管轄權。規則條文二十點二定明雙方合約中的仲裁條款的個別獨立性，也就是說即使合約應某些原因作廢，雙方間的仲裁協議並不會因合約的廢除而失效。規則條文二十點三指出所有挑戰管轄權的理據應盡可能在答覆仲裁通知時提出。否則，答辯人最遲必須在答辯書中否認仲裁庭的管轄權。如果申述人對答辯方作出的反申訴提出管轄權挑戰，其反對則需要在反申訴答覆中提出。

仲裁庭可以決定，是否有需要在仲裁申請書和答辯書之外，要求更多的書面陳述。[8]

規則條文二十二書面陳述的交換需在四十五天內完成，仲裁庭可以酌情延長有關時限。

規則條文二十三管理仲裁在審理階段時的證據安排。

按規則條文二十三點一，仲裁雙方有責任就其所依據的事實舉證。由於雙方均需提交證據，仲裁庭可能要求雙方提供一份證據概要，概要內應列出雙方依據的事實以及相應的文件證明。

仲裁庭可以就證人舉證作指示，包括制定合適的方法聽取一般和專家證人的證供。[9]仲裁雙方均可訪問證人。

仲裁庭可單方面委派專家證人就裁決糾紛提供協助。[10]

除非雙方同意，否則仲裁審訊過程全部保密。

規則條文二十三點十容許仲裁庭自行決定證據的處理。仲裁庭能決定是否跟隨法定的嚴格證據規則。仲裁庭能自行決定雙方提供的證據是否被接受、是否與爭議相關、是否重要和是否可信。

規則條文二十四賦予仲裁庭權力，於仲裁進行期間頒布臨時保護措施。臨時保護令將以臨時裁決的形式，令雙方採取相應的措施以確保和平衡雙方利益。

如當事人不遵從仲裁規則或仲裁庭所作出的指令，而又不能合理解釋抗命理由，仲裁庭有權強制性繼續仲裁並頒布最終裁決。[11]

當仲裁庭認為雙方已有合理機會陳述己方論點，仲裁庭便應宣布審理完結，按雙方所陳述的論點作為裁決的根據。[12]

如當事人知道（或理應知道）有人違反仲裁規則，便應即時向仲裁庭提出反對。[13] 在明知違規的情況下繼續仲裁可能被視為當事人就違規放棄反對權利。

V. 裁決 [14]

如仲裁庭由三位仲裁員組成，裁決應以眾數作準。[15]

仲裁庭在頒布最終裁決前有權頒布臨時、中期或部分裁決，並在非終局的裁決就仲裁費用作安排。[16]

所有裁決均應以書面頒布。[17] 頒布的裁決對仲裁當事人具最終約束力，故當事人有義務立即履行裁決命令。

裁決必須解釋所依據的理由，並由所有仲裁員簽注列明有關的時間地點。有效的裁決應附有香港國際仲裁中心的印章。

裁決必須按雙方於仲裁協議中所選擇的法律，或在雙方沒有同意的情況下，按於爭議最具密切關係的法律處理。[18] 只有在雙方同意的情況下仲裁庭才可運用「友好調停者」（amiable compositeur）或「公允善良」（ex aequo et bono）[19] 原則達致裁決。

規則條文三十二列明如雙方在仲裁終結前和解的處理辦法。

規則條文三十三至三十五指出雙方要求仲裁庭解釋、更正和補充裁決的權利。

規則條文三十六列明仲裁庭計算相關費用和收費標準。有關費用的計算可以在規則附帶的收費表中找到。

規則條文三十七列明雙方預付仲裁費用的安排。

VI. 其他條款 [20]

如糾紛涉及的金額不超過二十五萬美元，除非雙方另行同意，否則仲裁便應按照規則條文三十八點二所制定的簡易程序進行。

規則條文三十九提供了全面及詳細的保密條款，以確保仲裁過程以及當事人的身份得以保障。

規則條文四十列出了香港國際仲裁中心的免責條款。

第二部分　新加坡國際仲裁中心仲裁規則 [21]

新加坡國際仲裁中心於一九九一年成立，是一所獨立的非牟利機構，旨在為國際商貿提供中立的仲裁服務。[22]

最新的仲裁規則於二零一零年七月一日生效。

所有交予新加坡仲裁中心處理的仲裁均按其規則進行。[23] 如果規則所定與適用的法律有所衝突，則應以法律規定為準。

規則條文二就通知安排與時限提供仔細描述。所有與仲裁相關的通知、通訊以及建議均應以書面進行。通知送出後，按規則所定在同一日視為被對方收到。

仲裁經申訴人向中心主簿登記仲裁通知書展開。通知書內容須包括規則條文三所列出的要求。

抗辯人須在收到仲裁通知書後十四天內向中心主簿登記答覆書。答覆書須符合規則條文四所定的要求。

如果爭議的總金額（包括要求賠償、反指控以及雙方可抵銷的金額總和）不超過新加坡幣五百萬，仲裁雙方便可考慮在仲裁庭組成前要求仲裁按規則條文五所定的「快速程序」進行。[24]

按「快速程序」進行的仲裁通常由單一仲裁員處理。仲裁雙方和中心主簿可按糾紛的複雜程度或其他因素決定是否要求三位仲裁員聯合組成仲裁庭。[25]

仲裁員「必須保持獨立和中立，不得有任何為當事人代言辯護的行為」。[26] 中心主席有權委任仲裁員，在委任仲裁員時，主席必須確保該仲裁員有足夠時間處理仲裁事宜，並有足夠能力高速及高效率地達成裁決。

仲裁員在獲委任前必須向仲裁雙方、中心主簿以及其他仲裁庭成員披露任何可能令人對其中立性產生合理懷疑的情況。披露必須在合理時間內作出。[27]

如就仲裁員的中立性存有合理懷疑，雙方可以在收到仲裁員指定通知後十四日內申請要求仲裁員迴避。[28] 迴避的最終決定權在董事局委員會。委員會至少由兩名仲裁中心的董事組成。

仲裁庭應在徵詢當事人後根據雙方接受的方式進行仲裁。[29] 無論何種形式，仲裁庭均應確保仲裁能以一套公平、有效、經濟以及具終局性的環境下達成裁決。為達致以上原則，仲裁庭能決定審理事項的先後次序，將糾紛分階段處理，剔除重複或無關的證據，並指示當事人就某些重要的爭議點作針對性陳述。

如需要，仲裁庭應就書面陳述作指示。通常的陳述書包括申訴書、答辯書及其他補充文件。[30] 所有陳述書應附帶支持其內容的文件證據。如果有人違反仲裁庭指示，仲裁庭有權作出其認為適當的相應指示。

規則條文十八容許當事人自行決定仲裁地。在沒有相應約定的情況下，規則選用新加坡為首要仲裁地。仲裁庭有權按爭議的實際情況決定是否選用其他更合適的地方作為仲裁地。不論仲裁地的選擇如何，案件的實質審理可以在任何地方進行。

仲裁庭可以決定仲裁採用的語言，[31] 並可決定哪些文件應被翻譯成該語言。

仲裁雙方可以聘請具專業資格的法律代表或任何其他代表處理仲裁事項。[32]

規則條文二十一、二十二及二十三相應地定明就開庭審理、證人和專家證人，以及由仲裁庭委任專家事項作規定。

規則條文二十四賦予仲裁庭一系列的額外權利。仲裁庭可以在不抵觸相應法律的情況下行使這些權力；包括更正合同、裁定豁免權（律師或其他適用豁免權）。值得一提的是按規則條文二十四點十，仲裁庭可以勒令當事人「不得分散資產，確保仲裁程序中可能作出的裁決得到履行或執行」。

規則條文二十五沿襲了仲裁庭自裁管轄原則和肯定了合約中仲裁條款的獨立性。如果在仲裁庭組成前當事人對仲裁管轄權有異議，仲裁中心的董事委員會，將負責按表面證據，決定爭議是否隸屬仲裁管轄範圍。如果表面證據不支持爭議交由仲裁解決，所有仲裁過程將被擱置。

規則條文二十六容許仲裁庭頒布各種臨時保護措施。仲裁庭可以要求當事人交納保證金去換取相應的臨時命令。在仲裁庭組成前，當事人可按規則〈附則一〉所規定的緊急程序作出相應申請。

仲裁庭應按雙方同意的法律達致裁決。[33] 在雙方沒有選擇適用法律時，仲裁庭應按爭議本身決定合適法律。只有在雙方同意的情況下仲裁庭才可運用友好調停者（amiable compositeur）或公允善良（ex aequo et bono）原則達致裁決。

在仲裁庭認為當事人「不需要提交進一步的關聯性實質證據或陳訴書」時，便可宣布審理程序終結。[34] 在宣布審理終結的四十五天內仲裁庭便須向仲裁中心主簿呈交裁決草案。中心主簿可就裁決草案提出形式上的更改建議。在不影響仲裁庭自主決定權的前提下，主簿可提示仲裁庭注意實體裁決的某些內容。在仲裁中心主簿批准前，仲裁庭不能向當事人頒布任何裁決。

規則條文二十八點九規定當事人須承擔裁決結果，並須及時地履行裁決義務。條文規定就仲裁結果，雙方已在合法的情況下，無悔地放棄了任何形式的上訴權，承諾不會向任何國家的司法機構就裁決提出上訴、審查或追訴。至裁決日期起，裁決的結果是具終局性並對當事人有約束力。

規則條文二十九容許仲裁庭就裁決的文書錯誤作更改，並賦予仲裁庭作補充裁決的權利。

規則條文三十詳列了仲裁員收費、仲裁費用以及相應訂金的計算安排。規則條文三十三指出仲裁庭可以命令一方當事人在負擔仲裁費用外額外支付對方的法律費用。

規則條文三十四為新加坡仲裁中心的免責條款。仲裁的保密條款為規則條文三十五。

按規則條文三十六的一般安排，董事局主席、仲裁中心主簿和仲裁庭有權利解釋規則所沒有列明的事宜。行使以上權利的前提是確保仲裁能在公平、快捷和具成本效益的環境下達成裁決和其執行。中心主簿可在適當時候發布執行守則以確保仲裁規則能有效執行。

第三部分　倫敦海事仲裁員協會仲裁規則 [35]（LMAA Terms）

倫敦海事仲裁員協會於一九六零年成立，由一班來自波羅的海交易所的成員所組成。時至今天，倫敦海事仲裁員協會由正式會員和輔助會員所組成。

協會與香港和新加坡的仲裁中心不同之處是協會並不監管仲裁過程，協會的規則只供當事人作程序性的參考。

現行的協會規則在二零一二年一月一日實施。

規則的目的是制定一套公平、具效率和成本效益的程序，讓糾紛可以盡快透過仲裁解決。[36] 仲裁員按規則有責任公平及中立地就糾紛進行裁決，不可視其職責是為委任人服務。

仲裁展開日期以英國仲裁法一九九六年所定為準。[37]

仲裁雙方須同意採納規則作為仲裁守則。[38] 如雙方所委任的單一仲裁員，或仲裁庭所有成員均為海事仲裁員協會的正式成員，雙方則被視在採納協會規則為適用守則。

在協會規則適用，並在雙方沒有另行同意的情況下，適用於爭議的法律為《英國法》。[39]

仲裁過程由英國《仲裁法》監管。[40] 但如果仲裁地點不在英國，協會規則的應用則必須符合仲裁所應用的法律。

如果仲裁協議沒有決定仲裁員人數，仲裁庭應由三位仲裁員組成。協會規則第八段列出了委任三人仲裁庭的程序。簡單說，雙方各委派一位仲裁員，並由雙方仲裁員共同委派第三位仲裁庭成員。在雙方沒有另行指使的情況下，第三位仲裁員將充當仲裁庭主席。

協會規則段落九列出在委派了兩位仲裁員的情況下指派第三位裁判員的程序。裁判員的職責是了解仲裁內容並參與審案，但只在兩位仲裁員不能就裁決達成共識的情況下，取代兩位仲裁員的位置，就糾紛作單獨裁決。

仲裁庭的管轄權包括所有經雙方同意透過仲裁解決的爭議，以及涉及爭議及與其有關的事項。[41] 仲裁庭有權決定在何時以及如何處理相關事項。

仲裁庭決定所有程序與舉證事項。仲裁庭可按情況安排證供和陳詞；以口頭或書面形式呈上仲裁庭。[42] 因此，仲裁當事人應考慮同意仲裁以純書面形式進行，又或是要求仲裁庭開庭聽取證人供詞。

仲裁庭享有一切英國《仲裁法》所賦予的權力。另外，協會規則段落十四列出了一些額外的權利，供仲裁庭在適當時候用，以避免非必要的延誤和支出，並就爭議事項提供公平的裁決。舉例說，仲裁庭可以否決專家證人的需要，或是限制需要專家證人協助的事項。仲裁庭可以合併基於相同事實或法律基礎的糾紛進行審理。如果申訴人違反仲裁庭命令，不提交保證金，仲裁庭可以擱置仲裁的部分或全部內容等。

仲裁庭可以在正式審議案件前與當事人進行初期會議，[43] 讓仲裁庭了解案件的準備進度；讓雙方就審理的程序事項達成共識和容許仲裁庭作出其他指示等。就複雜的案件而言，初期會議是強制性的。一般來說，如果案件需要開庭五天或以上，便應進行初期會議。在某些個別情況下，雙方可能需要參與多過一次的初步會議。

在出席初期會議前，當事人應準備會議章程，[44] 並向仲裁庭提供與仲裁相關的文件；列表陳述一切雙方已經做出和將會作出行動，和列出希望仲裁庭作出的指示。雙方在列表中應估計審訊需時，並評估雙方是否就正式審理準備妥當。

協會規則十六處理雙方在收到裁決前達成和解協議的情況。

協會規則十八是處理休庭的安排。仲裁庭如需休庭，可就其費用和花費獲中期付款。

通常來說，裁決應在仲裁完結後的六個星期內頒布。[45] 在處理緊急爭議時裁決時間應相應地縮短。如果仲裁是純粹按書面文件進行裁決，若被問及，仲裁庭必須在收到雙方最終的書面陳詞時指出裁決需要的時間。

裁決需要指明原因。[46] 但雙方可以同意讓仲裁庭省略裁決原因。按英國《仲裁法》第六十九條，如雙方同意省去裁決原因，雙方則不可就裁決的法律問題進行上訴。即使雙方同意省去原因，仲裁庭依然會把裁決原因附錄在另一份文件上，交予仲裁當事人。這份裁決原因是保密的，雙方將不能在任何涉及裁決的程序中依賴裁決原因。

仲裁庭在達致裁決後應書面通知當事人。[47] 此時，當事人在取得裁決前應繳付仲裁庭的費用和支出。如果裁決在一個月內不被領取，仲裁庭可命令當事人的任何一方在十四日內付款並領取裁決。

協會規則段落二十五列出了更改裁決和作出額外裁決的程序。

仲裁庭可以在雙方不反對的情況下公開所作出的裁決。[48] 為確保雙方的資料保密，所有涉及雙方身份的裁決內文將被刪除。

如仲裁庭保留仲裁費用分配，仲裁當事人可在裁決作出後三個月內（或在仲裁庭容許的時間內）向仲裁庭申請安排有關事宜。[49]

就協會規則沒有觸及的事項，仲裁庭應按規則的整體精神酌情處理。[50]

協會規則附有四個附錄。

附錄一關於費用：仲裁員的委任費、中期費用、仲裁員在欠費下的離職權、開庭審理的預訂費、就仲裁裁決應提交的保證金、提早付款的會計以及住宿車馬費等。

附錄二附有協會仲裁的慣常程序。段落十一提出在雙方交換申訴書和抗辯書後的十四天內仲裁雙方需填寫一份問卷。雙方將透過問卷陳述仲裁庭主要需要處理的爭議重點、各方可能傳召的證人以及雙方希望仲裁應作出的指引。

附錄三是上述的仲裁問卷。

附錄四就評估在雙方有足夠準備的情況下，仲裁庭開審的合理時間。附錄段落三指出任何單一仲裁員如不能就開審日期提出指引便應該辭去職務。段落四交代仲裁庭不能按時開審時的情況。

第四部分　國際商會仲裁規則[51]
（ICC Arbitration Rules）

國際商會是一個在一九一九年於巴黎成立的非牟利機構。其成員包括國家代表、貿易組織以及私人公司等。組織以推廣全球商業貿易為宗旨。

國際商會有國際理事會和執行委員會。在一九二三年商會成立了國際仲裁法庭作為國際商會旗下的獨立仲裁機構。仲裁庭監管按國際商會仲裁規則進行仲裁。

現行的國際商會規則在二零一二年一月一日實施。

規則三列出了時間限制以及各項仲裁通知要求。

仲裁由申訴人向仲裁庭秘書處遞交仲裁邀請書開始。[52] 仲裁的正式開始日期是秘書處收到仲裁通知的日期。

通知格式應符合規則條例四（三）的要求並在遞交時交付相應的費用。秘書處可以就申請書的正確格式向申訴人提出時限。如果申訴人未能及時遞交合乎要求的仲裁邀請書，其案件將不被受理。

答辯方在收到由仲裁庭秘書處發出仲裁要求的三十天內需就通知內容作回應。回應的格式需符合規則條文五（一）內的要求。答辯方可申請延時答辯。答辯內容可包括反申索。如果答辯人有反申索，申索人須在收到其內容後三十天內就反申索作回應。

就仲裁庭管轄權的異議由仲裁庭自行裁決。[53] 商會秘書長有權將管轄權問題交由法庭處理。法庭會按表面證據考慮仲裁庭是否有管轄權。如果表面證據證明仲裁庭擁有管轄權,法庭則會把管轄權問題發還仲裁庭決定。

商會規則七至十就加入其它當事人、多方合約糾紛以及合併仲裁作安排。

仲裁員必須在所有時間保持公正中立。[54]

仲裁當事人可決定仲裁庭的人數。[55] 如果雙方不能同意仲裁員的人數,仲裁法庭會指派一位仲裁員進行審理,或在案情複雜的情況下委派三位仲裁員組成仲裁庭。當事人可自行委任仲裁員並向法庭尋求許可。若當事人不向法庭推薦委任法庭便會自行組成仲裁庭。當事人可按規則條文十四就仲裁員委任作出異議。

法庭在委派仲裁員的時候會按相關的國家委員會或團體的推薦作委任基礎。[56] 按規則條文十三(五),在合適情況以及仲裁雙方不反對的情況下,仲裁員的國籍將不會與當事人的國籍相同。

在仲裁庭組成後,商會秘書處便會在相關費用得到繳交的情況下,把案件所有文件轉交仲裁庭。[57]

法庭在雙方沒有協定的情況下會指定仲裁地點。[58] 但仲裁庭可自行決定在任何地方開庭審案和進行裁決。

如雙方沒有明文同意，仲裁庭應按照最適用於爭議的法律裁決。[59] 只有在雙方同意的情況下，仲裁庭才可以按友好衡平原則判案。

按規則條文二十二，仲裁庭必須盡全力按糾紛的複雜性和所涉及金額作出最具效率和符合成本效益的裁決。仲裁庭必須公平地確保仲裁雙方得到合理的機會陳述自己的觀點理據。相反，仲裁雙方有責任遵守仲裁庭所頒布的命令。

當仲裁庭收到案件後，便須在兩個月內與當事人共同草擬一份審理範圍書，交予仲裁法庭允許。[60] 審理範圍書應陳列所有仲裁庭需作裁決的事項。在法庭允許審理範圍書的內容後，仲裁雙方均不可在沒有仲裁庭批准的情況下加入新的申索事項。

在草擬審理書前後，仲裁庭應與仲裁雙方作案件管理會議。[61] 會議的目的是就仲裁的程序和時間制定路線圖。

按條文二十五仲裁庭需要在最短時間內確定案情事實。仲裁庭需要決定是否需要聽取證人（包括專家）的供詞，或者純粹就案情文件達成裁決。

在仲裁庭開庭審理結束，[62] 或雙方作最後陳述後，仲裁庭便會宣布審理終結，並向商會秘書處通知頒布裁決的日期。

規則條文二十八容許仲裁庭頒布臨時命令。按條文，即使當事人向法官申請臨時命令，其申請將不會被視為放棄仲裁協議或放棄仲裁庭所擁有的任何權利。

規則附件五容許當事人組成緊急仲裁庭。規則條文二十九列出了緊急仲裁庭的權力。如新加坡仲裁中心的緊急規則，此條文適用於在仲裁庭尚未組成之前所發生的，需要仲裁庭作臨時命令的突發事項。

按規則條文三十，仲裁庭有六個月的時間頒布裁決。時間從雙方簽注審理範圍書或法庭批准範圍書開始計算。法庭可在必要時主動延長限期，或在仲裁庭呈交合理要求後批准延期。

裁決必須附有合理解釋表明依據。按商會規則頒布的裁決被視為在仲裁的地方按裁決理由上定明的日期頒布。[63]

在頒布裁決前，仲裁庭需要先把裁決呈交仲裁法庭審核有關內容。[64] 法庭有權對裁決進行形式上的修改，或在不影響仲裁庭自主決定權的情況下提醒仲裁庭注意實體問題。此後，仲裁雙方便可在向商會繳交仲裁費用後得到裁決結果。[65]

裁決對仲裁雙方有約束力。[66] 當事人有責任及時地服從裁決安排。透過參與仲裁，雙方在法律上放棄任何形式的追索權。

規則條文三十五列出了裁決的修改、解釋以及退回條件。

規則條文三十六列出了需要繳交仲裁預付金的情況。仲裁費用分配在規則條文三十七找到。

規則條文三十八列出更改時限安排。按條文三十九，如雙方在發現仲裁有違規程序時，繼續參與仲裁，其參與被視作放棄就違規程序作出反對。條文四十為商會的免責條款。條文四十一說明在規則沒有提及的狀況下，仲裁庭應按規則的精神，盡力確保裁決能合法得到執行。

規則有五份附件。

附件一為國際商會國際仲裁院章程；

附件二為國際商會國際仲裁院內部規則；

附件三為仲裁費用和報酬表。報酬表詳列了仲裁的行政費用和仲裁員按糾紛多少所計算的收費；

附件四列出了數項管理仲裁的技巧，除附件四外，額外的案件管理技巧可在 *Techniques for Controlling Time and Costs in Arbitration*（ICC Publication No.843, 2007）冊子中找到。此冊可在 ICC 網站下載；

附件五為緊急仲裁規則。

第五部分 中國國際經濟貿易仲裁委員會仲裁規則 [67]
(CIETAC Arbitration Rules)

I. 總則 [68]

中國國際經濟貿易仲裁委員會（中國國際經濟貿易委員會仲裁庭）致力推廣透過仲裁解決國際經貿糾紛。

委員會管理透過其仲裁庭處理的糾紛。其決策機構包括董事、副董事和秘書。委員會的總部設在北京，並在深圳、上海、天津和重慶設有支部。支部運作由其秘書處負責，為總部授權管理仲裁。當事人可選擇把糾紛交予總部或支部處理。

現行的規則在二零一二年三月通過，在二零一二年五月一日實行。

委員會在雙方協定的基礎上接受契約性或非契約性的經濟貿易等仲裁糾紛。[69] 委員會受理的案件包括涉及國際性或國外的糾紛、涉及香港、台灣或澳門，以及國內爭議案件（涉及國內法定團體爭議等）。

仲裁雙方如協定把爭議透過委員會仲裁解決，則被視作同意透過委員會規則進行仲裁。[70] 但如果雙方同意透過委員會仲裁但就委員會規則進行了更改，經同意的更改會取締原本的規則，除非更改在法律上被視為無效。雙方亦可以應用另外的仲裁規則，在這情況下委員會的作用則變成單純管理仲裁。

按規則第四（四）條，中國法例要求仲裁協議指定一所經政府認可的仲裁機構。規則列明：「當事人約定按照本規則進行仲裁但未約定仲裁機構的，視為同意將爭議提交仲裁委員會仲裁」。

任何提議把爭議透過仲裁解決的條款都是仲裁協議。[71] 仲裁協議必須是書面記錄在「合同書、信件、電報、電傳、傳真、電子數據交換和電子郵件等可以有形地表現所載內容的形式」上。如申訴人在仲裁申請書中提到仲裁協議，而答辯人並不就仲裁提議的存在有異議，仲裁協議則被視為存在。

如果仲裁當事人對仲裁庭管轄權有異議，委員會可以就管轄權進行裁決，或把問題交由仲裁庭自行審理。[72] 就仲裁協議是否存的爭議，需要在仲裁庭進行第一次聆訊前，透過書面呈交仲裁庭。如果仲裁透過純書面解決，就仲裁協議是否存在的異議，必須在抗辯人呈交第一次正式抗辯前作出。

裁決按規則被視為在仲裁地點發出。[73] 仲裁雙方可自由決定仲裁地點。如果雙方不自行決定，仲裁地點則與管理仲裁的委員會相同。

條文八列出了文件通知須知以及其時限。

條文九要求仲裁雙方以誠信參與仲裁。

條文十指出如雙方不及時明確地就仲裁過程中的異樣提出反對，並繼續參與仲裁，即視其為放棄反對權力。

II. 仲裁過程 [74]

規則第二章分成三個部分：第一為仲裁通知、答辯和反請求（規則十一至二十一）；第二為仲裁員與仲裁庭（規則二十二至三十二）；第三為審理（規則三十三至四十五）。

按規則條文十一，仲裁由委員會秘書處收到仲裁申請展開。條文十二列出申請所需要的文件。委員會在收到有關文檔後會把仲裁申請、仲裁通知書和委員會屬下的仲裁員名單交給答辯人。

答辯人必須在收到仲裁通知後的四十五天內提交答辯書。答辯書的內容須符合規則條文十四（二）的要求。答辯人可在同一時間提交反請求。[75]

規則條文十七賦予委員會權利，在仲裁當時提出申請，和在所有有關人等同意的情況下把數個仲裁合併處理。如果委員會接受合併申請，仲裁會被合併為最早成立者。

規則條文二十定明在仲裁時，當事人可以聘請國內認可或海外的代表進行仲裁。相關的授權書須遞交委員會秘書處備案。

規則條文二十一賦予仲裁庭頒布臨時命令的權利。委員會有權把當事人所提出的保存現狀令申請按中國法轉介法院。仲裁庭亦可以按當事人申請頒布有關的臨時措施命令。

仲裁庭並不代表當事人。[76] 仲裁員在所有時間都必須保持公平獨立。

除非雙方另行同意，否則仲裁庭將由三位仲裁員組成。[77]

一般情況下，仲裁員會由委員會認可的仲裁員名單中選出。[78] 當事人可在相互同意的基礎上提選其他仲裁員，但提選需要經委員會主席批准。規則條文二十五、二十六和二十七就委任單一或三人仲裁員程序作了詳細的安排。作出委任時，委員會主席需考慮適用於爭議的法律、仲裁的地方和語言、仲裁雙方的國籍和其他有關的因素。[79]

按規則條文二十九，仲裁員必須披露任何可能使人對其獨立公正性產生合理懷疑的情況。就對仲裁員公正性所作出的異議須按條文三十所提供的程序進行。仲裁員可按條文三十一的程序被取締，而仲裁不會因仲裁員的退席受影響。

仲裁庭審理案件需按規則條文三十三至三十八所訂的程序進行。基本上，仲裁庭可按需要決定如何適當地審理案件。除非雙方另行協定，聆訊應在負責管理仲裁的委員會所在地進行（由北京委員會監管的仲裁應在北京進行聽證和聆訊）。在得到委員會秘書長同意的基礎下仲裁庭可安排聆訊在其他地點進行。仲裁庭可在任何地點進行裁決。

按規則條文三十六，聆訊應以閉門形式進行。如果當事人要求公開聆訊，仲裁庭可以考慮是否接受當事人的有關請求。在整個閉門仲裁過程中，所有有關人等（包括證人、專家證人和翻譯員）不得對外講及任何有關仲裁的事項。

規則條文三十九至四十一列出舉證程序。提出理據的一方有責任就理據所依賴的事實舉證。仲裁庭有權自主調查和搜證。仲裁庭亦可聽取專家意見，同時要求仲裁雙方提供有關的資料、文件、物件或貨品以便仲裁庭以及專家作校對、驗察或評估之用。雙方有責任配合仲裁庭的有關請求。

規則條文四十五容許仲裁庭在雙方請求或同意下充當糾紛的調停人。如果調停失敗，仲裁便可繼續進行。條文四十五（九）指明，任何雙方在調停過程中所透露的內容不能在仲裁中起任何作用。

III. 仲裁裁決 [80]

裁決必須在仲裁庭組成後六個月內完成。商會秘書長可按仲裁庭申請考慮延長裁決時間。

仲裁庭需獨立公正地按案情事實、協議規則、適用法律和國際慣例作裁決。[81] 裁決須說明申訴因由、爭議的案情、裁決的原因、結果、訟費的分配，以及仲裁日期和地點。雙方當事人可協議毋須仲裁庭在裁決提及爭議的因由。所有裁決必須附有仲裁協會的印章。

裁決對雙方有約束力，並不能就裁決在任何其他機構提出上訴或符合。

仲裁庭可以就爭議的某部分作出部分裁決。[82]

裁決的草稿必須交予仲裁委員會審核方能被仲裁庭簽注落實。[83] 在不影響仲裁庭獨立性的情況下，委員會可以就裁決內容，向仲裁庭指出任何委員會認為仲裁庭需要注意之處。

規則第五十條就分配訟費作規定。

規則第五十一和五十二條容許仲裁庭更改裁決和作出額外裁決。

裁決作出後，雙方應自動按照裁決內的時間表執行裁決。[84] 如果裁決內沒有制定時間表，則雙方應立刻行事。

IV. 簡易程序 [85]

規則第四章定明如果仲裁金額不超過人民幣二百萬或在超過時，在雙方另行協議的情況下，仲裁會以簡易程序進行。

V. 內地仲裁 [86]

規則第五章的條款適用於內地仲裁。

VI. 補充條款 [87]

第六章就其他事項，包括仲裁語言、仲裁費用與收費，以及條款詮譯等作安排。

如雙方沒有訂明仲裁語言，仲裁應以中文或其他仲裁委員會認為與案件適合的語言進行。[88]

仲裁委員會就條例有最終解釋權。[89]

第六部分　總結

本章節宏觀地總結了五款經常被採用的仲裁規則。明顯地，五款規則多有相同之處，這是因為它們都是根據基本的公平原則設計。由於規則的大同小異，仲裁員在面對一套不熟悉的規則時只要謹記上面就五款規則所作的總結，留意他們之間相同的結構，便會發覺其實所有的仲裁規則都是大同小異，並能很快的掌握新的仲裁守則。

概括地，一般的仲裁規則基本上會有以下的特性：

1. 大部分的規則開首都會就文件通知和時限定義；

2. 大部分的規則都以仲裁機構收到仲裁通知，或以答辯人收到仲裁通知書為仲裁開始日期；

3. 所有規則都要求仲裁員保持持平中立。規則會表

明如何委派仲裁員，並要求在介紹委任前披露任
何可能令人對其中立性產生合理懷疑的情況。有
些規則要求仲裁員在接受委任前確保他們有足夠
的時間在合理時間內就糾紛達成裁決。大部分的
規則都會列出反對仲裁員委任的方法；

4. 所有規則均承認仲裁庭的自裁管轄權，以及在綜
合契約中仲裁條款的單一獨立性。就自裁管轄權
的程序，有些規則把裁決權直接交給仲裁庭，其
他則授權予仲裁監管機構，研究是否有足夠表面
證據支持否決仲裁庭的管轄權；

5. 所有規則均要求仲裁按時以及在具成本效益的情
況下進行。仲裁庭必須讓雙方就理據作充分陳詞。
在符合以上兩個大前提下，仲裁庭可自行決定仲
裁的程序事項；包括呈交陳訴書、聽取證供和口
頭陳詞等。大部分的規則容許在雙方沒有同意的
情況下仲裁庭自行決定適用於爭議的法律；

6. 大部分的規則都定明決定仲裁地點的程序；

7. 大部分的規則都容許仲裁庭在最終裁決前，為確
保裁決得以執行而頒布臨時措施；

8. 在處理複雜案件時，很多規則都鼓勵仲裁庭召開
至少一次的案件管理會議。這容許雙方釐清案件

的主要爭議點，以及決定能最有效解決這些爭議點的程序；

9. 大部分規則都要求仲裁庭頒布書面裁決並提供裁決理由。大部分包含修改裁決以及要求仲裁庭解釋裁決的程序。有些規則要求仲裁應在收到雙方最後陳詞後的合理時間內完成裁決；

10. 大部分的規則定明雙方受規則所限，並承諾遵從裁決結果行事；

11. 大部分規則設有保密、棄權以及有關仲裁機構的免責條款；

12. 大部分規則均提供收費準則；

13. 仲裁規則的實施和監管十分多樣化，有些規則的實施由指定機構監管；有些則僅提供一套既定模式供當事人採用。當時人可按規則的特性，選擇最適合雙方需要的作為仲裁規則。

---

1. Art. 1.

2. 仲裁庭可在日後命令把文件翻譯成仲裁的協定語言。所以雙方應盡早把所有文件翻譯以交予仲裁庭。

3. See Art. 5.8.

4. Arts. 14-28.

5. Art. 14.3.

6. Art. 14.5.

7. Art. 14.6.

8. Art. 21.

9. Arts. 23.7 and 23.9.

10. Art. 25.

11. Art. 26.

12. Art. 27.

13. Art. 28.

14. Arts. 29-37.

15. Art. 29.1.

16. Art. 30.1.

17. Arts. 30.2-30.5.

18. Art. 31.

19. 這些詞語的基本意思是由仲裁庭按公正衡平原則裁決。

20. Arts. 38-40.

21. 有關規則，全文可在新加坡國際仲裁中心網址 www.siac.org.sg 下載。以下引用的條文為新加坡國際仲裁中心規則。

22. 新加坡國際仲裁中心冊子 "Why Choose SIAC"

23. Art. 1.

24. Art. 5，快捷程序陳列在 Art. 5.2

25. Art. 6.

26 Arts. 10.1 and 10.3.

27. Arts. 10.4 and 10.5.

28. Arts. 11, 12 and 13.

29. Art. 16.

30. Art. 17.

31. Art. 19.

32. Art. 20.

33. Art. 27.

34. Art. 28.

35. 規則可在 LMAA 的網址 www.lmaa.org.uk 下載。以下應用的規則段落為規則內的相應段落。

36. 段落三。

37. 段落四。

38. 段落五。

39. 段落六。

40. 段落七。

41. 段落十。

42. 段落十二。

43. 段落十五。

44. 段落十五（c）和（d）。

45. 段落二十。

46. 段落二十二。

47. 段落二十三和二十四。

48. 段落二十六。

49. 段落二十八。

50. 段落三十。

51. 規則全文可在 ICC 網址 www.iccwbo.org 下載。以下引述的條文為 ICC 規則的相應部分。

52. Art. 4.

53. Art. 6.

54. Art. 11.

55. Art. 12.

56. Art. 13.

57. Art. 16.

58. Art. 18.

59. Art. 21.

60. Art. 23.

61. Art. 24.

62. Art. 27.

63. Art. 31.

64. Art. 33.

65. Art. 34.

66. Art. 34 (6).

67. 規則全文可在 CIETAC 網址 cn.cietac.org 下載。以下引述條文為規則相應部分。

68. Arts. 1-10.

69. Art. 3 (1).

70. Art. 4.

71. Art. 5.

72. Art. 6.

73. Art. 7.

74. Arts. 11-45.

75. Art. 15.

76. Art. 22.

77. Art. 23.

78. Art. 24.

79. Art. 28.

80. Arts. 46-53.

81. Art. 47.

82. Art. 48.

83. Art. 49.

84. Art. 53.

85. Arts. 54-62.

86. Arts. 63-70.

87. Arts. 71-74.

88. Art. 71.

89. Art. 73 (2).

第四章　法庭與仲裁裁決的執行

此章討論香港法庭如何協助執行仲裁裁決。筆者將集中解釋《仲裁法例》第八十一條（《示範法》第三十四條）中的執行裁決條文，以及紐約條款第八十六、八十九和九十五中容許法庭拒絕執行裁決的法律細節。

第一部分解釋國際間如何透過《紐約公約》認可與互相執行仲裁裁決。第二部分為針對香港與新加坡的仲裁裁決執行概要。在亞洲，香港與新加坡被譽為是仲裁最優越的地點。在第二部分末段，筆者會思考法庭與仲裁庭之間的互動角色。第三部分討論一般在香港執行裁決可能遇到的問題。

第一部分　紐約公約 [1]

《紐約公約》（全名為《承認及執行外國仲裁裁決公約》），在一九五八年七月六日於紐約獲聯合國通過。至今有一百四十六個國家簽註執行。中國是其中一個簽註國，故香港和澳門均受惠於公約。在一九九七年七月一日前，由於香港是英國屬地，故公約在香港同樣有效。

公約篇幅不長，只有十六項條款。所有條款均為原則性，採納各國可就如何落實原則，按其實質需要透過司法機構和立法機關自行決定。[2] 但是，由於公約為國際性條文，在思考如何落實公約原則時，各國應互相參考執行方法，以達到一定程度的國際標準。

條文一闡明公約條款在跨國執行仲裁裁決的情況下適用。

條文二指出，契約國之間需互相承認，並協助執行任何將糾紛交於仲裁解決的書面協議。「糾紛」不一定源於合約，但其性質必須是可由仲裁所解決的。

「書面仲裁協議」沒有形式上的定義，但文件必須是帶有仲裁條文的合約，或單獨的仲裁協議。協議可以是一份經雙方簽署的仲裁合約、雙方的書信來往，又或是電報往來。

條文二（三）十分緊要。按條文，若雙方間存在有效的仲裁協議，契約國的法庭即有責任將糾紛交予仲裁解決。法庭必須尊重雙方的仲裁協議,除非法庭有足夠法律基礎裁定協議作廢或不能執行。[3]

條文三規定契約國必須承認仲裁裁決,並按公約條文就裁決予以執行。按公約達成的裁決在契約國的法庭內,應與本地裁決享同等待遇。

條文四就申請執行國外裁決的申請人提供簡單程序。申請人必須向法庭呈交經過有效認證的裁決正或副本,和呈交經有效認證的仲裁協議正或副本。如果裁決以外文寫成,申請人須就文件提供翻譯版本。

條文五是公約的精要條文,需全文列出:

> 「1. 被請求承認或執行裁決的管轄當局,只有在作為裁決執行對象的當事人提出有關下列情況的證明的時候,才可以根據該當事人的要求,拒絕承認和執行該裁決:
>
> > a. 第二條所述的協議的雙方當事人,根據對他們適用的法律,當時是處於某種無行為能力的情況之下,或者根據雙方當事人選定適用的法律,或在沒有這種選定的時候,根據作出裁決的國家的法律下述協議是無效的;或
> >
> > b. 作為裁決執行對象的當事人,沒有被給予指定仲裁員或者進行仲裁程序的適當通知,或者由

於其他情況而不能對案件提出意見；或

c. 裁決涉及仲裁協議所沒有提到的，或者不包括
仲裁協議規定之內的爭執；或者裁決內含有對
仲裁協議範圍以外事項的決定。但是，對於仲
裁協議範圍以內的事項的決定，如果可以和對
於仲裁協議範圍以外的事項的決定分開；那麼，
這一部分的決定仍然可予以承認和執行；或

d. 仲裁庭的組成或仲裁程序與當事人之間的協議
不符，或者當事人之間沒有這種協議時，與進
行仲裁的國家的法律不符；或

e. 裁決對當事人還沒有約束力，或者裁決已經由
作出裁決的國家或據其法律作出裁決的國家的
管轄當局撤銷或停止執行。

2. 被請求承認和執行仲裁裁決的國家的管轄當局，
如果查明有下列情況，也可以拒絕承認和執行：

a. 爭執的事項，依照這個國家的法律，不可以用
仲裁方式解決；或

b. 承認或執行該項裁決將和這個國家的公共秩序
相抵觸。」

條文（一）到（五）列出了法庭可拒絕執行裁決的原因。但要

留意的是，即使能證明（一）到（五）內的一個或多個原因，法庭都不一定要強制性地拒絕執行裁決，法庭就是否按（一）到（五）決絕執行裁決有很大的酌情權。

上述拒絕執行裁決理由的（一）與（二）與《仲裁條例》第八十一條（《示範法》第三十四條）、第八十六條（非公約和非國內的裁決）、第八十九條（公約裁決），以及第九十五條（國內裁決）內的拒絕理由相若。可是，按《仲裁條例》第八十六（二）（c）條；就非公約、非國內的裁決（在香港所作出的裁決便是非公約、非國內裁決），香港法庭有權在其認為公義的情況下拒絕執行，相反，法庭不能以同樣理由拒絕公約裁決。

與公約一樣，即使裁決抵觸了條文內容，《示範法》均給予法庭酌情權去考慮是否執行裁決。拒絕執行並不因裁決抵觸條文而被拒絕執行。

公約條文六容許執行法庭在裁決於仲裁庭被上訴時，暫時擱置執行裁決。

公約第七條承認和尊重國與國雙方或多方之間就互相承認和執行仲裁裁決協議。條文八至十一和十五就實行公約作出安排。

第十二條是公約生效日期；第十三條是契約國退出公約安排。

第十四條指出公約的效用是互相的。契約國只有在自己實行公約義務的情況下，方能要求其他國家相對按公約條款行事。

第十六條指出公約的合法文字。

大致上，公約的目的是容許仲裁裁決在契約國之間能够得到執行。如執行人能達到公約第四條的要求，除非回應方能按第五條內的拒絕內容提出反對執行，否則契約國有義務容許申請人在境內執行裁決。

在一百四十六個國家中執行裁決是仲裁非常具優勢的特質。裁決的執行比起要求法庭承認和執行外國法庭命令來得簡單快捷。

在公約條文五的幾個拒絕理由中，最常見的拒絕執行理據是「公共秩序」。大部分情況下有關方面都會找理由證明裁決的執行會影響公共秩序。[4]

直到近期，在香港取得的裁決很難在印度執行，儘管香港（中國屬地）和印度均是公約契約國。

這為希望在香港進行仲裁的印度當事人帶來難題。

問題的來源是，按印度在一九九六年通過的仲裁法案，公約國必須在《印度憲報》中刊登其《紐約公約》契約國身份。在刊登憲報前，即使是契約國的裁決都不能在印度執行。

中國在二零一二年三月十九日已於《印度憲報》內刊登其契約國身份。故香港裁決自此可按公約裁決資格在印度執行。

此舉解決了香港裁決在國際執行上的一個重大問題。

第二部分 執行合約

I. 友好和非友好的仲裁市場

仲裁是一個發展工業。很多國家（包括香港）均成立了仲裁中心。這些仲裁機構間存在强勁的競爭，各自推廣自己的優勢：包括城市能為仲裁提供的場地、設備和仲裁員的質素等。同時，仲裁必須得到當地司法機構認可，使裁決能在最沒有阻力的情況下得到執行。

地方司法機構對執行仲裁裁決的審核越少，則越被認為是「仲裁友好」地區。相反，法庭在執行裁決時介入越多，則越被認為是對仲裁「不友好」。按此評核守則，香港和新加坡常被評核為亞洲兩個最友好的仲裁地區。

II. 審核的必要

最近，即使是在香港和新加坡，很多人均提出法庭應在執行裁決時加以審核。有人認為這對仲裁發展有負面影響。

舉例，Peter Megens 在「新加坡仲裁與法庭：何去何從」[5] 一文中回顧了四個新加坡的近期案例，從中質疑新加坡是否依然是執行仲裁裁決的伊甸園。這四個案例分別是：*PT Perusahaan*

Gas Negara（Persero）TBK v. CRW Joint Operation[6] 和 AJT v. AJU[7] 的初審和上訴裁決。

Persero 是按國際商會仲裁規則進行的仲裁。雙方的合約按 FIDIC 建築合約條款（一九九九年第一版）起草，並包含仲裁條款。PGN（申訴人）在新加坡法庭要求上述仲裁的最終裁決。最終裁決的金額被按 FIDIC 合約條款組成的評核組織裁定為合理。

按仲裁庭的最終裁決，儘管仲裁庭已經作出裁決，裁決結果不影響雙方可把爭議帶到評核組織評核賠償金額。但是，按《示範法》條文三十四（二）（a）（ii）（公約條文五（一）（c）），PGN 抗辯仲裁庭的決定超越了其管轄權，原因是因為仲裁庭應先等待評核組織的審核，研究組織的決定是否合理，然後才頒布最終裁決。

在仔細研究 FIDIC 條文後，Ang J 以及上訴庭接納仲裁庭超越了其管轄權。兩級法院均認為在案中情況下仲裁庭只能頒布臨時裁決。由於仲裁庭沒有仔細審閱審核組織就賠償金額的定案，仲裁庭違反了其按 FIDIC 條款下所應該履行的責任。

在第二個案例中，AJT 是按新加坡仲裁中心規則進行的仲裁。在其裁決中，仲裁庭認為爭議雙方已經達成和解協議，毋須繼續仲裁。按和解協議，AJU 同意向泰國警方撤回其對 AJT 作出的欺詐和偽造指控。

在 AJU 撤回指控後，泰國警方停止了就案件的調查。可是，AJT 卻拒絕按協議終止仲裁。

AJT 向新加坡法院上訴，要求擱置仲裁庭承認雙方和解協議的終止仲裁命令。其原因是裁決有礙公共秩序。按 AJT 的理據，這是由於和解協議阻礙警方調查不可原諒的罪行（偽造以及使用偽造文件）。另外，AJT 陳詞說由於和解涉及貪污及舞弊，所以和解協議不能在泰國執行。

Chan J 認為裁決不應獲得法庭支持執行。他認為和解協議阻礙了泰國就不誠實罪行的執法，按泰國法律為非法協定（泰國是裁決的執行地）。故按國際禮讓原則，和解協議在新加坡應同等屬非法（新加坡為適用於合約的法律）。由於和解協議為非法協議，所以，承認其效力則對新加坡公共秩序造成影響。故 Chan J 最後擱置了仲裁庭的裁決。

上訴庭推翻了 Chan J 的決定。上訴庭認為 Chan J 不應質疑仲裁庭認為和解協議不違反泰國法的結論。這是因為仲裁庭的結論是事實性的。由於和解協議不涉及違法行為，則不會擾亂新加坡的公共秩序。

Peter Megens 就新加坡法庭對仲裁裁決的監管，與香港法庭在大部分案件中都支持仲裁裁決的態度相比較。[8] 他的結論是新加坡法庭可能比較願意把法庭自己的判決取代仲裁庭的判決。[9]

Megens 的結論是：[10]

「按所討論的案例，新加坡法庭在仲裁庭沒有明顯地扭曲法律，或在顯然犯錯的情況下質疑了仲裁庭的裁決。按此，新加坡法庭似乎想跟隨其他對仲裁不友好的國家。仲裁在不友好的情況下不能發展。希望新加坡不會繼續在這條路上走下去。按上訴庭在 *AJU v AJT* 的判決，看來上訴庭是希望制止原訟庭質疑仲裁庭的決定。

希望日後法庭在按《示範法》第三十四條或以公共秩序為由去審核仲裁庭裁決的時候謹記，《示範法》第三十四條以及公共秩序並不為上訴仲裁庭裁決提供簡易的法律藉口。」

筆者並不認為香港法庭跟 Megens 在新加坡所觀察到的有太大分別。

筆者列舉兩個近期在香港發生的案例。第一是 *Gao Haiyan and another v. Keeneye Holdings Ltd. and others*[11] 的原訟於上訴決定；第二是 *Pacific China Holdings Ltd.（In Liquidation）v. Grand Pacific Holdings Ltd*。[12]

Gao Haiyan 是一個西安仲裁委員會監管的仲裁。仲裁庭設有三名仲裁員。在頒布裁決之前，委員會的秘書長跟仲裁庭的其中一位成員嘗試與雙方進行調解。調解在西安的一家酒店內進行。與會人士除了兩位調解員外，還有一名 Z（一位與答辯人相關的人士）。會面期間，兩位調解人主動向 Z 提出答辯人支付二千五百萬人民幣以換取相關的股票以解決糾紛。調解員要

求 Z 向答辯人「做工作」令其接受和解提案。調解員事前並沒有就和解金額質詢申訴人的意見，而按證據，申訴人事前曾經透露不會接納和解。

答辯人拒絕了調解員的提議，仲裁因調解失敗而繼續。仲裁庭最後的裁決否決了答辯人的所有理據，並裁定答辯人所依賴的股份轉讓協議為無效。裁決中，仲裁庭「提議」申訴人可以支付五千萬人民幣給答辯人作為經濟補償。

當仲裁重開時，答辯人並沒有因仲裁員參與調解而即時抗議仲裁庭在審理案件時存在偏見。但是在得到裁決後，答辯人便向西安中級人民法院入稟因仲裁庭存在偏見而撤銷仲裁裁決。西安法院拒絕了答辯人的申請。

申訴人隨後希望在香港執行裁決。答辯人便以公共秩序為理由入稟香港法庭希望法庭拒絕執行受偏見影響的裁決在香港執行。

作為審理此案的法官，筆者認為證據不足以證明仲裁庭存在確實的偏見。但是，筆者覺得在西安酒店中與 Z 進行的晚餐調解安排，產生了令人生疑的表面偏見。筆者警告過，除非仲裁員非常小心，否則仲裁員參與調解往往會產生表面偏見的危險。

在審理案件時，筆者需要決定的是表面偏見是否觸犯香港（非西安）的公共秩序，筆者認為答辯人並不受西安法院的判決所限，可以在香港（作為裁決的執行地）向法院申請，以表面偏見為理由拒絕執行裁決。由於香港法庭通常不會執行在本港進行而受表面偏見所影響的裁決，筆者認為香港法庭亦不會容許在外地受到表面偏見影響的裁決在本港執行。外地的裁決（筆者當時想）不應該享有比本港裁決更優厚的執行待遇。因此，筆者容許了答辯人的申請並拒絕在本港執行西安的裁決。

上訴庭推翻了筆者的判決。上訴庭認為由於答辯人沒有在獲悉調解的情況後即時作出異議，其繼續參與仲裁應被視為是答辯人放棄以偏見為由去反對仲裁。此外，上訴庭亦提出是否存在表面偏見應按當地習俗而定，由於案中在西安進行的調解已經被當地法庭裁定沒有表面偏見，那麼香港法庭應該尊重西安方面的決定。

Pacific China 是按國際商會規則進行的仲裁。案中，PCH 上訴由三人仲裁庭所通過的裁決。上訴按《示範法》第三十四（二）（ii）和（iv）（《紐約公約》第五（一）(b) 和 (d)）提出。摘要地，上訴人認為仲裁庭沒有在裁決前給予合理機會讓 PCH 回應 GPH 就台灣法律呈堂的專家證供。因此，PCH 不合理地被拒絕依賴三個適用的台灣案例。此外，PCH 亦覺得仲裁庭不合理地拒絕聽取其就香港以及紐約法律的陳詞。

Saunders J 同意 PCH 所作出的三項程序性抗議。他認為如果仲裁庭循程序聽取 PCH 的陳詞，裁決的結果會有改變。因此，法庭應行使酌情權擱置裁決。

上訴庭推翻了 Saunders J 的決定。其理由是原訟庭應盡量尊重仲裁庭的案件管理決定。法庭不應在沒有嚴重程序失誤，導致當事人得不到公平審訊的情況下貿然介入仲裁程序。本案中 PCH 所提出的理據並不足以構成嚴重程序錯誤，而法官應該尊重仲裁庭的酌情權和仲裁本身的程序彈性。

按上述兩個案例，香港上訴庭是非常「仲裁友好」。在兩個案例中上訴庭均給予仲裁庭高度的自主性，並高度准許仲裁庭在案件管理上所作的安排。上訴庭提醒香港法庭不應輕易打擾仲裁庭的決定。相反，法官只有在極其嚴重和例外的情況下才應按《示範法》第三十四條推翻仲裁庭的裁決。

注意，在 *Pacific China* 一案中的法律原則與新加坡 *AJT* 所定的原則十分相似。

筆者認為香港和新加坡法庭在處理擱置仲裁裁決申請時的處理模式和手法沒有重大分別。

相似的原因很簡單：在所有執行《示範法》以及《紐約公約》的國家，申請人只能按條文所列明的理由提出申請，而法庭在審核這數個申請理據時，亦離不開數個既定的考慮。

無論如何考慮，法庭都必須審核仲裁的過程和裁決。在公約和《示範法》國家，真正的問題其實不是法庭是否應該審查仲裁，而是法庭如何審查仲裁。

實際上，在處理挑戰仲裁裁決時，法庭只有按三種方法處理證據。其一是單靠閱覽裁決後快速決定；其二是考慮有關挑戰理由的書面供詞，在不具盤問過程的情況下作判決；第三是通過全面審訊形式要求證人出庭作供和接受盤問後作出決定。

哪一個才適用於挑戰裁決的申請？

要考慮的實際因素是，挑戰裁決申請可能附帶大量的文件證據。舉例說，在 *Gao Haiyan* 一案中，除了有關調解前的背景、調解進行時的情況以及調解後的所發生事情的有關文檔和證人證供外，法庭更需要命令有關證人上庭接受盤問。

當然，法庭應按申請的個別情況作最適當的安排，但這句話在實際上如何操作？

只按裁決本身作判決，筆者認為在大部分情況下可能相對草率。在一般情況下，為保公平，當事人應該被容許就公約第五（一）條內的挑戰裁決理由呈上與理由相關的證據。

就如何審核證據，香港和新加坡法庭通常會按文件證據定案。法庭會單從證人的文件證供決定是否接受拒絕執行申請，不會要求證人上庭接受盤問。*Gao Haiyan* 是少數法庭容許證人上庭接受盤問的案例。

法庭不應該以事務指引，嘗試規管在處理拒絕執行裁決申請時法庭如何處理證據。有關申請所牽涉的實際情況變化太多，法庭不能就拒絕執行申請定下規範性的方程式。

當然，法庭可以鼓勵當事人在舉證時採取理性的態度。但是，如果當事人堅持呈交大量的文件，那麼法庭如何能在不給予雙方就呈堂證據陳詞的情況下公平地達至裁決？答案是法庭必需批准雙方陳詞。

至於要求證人上庭作供的審訊辦法，筆者則認為是只有在例外情況下才適用。

在提交拒絕執行申請時，當事人通常已經參與了一場產生裁決的審訊。如果雙方在執行裁決時，需要進行另一場決定裁決是否能被執行的審訊，額外產生的高昂訟費成本將令整個仲裁制度失去比例。合理的制度不可能要求當事人在執行裁決前再次經歷另一場持久的訴訟。如果仲裁裁決的執行要經過另一場審訊，仲裁將不可能發展成有效和快捷的解決紛爭辦法。

如上所言，法庭在多數情況下均會以文件證據作為處理拒絕執行申請的證據基礎。

即使法庭堅決地跟隨香港上訴庭在 *Pacific China* 和新加坡上訴庭在 *AJT* 所定下的不干擾政策，法庭仍然需要審閱申請人所呈堂以證明裁決不應該被執行的證據。

法庭依然需要審閱仲裁的過程以及裁決的理由，即使最後否決申請亦能向申請人解釋否決申請的理據。

法庭在處理拒絕執行裁決申請時，可能需要一至兩天的時間立即仲裁背景過程及裁決。即使是「仲裁友好」的國家亦不可能毫無保留地，在有反對的情況下容許裁決即時在境內執行。

如果法庭認為呈堂的證據與申請無關，則可透過訟費分配懲罰浪費法庭時間的當事人。舉例在香港，除非特殊情況，否則敗訴方需要以彌償基礎負擔勝方的訟費。

III. 審核時間

在 *Persero* 一案中，當事人在二零零六年二月簽署具仲裁協議的合約。審核組織在二零零八年十一月頒布決定，CRW 在二零零九年二月申請進行仲裁。仲裁在二零零九年十一月進行，其後 CRW 在二零一零年一月在新加坡法庭註冊。PGN 在二零一零年二月挑戰仲裁結果。Aug J 在二零一零年四月處理拒絕執行申請，並在二零一零年七月頒布判決。實際上，這件涉及美金一千七百二十萬的糾紛擾攘了兩年半方得到解決。而上訴庭的決定代表雙方需要經過另一場的仲裁去研究審核組織的評核。

在 *AJT* 一案中，仲裁通知書在二零零六年八月送出，雙方在二零零八年二月達成和解。仲裁裁決在二零零九年十二月頒布。AJT 在二零一零年七月申請拒絕執行仲裁裁決。上訴庭在二零一零年十一月下旬審理並在二零一一年八月頒布判決。所以，即使雙方達成和解協議，糾紛歷時五年都不得解決。

在 *Gao Haiyan* 中，仲裁在二零零九年七月開始，調解在二零一零年三月進行。仲裁在二零一零年五月繼續並在二零一零年六月產生裁決。西安法庭在二零一零年十月否決了答辯人的上訴。香港法庭在二零一零年八月頒布裁決執行令。筆者在二零一一年三月三十日審理拒絕執行申請並在四月頒布裁決。上訴庭在二零一一年十一月審理上訴並在二零一一年十二月允許上訴。雙方用了兩年半的時間去解決互相的糾紛。

在 *Pacific China*，仲裁要求在二零零六年三月發出，裁決在二零零九年八月頒布。Saunders J 在二零一一年二月審理拒絕執行申請並在二零一一年六月頒布判決。上訴庭在二零一二年三月聽取了上訴並在同年五月判決。糾紛歷時六年解決。

以上四個案例分別歷時二至六年不等。這已經是兩個在亞洲中最「仲裁友好」的地方了。

如果仲裁真正能帶給使用者快捷的解決糾紛方法，則必須縮短執行裁決所需要的時間。如果以上四個例子所需要的時間，代表一般仲裁所需要的時間，那麼仲裁的競爭力便會落後於透過專項法庭在香港進行的法庭訴訟了。從時間上計算法庭訴訟並不一定慢於仲裁過程。

那麼，仲裁是否不是有效的解決紛爭渠道？

筆者認為仲裁是有優點的。

上述四個案例並不代表日常經仲裁解決的商業糾紛。四個案例均涉及巨大金額。由於款項巨大，當事人可能覺得應作出戰略性拖延，此舉在經濟上可能有利於當事人。這些戰略性的技巧無論使用任何形式的解決方案都無可避免。

列舉的案例由於當事人的程序糾纏拖延日久。雙方用了很長的時間在法庭，透過訴訟和書信來往互相指責對方違反信用和欺騙自己。這些複雜的細節需要時間去處理。

不可爭辯的事實是，如果當事人願意花費大量時間和金錢，透過仲裁或法律程序拖延時間，以增強自己的談判優勢，在現行制度下很難杜絕和制止這種行為。

相比之下，在一般的商業糾紛中，如雙方希望就糾紛取得相對具最終性的結果，法庭訴訟可以提供相對快捷和具最終性的處理。特別是法庭能制定一套特定的系統，確保有公平的程序去處理就拒絕執行仲裁裁決的申請。

適合的程序需包含以下幾點重要事項：

1. 法庭應觀察並確定，所有有關仲裁裁決的申請都在最短的時間內獲得法庭制定一套適合該案件的審理程序指引；

2. 毫無理據的申請應早在頒布指引時被剔除，以確保無浪費金錢時間；

3. 申請應盡快獲得法庭審理，原訟庭最好能在給予案件指引後兩個月內處理申請，並在其後六個月內審理上訴申請；

4. 在時間越短越能盡快得到處理的前提下，法庭可考慮把聽取陳詞的時間限制在半天至一天，以方便排期處理；

5. 如表面案情涉及複雜的細節問題，法庭則應把聽取陳詞時間延長至兩天；

6. 為確保雙方能有合理機會向法庭解釋自己的陳詞，法庭應容許雙方在上庭陳詞之前，自由呈交書面陳詞；

7. 法庭應盡可能安排熟悉案件領域的法官處理拒絕執行仲裁裁決申請。

筆者同意以上七點對處理筆者所列舉的四個案例可能沒有太大的幫助。但是這些措施起碼應該能在處理一般案件是加快法庭的效率。

IV. 重新定義「仲裁友好」

事實上，法庭是否採取不干預政策對地區是否是「仲裁友好」並沒有太大的關聯。

仲裁並非單一以仲裁庭解決爭議。仲裁是否有效取決於整個紛爭解決過程是否能有效解決雙方的問題。這個過程包括法庭的參與、法庭為協助仲裁所提供的臨時濟助，以及處理執行仲裁裁決的申請等。就法庭是否干預仲裁的討論沒有意思，法庭的參與是整個仲裁解決爭議過程中的一環。

按此理解，法庭不應在是否干預仲裁的基礎上被評核是否「仲裁友好」，而是應該在法庭是否能在貫徹商業原則的情況下處理仲裁糾紛。

「商業原則」包括法庭慮及處理仲裁裁決的時間和成本。商人們不希望法庭關注每一項細節問題，重新審判雙方的糾紛。同樣，商人們亦不希望法庭在處理拒絕執行裁決申請時敷衍了事，輕視了地區在《示範法》和《紐約公約》內所承擔的責任。

法庭在每一個申請中都應審閱裁決內容。法庭是否拒絕執行裁決則是另一個問題。法庭應按香港和新加坡在 *AJT* 和 *Pacific China* 所定下的原則辦事，只有在仲裁庭有嚴重失誤的情況下，法庭方可按《示範法》和《紐約公約》內的拒絕執行條文否決仲裁庭的裁決。

法庭的最終決定權確保了仲裁的認受性。法庭的監察加強了仲裁庭的可信性，它確保仲裁是以公正公平的程序進行，而即使程序出現瑕疵，只要錯誤並不嚴重得有損公共秩序，仲裁裁決都可以在本港執行。

因此，筆者不提倡法庭每在跟仲裁庭持不同意見時便介入裁決，這是十分錯誤的想法。筆者所建議的是不必對法庭的介入過分敏感。法庭在處理嚴重錯誤的輔助角色正正是仲裁應該標榜，令使用者放心的優點。

V. 公眾對法庭的印象

筆者曾在牛津大學的民事程序科中向學生推廣香港法庭為何大力支持調解。筆者當時認為，由於調解在百分之七十的情況下都能協助當事人解決問題，調解是一個減低雙方訴訟成本相當有效的方法。

在學生的問答時間中，他們指出筆者的想法無視了爭議雙方的實際權利。他們認為，由於調解的成功取決於雙方之間的磋商和讓步，推廣調解否定了雙方的法律權利而過分依賴雙方的談判位置。按學生的想法，所有的事均可談判，而法律所賦予當事人的利益在談判過程中便淪為籌碼了。當事人很可能故意違約，並以其優越的談判位置而透過調解輕易地解決糾紛。

有些學生更認為如果調解的確如筆者所說的成功，那麼民事訴訟便沒有意義了。沒有了訴訟，法律的發展便會變得遲緩和不清晰。在調解主導的社會，法律會像馬克思所說的是失去意義，而法官將不能完成他們釐清法律的職責。

筆者不敢同意學生們的觀點（認為太過激進和欠根據），但與他們的對話卻令筆者反思。

筆者認為學生們的反應源於他們不希望看見法庭把裁定對與錯的責任承包給私人機構（例如調解員）。公眾希望透過法庭訴訟證明自己是正確的，即使訴訟包含了高昂的成本和可能造成重大的心理壓力。很多人都希望有上庭陳述己見的一刻，不願意折衷地透過相對便宜的方法和解。

在了解他們的心理後筆者對推廣調解的熱情稍有退減。但仍然覺得調解是有用和具成本效益的解決糾紛方法,但筆者同意不是每個人都接受調解,故法庭不可強行要求公眾使用自己不願意的方法行事。

筆者認為,仲裁在調解與訴訟兩極間取得平衡。

一方面,富經驗和能力的仲裁員能快捷有效地管理案件和按其專家知識達成裁決;另一方面,仲裁的過程有法庭把關,確保過程當中不會有嚴重的不公情況,基於法庭的輔助角色,公眾可放心把爭議交給仲裁解決,不必擔心權益受談判位置的強弱影響。

由於不同的仲裁使用者對法庭在其仲裁扮演的角色有不同需要,《仲裁條例》第九十九條容許仲裁當事人在仲裁協議中明文選擇條例附件中的條文是否適用。附件條文分配了法庭在仲裁中所扮演的角色。當事人可按條文自行選擇法庭參與的程度。當事人可選擇容許法庭就仲裁產生的初步法律問題進行判決(附表二條文三),容許法庭在發生嚴重不當事件時擱置仲裁庭的裁決(附表二條文四)、容許當事人在得到裁決後,如就法律問題不服裁決可向法庭上訴,或在向法庭上訴時是否先需要申請批准等。

由於仲裁使用者可自行選擇法庭的參與程度,故仲裁是可以滿足使用者希望法庭主持公義的訴求。調解當然亦有其優勝處，[13] 但卻不能滿足公眾對正確裁決的訴求。

第三部分　兩個香港裁決的問題

兩個近期的案例引發了業界就香港仲裁裁決認受性的討論。第一是終審法院在 *Democratic Republic of the Congo and others v. FG Hemisphere Associates LLC* [14]（剛果案）的判決；第二是原訟庭的 Stone J 在 *Hua Tian Long（No 2）* 的判決。[15]

I. 剛果案

Evergoinvest（仲裁當時人）在與剛果民主共和國的仲裁中勝訴，導致剛果民主共和國需要賠償巨大金額。勝訴後，Evergoinvest 將裁決的執行權賣給了 FG Hemisphere（申請人）。

取得執行權後，申請人入稟香港法庭在香港執行裁決。申請人申請攔截一筆由 China Railway Group Ltd.（CR）虧欠剛果的債務。CR 是在香港上市的中國公司。債務源自中國與剛果兩國所訂立的合約，由中國在剛果的發展項目換取中國在剛果的天然資源開發權。

申請人單方面向法庭取得了禁制令，阻止 CR 在申請人的申請有結果前付款給剛果。

剛果的陳詞是剛果國享有國家豁免權,故涉及主權的裁決不能在香港執行。剛果認為,按中國和香港的主權豁免法律原則,國家享有絕對豁免權,不受任何法庭裁決的影響。因此,香港法庭必須尊重豁免權並撤除有關的禁制令。

FG Hemisphere 的陳詞是,在香港,國家享有的是相對豁免權,而非絕對性。國家主權不能在純商業的糾紛上依賴豁免權。FG Hemisphere 的陳詞為本案純粹涉及商業糾紛,故剛果不能依賴國家豁免權抵賴其商業活動囤積的債務。

筆者在原訟庭審理初審時認為申請涉及的交易並非純是商業活動,故不論國家豁免權是否絕對性,FG Hemisphere 都不能在香港執行裁決。按此原因筆者撤銷了禁制令。

上訴庭大比數推翻了筆者的裁決(Yuen JA 同意筆者的判決)。大比數認為,按香港法,國家主權僅享有相對性豁免權。上訴庭大比數裁定案件的交易有可能是純商業的,故恢復了禁制令。

上訴到終審法院,大比數認為(Bokhary J 和 Mortimer NPJ 少數反對)香港應該跟隨中國採用外交絕對豁免權。終審法院亦大比數認為剛果參與仲裁不足以構成放棄豁免權,故 FG Hemisphere 不可以在香港執行裁決,攔截屬剛果的債項。

在剛果案判決之後,業界認為所有涉及國營企業的商業仲裁裁決(無論是否在香港進行)都會因國家豁免權而不能執行。

筆者不認為這是對剛果案的正確了解。

即使假設國營企業是國家豁免權所包括的部分，國營企業都不能依賴豁免權去逃避裁決責任。原因是國家豁免權只能是在涉及兩個國家的情況下方才適用。

在上例中，國營企業是在中國領土（香港）的法庭被申索，訴訟並不涉及另一個主權國。作為中國的商業組織，國營企業如何可以被豁免與本國法庭的命令？

比較下，在剛果案中，剛果國是在中國領土上引用豁免權。由於案件涉及兩個國家主權，故法庭必須考慮剛果是否就所有案件均可享有豁免權。

因香港法庭與國營企業同屬一個國家主權，故在涉及國營企業的訴訟中「國家豁免權」根本不適用。

換一個角度分析剛果案，在被告人享有國家豁免權的情況下，當事人是否絕無辦法去執行裁決？這個問題在所有採用「絕對豁免權」的國家均會碰到。

要在豁免方身上取得保障，便應從仲裁開始之前籌劃。在仲裁開始前，申訴人可以按《仲裁條列》第三十五條，（《示範法》第十七條）向仲裁庭申請臨時保障。

具體地，當事人可以向仲裁庭申請頒令被告妥善保存某些資產，以確保裁決得以執行。事實上，申訴人是在向被告索取保證金。舉例申訴人可要求仲裁庭頒令要求被告（享有豁免權的一方）把一定金額存入第三方保管，並要求第三方承諾去保管金額以至仲裁庭頒布裁決，便按裁決指示發放金額。

當然，這並不保證仲裁庭會依申請照章頒令，即使頒令，被告也不一定會按令行事。可臨時命令至少容許仲裁庭在被告違令的時候採取制裁行動，如禁止被告在按令行事前在仲裁中舉證或發言等。

在要求保證金的同時，申訴人應留意仲裁庭可能要求申訴人同時提供保證金以確保雙方公平享有裁決執行的保證。

II.「華天龍」案

這是一樁針對船隻「華天龍」的海事案件。「華天龍」是中國交通部旗下廣州打撈局的船隻。案中申訴人控告船主違反租船合約，並在香港扣留船隻作為保證金。

打撈局最初以豁免權為理由申請撤銷案件，但理據隨即被Stone 法官拒絕。法庭指出，被告是中國境內機構，不涉及外來主權，故豁免權並不適用。[16]

打撈局指，即使主權豁免不適用，作為國家政府機構，打撈局在港享有與回歸前「皇室豁免權」的對等地位。打撈局的論據是，在回歸後，中國政府繼續按《普通法》享有相當於當年英國政府享有的豁免訴訟地位。

法庭接納了打撈局的論點。

雙方爭議點主要圍繞官方法律程序條例（Cap 300）第三條：「針對官方提出的申索，可按照本條例的條文採取針對官方的法律程序以強制執行該項申索，毋須總督的同意。」案中雙方主要爭議上述條列有否在一九五七年生效時同時廢除《普通法》中的「皇家豁免權」。

法官認為，在回歸以前，香港的「皇家」機構有二：港英政府以及英國政府。官方法律程序條例只取消了港英政府的豁免權，卻沒有取締英國政府的訴訟免疫權。這是因為作為香港立法機關，當時的立法局沒有權利透過立法取消屬英方的豁免權。

按法理，中央政府在回歸後繼續享有與英國政府一樣的豁免權。[17]

但法官認為，即使被告可能受惠於豁免權，被告人在案中的行為，已證明被告人已經放棄了豁免權，故判被告人敗訴。

抗辯人就 Stone 法官的判決進行了上訴。但在上訴有結果前雙方就案件達成了協議。故自回歸後，上訴庭並未有機會就「皇家豁免權」進行審理。

追溯普通法，「皇家豁免權」源於中世紀「皇權不能犯錯」的普遍思維。從一般的角度看，在現代社會中應用來自中世紀的皇權概念似乎有所不妥。尤其是現代政權從歷史或原則上均與「皇權」連不上關係。

不過，縱使 Stone 法官的判決並不完美，從法律上中央政府仍然在香港擁有豁免權。雖然上訴庭並未確認或反對，但 Stone 的第一審裁決仍然有相當的參考性。

那麼，在「華天龍」的判決是正確的前提下，判決對商業仲裁有甚麼影響？

首先要注意的是此案中香港就處理案件的司法管轄權。「華天龍」是訴訟人申請在香港水域中扣留的。除此之外，香港與案件沒有其他關聯。申訴人租用船隻的目的是在越南和馬來西亞水域活動，而被告打撈局則除了是船主外，在香港沒有任何資產。

第二，Stone 法官在判詞中把中央政府機構分開兩種類型：

1. 中央政府的直接分支機構，並負責進行政府工作；和

2. 機構擁有與中央政府分開的獨立身份，並以其獨立身份進行商業活動。

法官在判詞中指明，豁免權只適用於第一類的政府機構；第二類的機構並不隸屬政府豁免權範圍內。[18]

按判決，在香港從事商業活動的國營企業並不享有豁免權。企業擁有獨立於國家政府的法律身份。縱使中央政府持有企業的股份，企業由於不是執行政府事務，故並不擁有豁免權。

這跟法庭在「華天龍」案中決定打撈局是交通部的一員有所分別。

「華天龍」是亞洲最大的起重機吊船，打撈局透過擁有和使用船隻參與各項搜救和打撈工作，參與並行使中央政府賦予的權力和責任。打撈局和交通部隸屬中央政府的一部分，沒有獨立的身分。

在上述原則上，Stone 法官認為打撈局是享有豁免權的機構。

第三，按香港《基本法》第二十二條：[19]

「中央各部門、各省、自治區、直轄市在香港特別行政區設立的一切機構及其人員均須遵守香港特別行政區的法律。」

筆者解讀第二十二條的意思是，當負責執行中央政府事務的國營機構在香港成立辦事處或進行活動，這些機構必須遵守香港法律。如是者，在香港設有辦事處，或是進行活動的機構在原則上不能擁有豁免權。這是因為香港法律要求他們執行法庭指令，就違反商業協議賠償對方的損失。

第四，《仲裁條例》第六條表明條例適用於「政府及中央人民政府在香港特別行政區設立的機構」。

就《基本法》第二十二條和《仲裁條例》第六條的規定，無論「皇家豁免權」是否在回歸後繼續生效，任何國家機構在香港成立辦事處，便受到《仲裁條例》所規管，包括條例第七十三條就裁決對於訴訟雙方具有約束力。

綜上所述，無論「皇家豁免權」在回歸後是否生效，豁免權在執行仲裁裁決的案件中並不適用。任何中央政府機構一旦在香港成立辦公處,該辦事處便受《基本法》第二十二條和《仲裁條例》的第六條所規定,受香港法庭的管轄和法庭命令的約束。即使「華天龍」的理據成立,所謂的豁免權只適用於中央政府沒有在香港設有辦事處的公共機關。

第四部分 總結

本章討論了法庭如何承認和執行裁決。

需要注意的要點如下:

1. 除非裁決嚴重和明顯違反《仲裁條例》第五條的規定,否則法庭不會輕易干擾仲裁庭的裁決;

2. 按《示範法》和紐約公約,法庭需應申請人申請要求審察裁決。審察需要時間,但法庭應建立程序確保審察不要消耗過長的時間;

3. 仲裁的優勢是富有彈性。仲裁協議能按雙方的要求制定法庭就糾紛所扮演的角色。雙方在協定仲裁協議時按需要採用《仲裁條例》所定的選擇性條款;

4. 「主權豁免」只有在申訴人要在香港執行涉及國外主權國的裁決時才會產生麻煩。大部分的仲裁案件不會受剛果案的影響。即使被執行人是外國主權國，當事人均可在仲裁前向仲裁庭申請要求對方存入保證金避免執行上的不方便；

5. 「皇家豁免」只有在被執行人是中央政府沒有在香港設辦事處的情況下適用。大部分的案件不會因「華天龍」一案在香港失去執行權。

---

1. 公約有五種語言的官方版本（英文、法文、西班牙文、俄文和中文）。有關公約全文可在 newyorkconvention.org 網址下載。該網站提供很多有關公約的資訊，包括公約國就施行公約的案例。以下所引用的條文為公約的相應的條文。

2. 仲裁進行的國家通常稱為「監察國」，而申請執行裁決的國家則通常稱為「執行國」。

3. 參照第八條（《示範法》第八條）的相約條款。

4. 參照第一章第二部分（II）部分就法庭就有關公共政策的討論。

5. [2012] 78 Arbitration 26.

6. [2010] 4 SLR 672 (Ang J); [2011] 4 SLR 305 (Chao, Phang, Rajah JJA).

7. [2010] 4 SLR 649 (Chan J); [2011] 4 SLR 739 (Chan CJ, Phang and Rajah JJA).

8. *Loc. cit.*, p.35.

9. *Ibid.*, p.33.

10. *Ibid.*, p.36.

11. HCCT 40 of 2010, 12 April 2011 (Reyes J); CACV 79 of 2011, 2 December 2011 (Tang VP, Fok JA, Sakhrani J).

12. HCCT 15 of 2010, 29 June 2011 [Saunders J]; CACV 136 of 2011, 9 May 2012 [Tang VP. Kwan and Fok JJA].

13. 筆者會在以下篇幅詳細討論調解細節。

14. FACV Nos. 5, 6 & 7 of 2010, 8 June 2011 (Bokhary, Chan and Ribeiro PPJ; Mortimer and Mason NPPJ).

15. [2010] 3 HKLRD 611.

16. 判詞的第二十九段

17. 判詞的第八十八段

18. 判詞的第九十八段

19. 感謝 Val Chow 向筆者指出相關條文。

第五章
調解的簡議和仲裁未來發展

本章比較調解與仲裁兩種私人解決爭議的方法。第一部分解釋調解的法律結構和有關的案例。第二部分比較調解與仲裁的利弊。最後是展望調解和仲裁兩方面的發展。

第一部分　調解

I. 現行制度下香港的調解程序

調解是透過中立的第三者協助雙方就糾紛達成和解。

按爭議[1]本質，調解員會與糾紛雙方共同或單獨會面，尋求可能的和解方案。在一般涉及兩方面（A 與 B）的調解可能會按以下方法進行：

1. 調解員與 A 和 B 進行初步會面；

2. 調解員單獨會見 A 與 B，嘗試了解雙方願意和解的條件；

3. 在單獨會面時，調解員嘗試取得 A 或 B 授權向另一方提出和解方案。在沒有授權的情況下，所有與調解員單方面的對話內容是絕對保密的。調解員必須在透露任何單方面對話內容時向當事人取得相應的授權；

4. 調解員來回於 A 和 B 之間，嘗試把雙方的分歧縮小；

5. 如果調解員認為 A 和 B 接近達成和解方案，便可以召開雙方會議並討論和解方案的細則，在雙方同意所有細節後，雙方便可以簽署和解協議；

6. 如果調解員覺得和解並不可能，他應通知調解雙方並終止和解；

7. 雙方的律師可以在調解過程中參與協助其當事人。

調解的成功率大概有百分之七十。有經驗的調解員通常能在調解首天便能判斷雙方是否能達成和解。因此，在很多情況下，訴訟不應該因為雙方正在進行調解而擱置。[2]

相比訴訟，調解省時快捷得多。

相比訴訟，在調解過程中雙方更能就自己真正的想法與調解員溝通。當事人毋須考慮其想法在法律上是否成立。調解員可以協助當事人雙方按其想法尋求和解。

在訴訟中，雙方的想法通常不是法庭考慮的事項。法庭是按法律判案的。即使勝訴，法庭在頒布濟助時不可能偏離法規而按雙方的意願辦事。

舉例說，雙方可在調解中同意就某事項道歉和賠償，但法庭則只能命令敗訴方作金錢補償，一般法庭是沒有權利要求敗訴方道歉的。

透過近期香港事務律師與大律師專業守則的更改，律師有責任就調解的合適性向當事人提供建議。因此，如律師在處理案件時不了解或不考慮調解是否合適，便違背專業操守了。

在 *Chevalier（Construction）Co. Ltd v Tak Cheong Engineering*

Development Ltd.[3] 一案中，林法官强調律師必須在當事人參與調解前向其提供案件分析，並解釋訴訟的利弊。林法官批評此案律師向當事人誇大了勝訴的可能性，導致當事人對案件產生不切實際的幻想。

筆者認為調解適用於絕大部分的案件。[4] 即使雙方曾作出持久的訴訟，調解都能有效的協助雙方達成和解。

調解員在調解過程中扮演關鍵角色。調解員的協助令雙方放下不必要的姿態並真誠表達其希望得到的結果。這些結果很可能是他們不能從訴訟中得到的。

調解員在雙方當事人之間來回傳達建議和反建議是處理商業糾紛很好的方法。這方法同樣適用於非商業的糾紛之中。在很多國家，調解在解決婚姻糾紛中都取得具鼓舞性的結果。沃爾夫法官（英國高等法院前首席法官及香港終審法院非常任法官）在二零零八年十二月在香港的一個法律界會議中提到，調解甚至能被應用在司法覆核的案件中。

綜上所述，香港法院非常致力推動調解的發展。法院認為，如果糾紛能透過調解解決，當事人實不應纏繞法庭，浪費有限的公共資源和法庭時間。

除推廣外，法院同時亦透過二零一零年一月一日生效的實務指引採取實際措施。

實務指引有數個目的。它強調所有在調解中發生的對話均享有法律保密權。[5] 它指出如果當事人無理拒絕調解，拒絕方即使最終勝訴亦可能在訟費分配上受到處罰。它就希望進行調解的當事人作出了程序上的指引。

按指引，當事人 A 會透過書面邀請當事人 B 就糾紛的全部或整個部分進行調解。如果 B 同意，需書面同意邀請。在書面同意後雙方便能進一步商討調解的細節。如果 B 拒絕調解，他必須在調解回應書中填上拒絕的理由。

按指引產生的文件需向法庭備案。這樣容許法庭監管案件是否透過調解結案。這亦為將來可能發生的訴訟留了證據，在法庭分配訟費時可看到當事人是否無理拒絕調解。

備案的文件也顯示雙方之間所同意的「調解最低目標」。在雙方達成目標的基礎下，雙方不會遭訟費懲罰。

甚麼是適當的最低調解目標？在 *Hak Tung Alfred Tang v. Bloomberg LP and another* [6] 一案中，時任聆案官的龍劍雲提出基本的調解目標應該是參與至少一次的具體調解會議，會議的時間應由調解員所訂。

意外地，許多當事人不能同意調解員的合適人選，需要邀請法庭就委任人下決定。同在 *Upplan Co. Ltd. v. Li Ho Ming and another* [7] 一案中，任聆案官的龍劍雲指出了法庭在委任調解員時會考慮的因素，包括糾紛的性質、金額、費用與調解員是否有時間等。

在申請由拒絕調解一方支付懲罰性訟費時，拒絕調解方需解釋合理的拒絕原因。[8] 邀請調解方並不需要證明調解有合理的成功可能。

基於調解對訟費的影響，很多人會敷衍進行調解以確保不會在訴訟後獲判懲罰性訟費，藉此拖延訴訟。

通常，當事人 A 會指示律師在參與數個小時的調解終止談判。在香港，調解的費用首兩小時大概是港幣二千五百元（包括準備），之後每小時港幣五百元。所以，付出港幣二千五百元進行調解等於是購買了訟費上的保險。

上述的虛假性調解是否令法庭的實務指引變得有名無實？

筆者不同意這消極的看法。當事人的法律代表有責任協助法庭解決糾紛。他們有義務確保當事人不濫用調解，並純粹視其為預防懲罰性訟費的例行公事。如只把調解視為例行公事，雙方只會徒添訴訟成本，到頭來反費時失事。

同時，法庭期望律師們拒絕和譴責當事人採取純戰略性的行動。

在涉及無法律代表的案件中，濫用調解事務指引的行為相對難以監察。縱使如此，當事人都需謹記無誠意地參與調解並不符合經濟原則，並會延遲解決爭議的時間。

II. 《調解條例》（Ord. No. 15 of 2012）

立法會在二零一二年六月二十一日通過《調解條例》，條例正待律政司定期實施。

《調解條例》的目的是提倡、鼓勵和促進以調解方式解決爭議。[9]

「調解」一詞在條例第四章被定義為：

「一個或多於一個分節構成的有組織程序，在該等分節中，一名或多於一名不偏不倚的個人在不對某項爭議或其任何部分作出判決的情況下，協助爭議各方作出下述任何或所有事宜 ——

　　　　1. 找出爭議點；

　　　　2. 探求和擬訂解決方案；

　　　　3. 互相溝通；

　　　　4. 就解決爭議的全部或部分，達成協議。」

定義中「不偏不倚」的便是調解員。

《調解條例》適用於在香港進行的調解程序，無論過程是全部在香港進行又或是部分在香港進行。調解雙方亦可通過協議指明調解按香港《調解條例》進行。[10]另外，《調解條例》亦適用於與調解相關的通訊。

在條例第二章提到的調解協議是：「指兩人或多於兩人所訂立的書面協議，同意將他們之間的爭議交付調解。」協議可以以電子形式存在。

在條例第二章提到的「調解通訊」的定義為：在調解過程中「（a）說出的任何說話或說出的任何行為；（b）擬備的人和文件；或（c）提供的任何資料。」這定義並不包括雙方的調解同意書或在調解後雙方就糾紛所達成的整個或部分和解協議。

《調解條例》適用在所有在第五（一）章內所提出的情況。[11]條例不設時效，即是無論調解是在條例生效前或生效後進行均受條例監管。

除了在附件一內所列出的例外情況，香港政府同樣受《調解條例》所規管。[12]總括而言，附件一內的例外情況主要涉及按現行法例所進行的調解（例如《勞資審裁處條例》（Cap. 25）、《婚姻制度改革條例》（Cap. 178）、《性別歧視條例》（Cap. 480）、《殘疾歧視條例》（Cap. 487），以及《種族歧視條例》（Cap. 602）。仲裁員需知道按《仲裁條例》第三十二章所進行的調解仲裁並不受調解條例所限。

調解條例第七章容許任何人協助當事人進行調解，故即使當事人代表並非律師或大律師，其充當調解代表均不違反《法律執業者條例》（Cap. 159）。

《調解條例》的關鍵在第八至十章。第八至十章指出調解通訊的保密性，並就這些通訊是否能在法庭作為證據提出規定。

基本上，調解通訊是保密的。故此，任何人只能在《調解條例》第八（二）和八（三）適用的情況下方能透露在調解過程中所獲得的通訊。

《調解條例》第八（二）章列出可以在沒有法庭容許的情況下把調節通訊呈堂的情況：

在下述情況下，任何人可披露調解通訊 ——

1. 所有下述人士均同意作出該項披露：

   i. 有關的調解的每一方；

   ii. 有關的調解的調解員，如有多於一名調解員，則每名調解員；及

   iii. 作出該項調解通訊的人（如該人並非有關的調解的任何一方或調解員）。

2. 該項調解通訊的內容，是公眾已可得的資料（但僅因非法披露才屬公眾可知的資料除外）；

3. 該項調解通訊的內容，是假若無本條規定，便會符合以下說明的資料：受民事法律程序中的文件透露規定所規限，或受其他要求當事人披露他們管有、保管或控制的文件的類似程序所規限；

4. 有合理理由相信，為防止或盡量減少任何人受傷的風險，或任何未成年人的福祉受嚴重損害的風險，作出該項披露是必須的；

5. 該項披露是為研究、評估或教育的目的而作出的，並且既沒有直接或間接洩露該項調解通訊所關乎的人的身份，亦相當不可能會直接或間接洩露該人的身份；

6. 該項披露是為徵詢法律意見而作出的；或

7. 該項披露是按照法律施加的要求而作出的。

在獲法庭批准的情況下，調解通訊可在三種情況下被披露：

1. 執行或質疑經調解的和解協議；

2. （如有人提出、指稱或申訴，而針對的是調解員所作出的專業失當行為，或任何以專業身份參與有關的調解的其他人所作出的專業失當行為）就該指稱或申訴提出證明或爭議；或

3. 有關的法院或審裁處認為在有關個案的情況下屬有理由支持的任何其他目的。

按《調解條例》第九章，調解通訊只有在獲法庭許可的情況下方能被作為呈堂（包括仲裁）證據。在證據被應用在仲裁情況下，申請應該在原訟法庭提出。[13] 在考慮是否允許調解通訊未

呈堂證據時，法庭會考慮：

1. 該項調解通訊是否可以根據第八（二）條披露，或是否已經如此披露；

2. 披露該項調解通訊或接納該項通訊作為證據，是否符合公眾利益，或是否有助於秉行公義；及

3. 有關的法院或審裁處認為屬相關的任何其他情況或事宜。

業界曾希望《調解條例》會協助統一調解員的執業要求，並提供一套調解員需要遵守的專業守則。可是現行條例並沒有提供有關的指引，要留待以後的立法討論。

第二部分　調解與仲裁的比較

在本節，筆者簡單比較調解與仲裁的分別。

首先，就保密性而言，仲裁與調解均受保密條款所保障。

筆者已經提過《調解條例》中的相關保密條例，《仲裁條例》中的保密條例可在第十七和十八章中找到。

按第十七章，涉及仲裁的法庭程序均閉門進行。但是法庭在諮詢雙方後可把判決個別內容公開。任何公開的判決內容不可洩漏任何有關仲裁（包括雙方身份）的細節。

第十八條禁止涉及仲裁的所有人士在沒有當事人雙方同意的情況下出版、透露或傳達任何涉及仲裁或其裁決的資訊。第十八（二）條容許仲裁人在三種情況下單方面透露仲裁資訊。這三個情況為：

1. 該項發表、披露或傳達，是 ——

    i. 為保障或體現有關一方的法律權利或利益；或

    ii. 為強制執行或質疑該款所提述的裁決，而在香港或香港以外地方的法院或其他司法當局的法律程序中作出的；

2. 該項發表、披露或傳達，是向任何政府團體、規管團體、法院或審裁處作出的；而在法律上，有關一方是有責任作出該項發表、披露或傳達；或

3. 該項發表、披露或傳達，是向任何一方的專業顧問或任何其他顧問作出的。

《調解條例》和《仲裁條例》的保密條文相似甚多。概括來說，適用於仲裁保密的條款比調解的少，範圍亦相對的窄。

第二，儘管香港的法律架構導致濫用調解的情況，同樣的濫用情況則不大會在仲裁中發生，因在仲裁中違反仲裁庭命令會招致嚴重的後果。

第三，調解亦需要案件管理。例如在調解正式展開前雙方與調

解員可選擇透過會議釐清雙方在調解需要處理的實質問題。

但是，一般而言，調解的程序是透明及彈性的，隨雙方談判的進展，調解員會採取不同的方法協助雙方達成雙贏的調解方案。

比較下，案件管理對仲裁則非常重要。案件管理協助仲裁各方面釐清和了解案件的確實爭議點，並協助仲裁庭決定各個爭議點應如何舉證。案件管理為調解提供確實時間表，協助仲裁庭按時審案，不會因延時而提高訟費成本。

第四，法庭不會輕易探討在調解的細節。除了在《調解條例》內明文規定的情況外，法庭會尊重調解的保密性，並不會容許調解內容呈堂。

相對地，筆者認為在仲裁過程中法庭和仲裁庭之間有互補的關係。法庭確保仲裁是在公平的程序下所進行，並在仲裁產生重大的法律或事實錯誤，導致裁決欠公平的情況下介入更正結果。當然，法庭給予仲裁庭相當高的自主權，但在適當時法庭會毫不猶豫地仔細審理裁決是否正確。

第五，透過調解達成的和解協議具法律效力，可轉換被當成法庭命令（Tomlin Order）執行。

法庭命令的作用是令法庭擱置涉及糾紛的所有法律程序。由於雙方達成了和解協議，法庭會在雙方尊重和願意執行協議的基礎下擱置法律程序，如果雙方違反和解協議，另一方則可要求法庭命令違約方執行和解協議內容。

法庭命令為執行和解協議提供了許多方便，當協議雙方卻不能在香港以外的地方執行協議。

仲裁裁決可以按《仲裁條例》當作法庭命令執行。此外，按《紐約公約》，仲裁裁決被一百四十六個國家承認並容許仲裁裁決在其境內執行。

第六，仲裁和調解可同時進行，但如果調解員和仲裁員為同一人，則必須相對小心確保程序公正。

仲裁和調解由同一人進行是有風險的，調解中雙方在與調解員單獨會面時，應鼓勵他們暢所欲言，坦白說出當事人希望得到的結果。如果調解人在調解失敗後同時充當仲裁人，兩個角色間則會產生極大的利益衝突。最起碼，仲裁員是不應單獨會見當事人的。

充當過調解員的仲裁員在調解過程中必知道雙方的保密資料，在這情況下仲裁員如何在仲裁時保持中立？

要保持中立，仲裁員便可能要違反調解員的保密責任，把其所知保密資料告知雙方，以免在不公開公正的情況下作出裁決。

按《仲裁條例》第三十三條，仲裁員可在雙方當事人書面同意下兼當調解員。但如果調解未能產生和解協議，而爭議需要透過仲裁繼續解決，仲裁員則必須向各方透露在調解過程中獲悉，認為對仲裁有關鍵性的資料。

自然衍生的問題是，仲裁員如何知道哪些在調解過程中所透露的機密資料會對仲裁產生關鍵作用？不同的資料可在仲裁過程中有不同程度的重要性。因此，仲裁員很難拿捏，如何披露就從調解過程中取得的資料。兼任調解員的仲裁員也會因此活在偏見的陰影中。

基於仲裁與調解在結構上所存在的矛盾，香港的仲裁員普遍不傾向接受調解仲裁的委任。相反，調解仲裁在國內則相對普遍。

第三部分　仲裁的發展

筆者認為仲裁在訴訟外提供了相當有效的糾紛解決渠道。仲裁相比訴訟更能節省時間和成本。但是，仲裁的效率終究取決於仲裁員的辦案能力，他們必須時刻保持中立和效率。和生活中其它事情一樣，每個人的方法能力都不會是一樣的。

仲裁可以有許多形式，它跟人與人之間所產生的矛盾一樣層出不窮。某些仲裁可能涉及極多複雜的專業和技術性問題，而其他的可能只是要求仲裁員公平地分配一項產業，並不是每個仲裁都涉及法律，更遑論是艱深的法律論點了。

所以，雖然法律知識和訓練對成為仲裁員有一定的幫助，筆者並不認為法律知識是成功仲裁員所必備的。最重要的是仲裁員能否在仲裁過程中時刻保持中立和採取開放的態度，給予雙方合理機會就爭議作解釋和陳詞，並嘗試用合理時間去理解雙方的論點。

這當然是易說難為的。但能做到中立開放並不需要任何專業法律技巧。中立開放需要的是仲裁員擁有耐性、專注力、智慧和公平原則。這些特點是每個人都可擁有的，所以筆者認為每個人都可以成為成功的仲裁員。

筆者透過此書道出一些仲裁員應該思考的事項，而不是希望每位讀者都同意本人的觀點。重要的是希望成為仲裁員的讀者起碼能夠理解和思考在仲裁中重複出現的問題，並以此書為起點去思考解決問題的方法。筆者所希望的只不過是提出，無論如何，仲裁員均應公平、及時以及按具成本效益的方法解決爭議。

近年，調解被廣泛推崇為解決爭議的好辦法。

的確，相比仲裁，調解更能彈性處理雙方糾紛。調解具靈活結構，能以低成本迅速協助雙方解決爭議。

但調解亦有其缺點。例如調解不能滿足人們希望透過法律伸張公義的心理需求，這訴求並非金錢所能衡量的。

很多人希望通過法庭的判詞去宣布他們的權利。筆者覺得仲裁可以有效的滿足人在這方面的需要。這也是本人堅信，在仲裁員有效持平地辦案的情況下，仲裁的前景是十分可觀的。

總括而言，仲裁具有相當大的潛力。《仲裁條例》是重要的開始，但只是一個開始。

1. 筆者在本章形容調解的概念源於《淺談新民事司法訴訟》第六章的內容，並更新了案例的發展。

2. 不過，法庭不會單純因為雙方正進行調解而自動擱置訴訟。在 *Faithbright Development Ltd v Ng Kwok Yuen and others* HCA No.9058 of 1999, 20 Sept. 2010 一案中，時任聆案官的龍劍雲指出，法庭在考慮是否在調解期間擱置訴訟，取決於案件所有有關因素。例如，如果法庭發現雙方有拖延訴訟的傾向，則大部分情況下不會擱置訴訟進度。

3. HAC No. 153 of 2008, 8 June 2011（第二十段）。林文瀚法官指出，尤其是在建築工程糾紛中，雙方自定的排解程序往往比透過法庭訴訟有效和快捷。因此，涉及爭議的各方均應考慮有關的選擇。建築糾紛所衍生的工程延誤可影響工程的整體進度，從而產生高昂的訟費和違約金。適合的自定排解程序能有效縮短解決糾紛的時間，並避免影響到工程整體進度。當事人可以同意暫時遵從排解人的決定，直到工程完成為止。其後，若雙方就排解的決定有爭議，便可向法庭申請重新審核有關的決定。

4. 在 *Incorporated Owners of Shatin New Town v Yeung Kui* CACV 45 of 2009, 於二零一零年二月五日的判決內，張澤祐法官（石仲廉法官與倫明高法官同意判詞）在判詞第八段指出，在涉及如何正確詮譯樓宇公契的案件中，業主立案法團有權拒絕進行調解。原因是詮譯公契涉及法律問題，而法團有法律責任正確施行共契條款，其範圍不止涉及答辯人，而是關乎樓宇所有業主的利益。故法庭訴訟是正確的辦法。

5. 此原則在 *Champion Concord Ltd v Craigside Investments Ltd and Others* FACV Nos. 16 & 17 of 2010, 於二零一一年五月十七日的判詞中被終審法院肯定。李義法官在判詞第十七段中提出，調解過程享有絕對的保密性，這是普遍接受和適用的原則。只有在少數極其特殊的例外情況下，法庭方會容許抵觸保密原則的證據呈堂。就法庭如何處理調解保密性的方法，可參考早期案例 *Wu Wei v. Liu Yi Ping* HCA No. 1452/2004, 於二零零九年一月三十日頒下的判詞（暫委法官黃國瑛資深大律師）。不過，要注意該案是在新的《調解條例》施行前判決的。

6. HCA No. 198/2010, 二零一零年七月十六日（第十三至十五段）。

7. HCA no. 1915 of 2009, 二零一零年八月五日，在 *Resource Development Ltd v Swanbridge Ltd*, HCA No. 1873 of 2009, 龍劍雲司法常務官於二零一零年五月三十一日頒下的判詞第六段中提到，在一切均等的情況下，調解員的收費是委任調解員最重要的因數。

8. *Golden Eagle International (Group) ltd. v. GR Investment Holdings Ltd.* HCA 2032 of 2007, 25 June 2010 (林文瀚法官).

9. MO s. 4 (1).

10. MO s. 5 (1).

11. MO s. 5 (2).

12. MO s. 6.

13. MO s. 10 (3)(e).

鳴謝

本書內容源於二零一二年一至二月期間,筆者分別在香港海事法協會和香港大學所作的演講。筆者對這兩所機構一向以來的支持和鼓勵十分感激。特別鳴謝 Steven Wise 先生和 Peter Mills 先生(海事協會的兩位現任和剛退任的秘書長)幫助協調有關演講的事情。亦感謝王則左先生慷慨向參與演講的賓客送贈了他所撰寫的《仲裁條例註解》。

本書第一章是筆者於二零一一年在悉尼舉行的亞太區司法機構會議中演講講詞的改篇。該會議由新南威爾士、香港和新加坡的司法機構聯合舉行,筆者在該會議中獲益良多,更深切地了解到香港、新南威爾士、澳洲、新加坡和其他地方等地區就仲裁事宜在施法上的分別。

本書第二章第二部分的內容來自筆者在二零一二年五月,應香港仲裁司學會和香港法律專業學會邀請,在 International Arbitration in Hong Kong: Some Issues and Recent Development 會議中就仲裁的臨時濟助申請所作出的演講。筆者感謝兩所機構的信任和邀請。

本書第四章第二部分內容來自筆者在二零一二年九月在香港 CIETAC 開幕典禮上就《法庭向仲裁提供的援助》的演講詞。感謝香港律政司和香港 CIETAC 的邀請。會上，筆者從楊弘磊法官的演講「海外裁決如何在國內執行」之演講中獲益良多。

同時，亦十分感謝陳星楠先生抽空將本書翻譯成中文，並交予香港三聯書店出版。

本書承蒙多方協助，篇幅有限未能一一致謝，但筆者亦十分感謝他們。當然，本書所有的不足處皆源於我。

有三位人士筆者必須特別鳴謝，他們是：Micheal Delaney 先生、Robin Peard 先生和楊良宜先生。Micheal Delaney 先生在筆者剛成為大律師時，勇敢委任筆者代表客人參與本人人生第一次仲裁。Robin Peard 先生在一九八一年暑假，筆者充當暑期實習生時教導了本人仲裁的基礎知識。楊良宜先生多年來多次邀請筆者向他的門生演講，並容許筆者選擇自己喜歡的題目。在這些機會中，筆者與楊先生和他的同僚和學生的豐富交流，有助筆者釐清很多對仲裁法的思維。

筆者希望以上三位不介意本人把此書獻給他們。

Anselmo Reyes

香港

二零一二年十月十五日

HOW TO BE AN ARBITRATOR: A PERSONAL VIEW

Chapter 1
A Framework for Hong Kong Arbitration

A framework for Hong Kong arbitration is to be found in the Arbitration Ordinance (Cap.609). This chapter introduces the main provisions of the statute in Section A. It illustrates in Section B how those provisions might apply to answer some basic questions which typically arise in connection with any arbitration. The object is to give the reader a feel for the practical application of the statute. That feel will serve as the foundation for later chapters which will examine specific aspects of the arbitration process in greater detail.

A. The Arbitration Ordinance

The Ordinance was enacted on 11 November 2010 and came into force on 1 June 2011. Subject to transitional provisions in the new Ordinance concerning arbitrators appointed and arbitrations commenced before June 2011, the old Arbitration Ordinance (Cap.341) has been repealed and is no longer in effect.

I. Preliminary matters

The Ordinance functions as a self-contained code governing arbitrations (whether domestic or international in subject matter) held in Hong Kong.

The UNCITRAL Model Law as amended on 7 July 2006 has force of law in Hong Kong as a result of the Ordinance coming into effect.

Commercial arbitration is a global phenomenon. The United Nations Commission on International Trade Law (UNCITRAL) first promulgated the Model Law on International Commercial Arbitration in December 1985 with a view to unifying the law regulating commercial arbitrations wherever in the world they might take place. Since then, more and more states have adopted the Model Law as the standard by which arbitrations within their boundaries are to be conducted.

However, the Model Law does not merely set out rules for the conduct of arbitrations within a state. It also provides for the enforcement of foreign arbitration awards in a given state which has adopted the Model Law.

Different states may "pick and choose" from among the provisions of the Model Law when adopting the same for use in their particular jurisdiction. Nonetheless, there will inevitably be a substantial degree of sameness (with only slight variation) in the provisions of the Model Law adopted by different states.

Such an outcome will only benefit international commerce as the last thing that persons engaged in business transactions would want to discover is that the laws regulating arbitration and the enforcement of awards in an outside jurisdiction in which they do business are radically different from the laws which they are accustomed to in their home country. The fewer surprises there are for persons doing business in a foreign state, the more willing they should be to expand their investment in that state.

Previously under the old Ordinance there were separate rules for "domestic" and "international" arbitrations. Subject to transitional arrangements, the distinction between "domestic" and "international" arbitrations may be regarded as obsolete. Arbitrations here are now all governed by the Model Law as enacted by the new Ordinance. This unitary regime is the major reform under the new Ordinance.

Section 3[1] identifies the objective behind the reforms introduced by the new Ordinance. The objective is "to facilitate the fair and speedy resolution of disputes by arbitration without unnecessary expense".

To achieve that objective, arbitrators and the Court must bear in mind 2 cardinal principles. The first is that "subject to the necessary safeguards that are necessary in the public interest, the parties to a dispute should be free to agree on how the dispute should be resolved". The second is that "the Court should interfere in the arbitration of a dispute only as expressly provided for in this Ordinance".

The first principle gives priority to the parties' agreement to go to arbitration (rather than Court litigation) to resolve their differences. The parties should only approach the Court for assistance to the extent necessary in order to give effect to their agreement to arbitrate.

The second principle complements the first. There may be times when a party (or possibly both parties) will have to seek the Court's assistance to give effect to the agreement to arbitrate. In such situations, the Court's approach will be to intervene as little as possible and, even then, it will only intervene to the extent permitted by the Ordinance. The Court will avoid putting itself in the situation where the Court (as opposed to an arbitral tribunal) is resolving the parties' substantive dispute.

Section 5 (which applies in place of Model Law Art.1 (Scope of Application)) provides for the Ordinance to regulate any arbitration in Hong Kong. This will be regardless of where the agreement to arbitrate was made.

For arbitrations which take place outside Hong Kong, only certain sections will apply. Those sections are ones which common sense would expect to apply. Thus, for example, s.20 (concerning Court proceedings commenced here in breach of an agreement to arbitrate); ss.21, 45 and 60 (conferring a power on the Court to make interim orders in aid of arbitration); and s.61 and Part 10 (concerning the enforcement in Hong Kong of a tribunal's orders and awards) will be applicable.

Section 6 provides that the Ordinance will apply to "the Government and the Offices set up by the Central People's Government" in Hong Kong. I will examine this section in more detail in Chapter 4 when discussing the potential impact on arbitration in Hong Kong of the decision in The "HUA TIAN LONG" (No.2)[2] (holding that Offices of the Central People's Government enjoy an immunity from suit in Hong Kong analogous to the immunity formerly enjoyed here at common law by Offices of the British Colonial Government).

II. General provisions

Section 8 replaces Model Law Art.2 (Definitions and Rules of Interpretation) with the definitions and principles of interpretation found in s.2 of the Ordinance.

More importantly, s.9 supplements the definitions in s.2 with the principle of interpretation found in Model Law Art.2A. This useful principle of interpretation requires that, in construing the Model Law, "regard is to be had to its international origin"; to "the need to promote uniformity in its application"; and to "the observance of good faith". Further, "questions ... which are not expressly settled [by the Model Law] are to be settled in conformity with the general principles on which this Law is based".

Section 10 enacts Model Law Art.3 (Receipt of Written Communication). It provides that written communications are deemed to have been received once delivered. As for instantaneous means of communication (for instance, e-mail and fax), ss.10(2) and (3) modify Art.3 by stipulating that such type of communication will be deemed to have been received on the day on which the message is sent, provided there is "a record of receipt of the communication by the addressee".

Section 11 enacts Model Law Art.4 (Waiver of Right to Object). The parties can agree to derogate from parts of the Model Law.[3] Where an arbitrator deviates from the procedures in the Model Law without the parties' agreement and the Model Law permits such derogation, then objection to the non-compliance must be made without "undue delay". If instead a party proceeds with the arbitration, that party will be deemed to have waived any right to object.

Art.4 is an extremely compact and cryptic provision. Although not entirely clear, the implication appears to be that, where an arbitration deviates from the Model Law in a way that is not permitted, a party who fails to object promptly will not be deemed to have waived the right to object at a later time. This is presumably because an arbitrator does not have jurisdiction to depart from mandatory provisions of the Model Law and the parties cannot, by mere silence or waiver, confer upon the arbitrator a jurisdiction which the latter does not have under the Ordinance.[4]

Section 12 enacts Model Law Art.5 (Extent of Court Intervention). It insists that "no Court shall intervene except where so provided in this Law".

Section 13 designates the Court and the Hong Kong International Arbitration Centre (HKIAC) as the bodies to assist or supervise arbitrations in accordance with the Model Law. The HKIAC is a company limited by guarantee which administers arbitrations and provides facilities and other services for arbitration in Hong Kong.

Section 14 states that the Limitation Ordinance (Cap.347) applies to arbitrations in the same way that it applies to actions in Court.

Section 14(3) deals with the situation where an arbitration agreement provides that no cause of action will accrue until an award is made. Such a provision is sometimes known as *a Scott v. Avery* clause, after a famous 19th century case[5] in which the provision featured. The clause may prevent a person from immediately suing the other party in Court for breach of contract. But one ignores the clause for the purposes of calculating limitation (that is, whether the time allowed by the law for commencing a Court action has expired)–time runs from the moment when a cause of action would normally have arisen in the absence of the clause.

Section 14(4) clarifies that, where an award is set aside, the period between commencement of arbitration and the setting aside, is excluded from any time limitation calculation.

Section 16 stipulates that Court proceedings relating to arbitrations are heard by the Court in chambers (not open to the public). But the Court may override this rule of its own motion or upon the application of a party. This provision ensures that arbitration proceedings remain confidential, even where a party seeks the Court's assistance to enforce an arbitration agreement or challenge the conduct or award of a tribunal.

The confidentiality conferred by s.16 is reinforced by s.17 which governs the reporting of Court proceedings under the Ordinance. In addition, s.18 prohibits, save in limited circumstances, the disclosure of information relating to arbitral proceedings or to the contents of an award.

For the purposes of establishing the practice or principles to be followed in connection with arbitration proceedings, the Court may decide to publish its Judgment in relation to a given arbitration. When so doing, the Court will usually redact its Judgment. The published version would then focus on legal principle, rather than disclose details of the arbitration (including the names of the parties involved).

III. Arbitration agreement

Section 19 enacts the definition of arbitration agreement in Option I of Model Law Art.7 (Definition and Form of Arbitration Agreement). Option I defines an "arbitration agreement" as "an agreement … to submit to … in respect of a defined legal relationship, whether contractual or not". Option I adds that: "An arbitration agreement may be in the form of an arbitration clause or in the form of a separate agreement." [6]

The remainder of Art.7 provides that, for the Ordinance to apply, an arbitration agreement must be in "writing". It then defines what constitutes "writing". The definition is wide. For instance, it includes "information generated, sent, received or stored by electronic, magnetic, optical or similar means".

Section 19(1) extends the definition of "writing" in Art.7 by stipulating that an arbitration agreement is in "writing" if it is contained in a document "whether or not the document is signed by the parties to the agreement". But the agreement must have been recorded in the relevant document by a person (including someone not a party to the arbitration agreement) with the authority of the parties.

Section 20 enacts Model Law Art.8 (Arbitration Agreement and Substantive Claim before the Court). It deals with the situation where Court proceedings are initiated in breach of an arbitration agreement. If the defendant objects "not later than when submitting [a] first statement on the substance of the dispute", the Court must stay the Court proceedings and insist on the dispute being resolved by arbitration. The Court normally has no discretion in the matter. Unless it finds that the agreement is "null and void, inoperative or incapable of being performed", the Court must stay the litigation and leave the parties' dispute to be resolved by an arbitral tribunal.

Exceptionally, even if an arbitration agreement is binding and operative, the Court retains a discretion, whether or not to grant a stay, if a claim falls within the jurisdiction of the Labour Tribunal.

In Admiralty (that is, shipping) matters, the Court may make a stay conditional on the lodging of security by a defendant. Where a Court grants a stay, it may also order that any security or bail put up in connection with a vessel be held as security for the satisfaction of an award.

Note that the Court's duty to stay a dispute brought before it by a plaintiff P against a defendant D in breach of an arbitration agreement between P and D, is qualified by s.19(3). The latter provision brings into play Control of Exemption Clauses Ordinance (Cap.71) (CECO) s.15.

CECO s.15 offers P a measure of protection where P has bought goods as a consumer from D. Where P has dealt with D as a consumer, an arbitration agreement in relation to the purchase can only be enforced in 2 circumstances. The first is where P has agreed in writing, following the occurrence of the dispute with D, to go to arbitration in relation to that dispute. The second is where P has previously gone to arbitration, pursuant to the purchase agreement, in respect of some other difference with D.

Where the Court stays the parties to arbitration pursuant to Art.8, the Court's decision will not be subject to appeal. In contrast, a party may seek leave to appeal against a refusal to stay proceedings to arbitration. This is again a manifestation of the cardinal principle that, as much as possible, the Court should hold the parties to their agreement to resolve disputes by arbitration, rather than litigation.

Section 21 states that, both before and during arbitrations, a party may seek interim relief from the Court.

IV. Composition of arbitral tribunal

Section 23 enacts Model Law Art.10(1) (Number of Arbitrators). The parties are free to set the number of arbitrators. Where they are unable to agree on how many arbitrators there should be, the number will be 1 or 3 as decided by the HKIAC.

Section 24 enacts Model Law Art.11 (Appointment of Arbitrators). It gives detailed provisions for the appointment of arbitrators, especially where the parties fail to agree procedures or do not comply with agreed procedures.

Section 25 enacts Model Law (Art.12) (Grounds for Challenge). On appointment, an arbitrator is required to disclose "any circumstances likely to give rise to justifiable doubts as to ...

impartiality or independence". An arbitrator's appointment may be challenged if there are "justifiable doubts as to ... impartiality or independence". The arbitrator may be removed where one "does not possess qualifications agreed to by the parties". But, where a party has appointed an arbitrator, a challenge may be in respect of matters which the party became aware after the arbitrator's appointment.

Section 26 enacting Model Law Art.13 (Challenge Procedure) explains how to challenge the appointment of an arbitrator. It also states the effect of a challenge.

Sections 30 and 31 enable a tribunal with an even number of arbitrators to appoint an umpire. The parties or (if they fail) the arbitrators are free to agree what the umpire's functions are to be. Section 31 provides for an umpire to replace the tribunal where the latter cannot reach any agreement in relation to a matter in dispute.

Sections 32 and 33 concern mediation in aid of arbitration (sometimes known as "med-arb"). [7] The provisions enable an arbitrator to act both as mediator and (in the event that mediation fails) as arbitrator. A person may be mediator and arbitrator in a matter where the arbitration agreement so allows, or where the parties later agree in writing. Before proceeding with an arbitration, however, a mediator turned arbitrator must disclose to the parties such confidential information obtained in the mediation as the arbitrator considers "material to the proceedings". "Mediation" is defined in s.2 to include conciliation.

V. Jurisdiction of the arbitral tribunal

Section 34 enacts Model Law Art.16 (Competence of Arbitral Tribunal to Rule on Its Jurisdiction). A tribunal may rule on its own jurisdiction. A challenge to jurisdiction must be mounted "not later than the submission of the statement of defence". The mere fact that a party has appointed an arbitrator will not preclude a jurisdictional challenge by that party.

It is important to understand the thinking underlying Art.16.

An agreement to arbitrate may exist as a free-standing contract or as part of some longer contract.

In the latter case, the agreement to arbitrate is treated by the law as "autonomous" or independent. This means that, if for some reason (say, mistake, misrepresentation or fraud) the longer contract is or becomes void, the agreement to arbitrate contained in the longer contract may still be valid. The law treats the enforceability of the agreement to arbitrate as a separate issue from the validity of the longer contract (minus the agreement to arbitrate).

This autonomy of the agreement to arbitrate is the reason why an arbitrator may rule on the validity of the longer contract (for example, whether that contract has been vitiated by mistake, misrepresentation or fraud) without undermining the jurisdiction (to settle the parties' dispute) conferred on the arbitrator by the agreement to arbitrate. In the absence of this principle of the autonomy of the arbitration agreement, there would be a contradiction. In ruling that the longer contract was void, the arbitrator would at the same time be annulling the arbitration agreement which forms the basis of his or her jurisdiction to declare the contract void.

The arbitrator would of course still have to determine whether he or she has jurisdiction to act as arbitrator under the terms of the autonomous agreement to arbitrate. Art.16 thus specifically confers on the arbitrator the competence to rule on his or her own jurisdiction to arbitrate pursuant to the agreement to arbitrate. This is sometimes referred to as the "competence-competence" principle. That is, an arbitral tribunal has the "competence" to rule on its own "competence" or jurisdiction to determine the parties' disputes.

But a ruling by the arbitrator on his or her competence to act as arbitrator under an alleged agreement to arbitrate cannot be the final word on the question of jurisdiction. The Court must have the final say on the matter, since the arbitrator could be wrong on the question of his or her jurisdiction to arbitrate. Where then the tribunal decides that it has jurisdiction, a party may still appeal to the Court against the ruling. The Court's decision on the matter will be subject to no appeal.

In contrast, where a tribunal rules that it has no jurisdiction to arbitrate, there is no appeal against that decision to the Court. The Court would then have to determine the substance of the dispute.

VI. Interim measures and preliminary orders

Section 35 enacts Model Law Art.17 (Power of Arbitral Tribunal to Order Interim Measures). It enables arbitrators to grant interim measures to maintain or restore a status quo; to prevent action likely to cause current or imminent harm; to preserve assets out of which an award may be satisfied; or to preserve material evidence.

Section 35(2) is cryptic. It merely states: "An interim measure referred to in Article 17 … is to be construed as including an injunction, but not including an order under section 56."

Section 56, on the other hand, confers general powers on an arbitrator for the conduct of an arbitration. For example, it enables an arbitrator to give orders for security for costs; discovery; the giving of evidence by affidavit; and the inspection and preservation of property.

There is on the face of things a significant overlap between Art.17 and s.56. Why should that be the case? I shall suggest an answer to this conundrum in Chapter 2. For the moment, it should be noted that, although there is overlap, Art.17 and s.56 are not identical in the powers they confer. The Art.17 powers seem wider in scope than those under art 56.

Section 36 enacts Model Law Art.17A (Conditions for Granting Interim Measures). This states the test for granting an interim measure. The test entails balancing the harm that would result from the refusal of a measure against the harm that might ensue from the grant of the same. Where the former harm outweighs the latter, interim relief should *prima facie* be given. But the test also requires a tribunal to assess whether the requesting party has a "reasonable possibility" of succeeding on the merits.

By s.37, requests for interim measures can be made *ex parte*, that is, unilaterally by application to the Court in the absence of (and sometimes without even informing) the other party.

Sections 39 to 42 make specific provisions for the various interim measures which a tribunal can direct. In particular, an arbitrator may require a party in whose favour an interim measure is granted to provide security or may order that party to pay to the other party the costs and damages attributable to the grant of the measure.

Section 45 empowers the Court to grant interim measures in aid of arbitrations taking place inside or outside Hong Kong. In relation to an arbitration in Hong Kong, the Court's jurisdiction is concurrent with that of the arbitral tribunal. Where proceedings have been or will be commenced outside Hong Kong, the Court may only grant an interim measure if the arbitration is "capable of giving rise to an ... award (whether interim or final) that may be enforced in Hong Kong" and the interim measure is of "a type ... that may be granted in Hong Kong ... by the Court".

Section 45(6) enables the Court to grant an interim measure in relation to non-Hong Kong proceedings even where the relevant dispute would not give rise to a Hong Kong cause of action.

VII. Conduct of arbitral proceedings

Section 46 requires that parties be "treated with equality".

An arbitral tribunal must therefore be independent, fair and impartial. The tribunal must give the parties "a reasonable opportunity [8] to present their cases and to deal with the cases of their opponents". The tribunal needs to use procedures that are "appropriate to the particular case" and which avoid "unnecessary delay or expense". Such procedures should then "provide a fair means for resolving the dispute".

Section 48 enacts Model Law Art.19 (Determination of Rules of Procedure). The parties are free to agree on the procedure to be followed by a tribunal. If they do not agree, the tribunal may conduct the arbitrations "in the manner that it considers appropriate".

An arbitral tribunal should not be regarded solely as a surrogate Court bound by the formal rules of evidence used in Court proceedings. One of the advantages of arbitration is supposed to be its informality. Therefore, in many cases, it may be appropriate (and cheaper!) for the tribunal to adopt a more relaxed attitude to the proof of relevant facts.

Sections 49 to 63 deal with the conduct of the arbitration by the arbitrators and, where necessary, with the assistance of the Court. For example, s.50 deals with the language of the arbitration; s.51 provides for statements of claim and defence; and s.52 concerns the oral or written conduct of proceedings. Where a party is in default, an arbitrator may make peremptory orders (that is, penalising the party in default for noncompliance) under s.53. The tribunal may appoint experts to prepare reports or assessors to assist in technical matters.

I have mentioned the arbitrators' powers under s.56. One should also note that a tribunal may not order security for costs by reason only that a party is ordinarily resident or has been incorporated outside of Hong Kong. It is also worth bearing in mind that s.56(8) empowers a tribunal to administer oaths to witnesses and to "direct the attendance … of witnesses in order to give evidence or to produce documents or other evidence".

Section 57 empowers a tribunal to limit the amount of recoverable costs.

Section 58 gives an arbitrator power to extend the time in which a party may commence arbitral proceedings or any other dispute resolution procedure (such as mediation) that needs to be exhausted before an arbitration can commence.

Section 59 enables a tribunal to dismiss a claim where a claimant has "unreasonably delayed" in pursuing a claim.

Section 60 allows the Court to make orders for the inspection and preservation of evidence and for the conduct of experiments on property. These mirror the arbitrators' powers of which examples have already been mentioned. But the Court's powers are wider in that it may make such orders even in connection with non-Hong Kong arbitrations.

Under s.61, with leave of the Court, an arbitrator's interim directions and orders may be enforced in the same way as orders and directions of the Court.

Section 63 provides that the prohibitions in the Legal Practitioners

Ordinance (Cap.159) against unqualified persons practising as a barrister or solicitor do not apply to arbitral proceedings. Consequently, anyone may do anything (including advise or appear as an advocate) in relation to an arbitration. The rationale is that, because arbitration is a private means of dispute resolution, a party should be free to instruct whomever that party wants to act on its behalf in an arbitration.

VIII. Making of an award and termination of proceedings

Section 64 enacts Model Law Art.28 (Rules Applicable to the Substance of the Dispute). Arbitrators are to decide a dispute in accordance with the law chosen by the parties. A choice of law clause in an agreement is to be construed by the Hong Kong Court, absent an express provision to the contrary in the parties' agreement, solely as a reference to the substantive law of a foreign state X (that is, exclusive of X's conflict of law rules). This avoids the problems of *renvoi* or transmission, namely, the situation where X's conflict of law rules stipulate that Hong Kong law or (alternatively) the law of some other foreign state is to apply.

Section 64 provides that a tribunal "shall decide *ex aequo et bono* ... only if the parties have expressly authorised it to do so". The expression *ex aequo et bono* refers to generally accepted principles of fairness and justice, as opposed to the laws of any particular state.

By s.65 (enacting Model Law Art.29 (Decision-making by Panel of Arbitrators)), decisions must be reached by a majority of tribunal members, although questions of procedure may be decided by a presiding arbitrator.

Section 67 enacts Model Law Art.31 (Form and Contents of Award). This requires an award to be in writing signed by the arbitrators (or at least a majority of them). It requires that an award state reasons unless the parties have agreed otherwise.

Art.31(4) imposes an obligation on the arbitrators to deliver a copy of the award to each party. But by s.77, that obligation can be made subject to the full payment of the tribunal's fees and expenses. It is usual for an award not to be released to the parties until the tribunal's fees have been fully paid.

Section 69 enacts Model Law Art.33 (Correction and Interpretation of Award, Additional Award). The provision enables a party to request an arbitrator to correct clerical or typographical errors in an award. It also enables the parties, by agreement, to request the arbitrator to give an interpretation of a specific point of the award.

The provision further empowers an arbitrator to review an award of costs made in ignorance of information (such as a settlement offer) which the arbitrator ought to have taken into account. Usually, a tribunal will not be told of a settlement offer until after an award has been published. Thereafter, having been told of the offer to settle, the tribunal may wish to revise any determination on the incidence of costs in its published document. The ability to revise its award on the question of costs enables a tribunal to cater for the possibility where the winning party would have been better off by accepting a settlement offer.

Costs are normally awarded in favour of a winning party. But, where costs have been needlessly incurred only because the winning party refused to accept a generous settlement offer, the tribunal may think it just to deny the winning party its costs from the date when it ought reasonably to have accepted the other side's offer.

Section 70 empowers a tribunal to award any remedy or relief that a Court could have ordered. But the tribunal can only order specific performance of a contract if the contract does not relate to land or an interest in land.

Section 71 allows arbitrators to make awards at different times on different aspects of a dispute.

Section 74 confers on arbitrators a wide discretion in the award of costs.

Section 78 makes the parties jointly and severally liable for the tribunal's reasonable fees and expenses.

Section 79 enables an arbitrator to award interest.

IX. Recourse against award

Section 81 enacts Model Law Art.34 (Application for Setting Aside as Exclusive Recourse against Arbitral Award). This stipulates the limited grounds on which an award may be set aside by the Court.

Those grounds are that a party was under some incapacity; that the arbitration agreement was invalid under some proper law; that a party did not have proper notice of the arbitration or was unable to present its case; that the award falls outside the scope of the parties' submission to arbitration; that the tribunal was improperly constituted; that the subject matter of the arbitration was not capable of being settled by arbitration under the law of Hong Kong; that the award is in conflict with public policy.

A party has to challenge an award within 3 months from the date of receiving it.

X. Recognition and enforcement of awards

Section 84 allows an award to be enforced as a judgment of the

Court provided leave is first obtained. In other awards, by the simple procedures set out in Part X of the Ordinance, arbitration awards may be converted into judgments of the Court.

By s.85, an application for leave to enforce an award which is neither a Mainland award nor an award governed by the New York Convention must include original or certified copies of the award and arbitration agreement. A Hong Kong arbitration award would fall within this category of awards which are neither Mainland awards nor Convention awards.

The New York Convention was promulgated by the United Nations Conference on International Commercial Arbitration in 1958. It concerns the recognition and enforcement by a domestic Court of foreign arbitral awards. It enables an arbitration award made in a state A which is a party to the Convention to be enforced with a minimum of formality in a state B which is also a party to the Convention.

Normally, it will not be easy to enforce a judgment obtained from the Court of one country A in another country B. One will typically have to convert the judgment of the Court in country A into an order or judgment of a Court in country B. Such conversion may require complex procedures to be followed and may, as a result, necessitate time-consuming litigation in country B.

In contrast, the recognition and enforcement procedures which signatories to the New York Convention are bound to implement should make it easier and simpler for awards to be enforced even across national boundaries. This capacity for ready enforcement across national boundaries is one of the advantages of arbitration.

The PRC (including Hong Kong) is a party to the New York Convention, as are many other states.

Hong Kong awards obviously cannot qualify as "foreign" arbitral awards in Hong Kong. Further, since Hong Kong is part of the PRC, it follows that Mainland awards cannot be treated as "foreign" arbitral awards by the Court here. Consequently, the Ordinance distinguishes 3 categories of awards for the purposes of enforcement: Convention awards, Mainland awards and non-Convention awards (including Hong Kong awards).

A Mainland award is defined in s.2 as "an arbitral award made in the Mainland by a recognised Mainland arbitral authority in accordance with the Arbitration Law of the People's Republic of China". A "recognised Mainland arbitral authority" is "an arbitral authority that is specified in the list of recognised Mainland arbitral authorities published by the Secretary for Justice".

Section 86 provides that leave to enforce a non-Convention award "may" (not "must") be refused on certain grounds. Such grounds are similar to those allowing recourse against an award in the Court set out in s.81.

But there is one additional ground that is found in s.86(2)(c). The Court may refuse enforcement of a non-Convention award as a judgment of the Court "for any other reason the Court considers it just to do so".

Section 87 allows a Convention award to be enforced under the s.84 mechanism just described or directly by action in Court. But, in any event, a Convention award is binding "for all purposes on the persons between whom it was made, and may accordingly be relied on by any of those persons by way of defence, set off or otherwise in any legal proceedings in Hong Kong".

Enforcement of a Convention award may only be refused in limited circumstances. Those are identical to the narrow grounds for recourse against an award set out in s.81. Note that the additional ground for nonrecognition found in s.86(2)(c) does not apply to Convention awards.

Section 92 allows Mainland awards to be enforced by action in Court or in the manner set out in s.84. A Mainland award is also to be treated as binding on the parties for all purposes in any event.

Section 93 provides that a Mainland award may not be enforceable if an application has been made to enforce it in the Mainland. But if an award has not been fully satisfied in the Mainland despite an application to enforce it there, the award may be enforced in Hong Kong to the extent not satisfied.

Section 95 sets out the grounds for refusing enforcement of a Mainland award. Those are identical to the grounds for refusing enforcement of a Convention award. The additional ground for refusing recognition found in s.86(2)(c) does not apply to Mainland awards.

XI. Provisions that may be expressly opted for and automatically apply

By s.99 the parties may expressly agree in an arbitration agreement that certain sections of Schedule 2 of the Ordinance are to apply. For a limited time (up to 6 years), subject to any agreement to the contrary, all provisions of Schedule 2 will apply where the parties have stipulated that arbitration pursuant to their contract is to be treated as "domestic arbitration".

Section 101 deals with opt-in and opt-out provisions in construction subcontracting cases. This section was enacted in response to concerns in the building industry that old standard construction contracts (based on the distinction between international and domestic arbitration agreements which featured in the old Arbitration Ordinance) would continue to be in use long after entry into force of the new Ordinance.

Some opt-in provisions worth considering for inclusion in an arbitration agreement under s.99 are as follows:

(1) Sch.2, s.2 (allowing arbitrations to be consolidated);

(2) Sch.2, s.3 (empowering the Court to decide preliminary questions of law in connection with an arbitration);

(3) Sch.2, s.4 (allowing an award to be challenged on the ground of serious irregularity);

(4) Sch.2, s.5 (allowing an appeal to the Court against an arbitral award on a question of law);

(5) Sch.2, s.6 (allowing applications for leave to appeal against an arbitral award on a question of law).

These opt-in provisions enhance the flexibility of arbitration as a means of dispute resolution. The parties to an arbitration agreement can in their contract choose specific provisions as their needs require. The parties' arbitration agreement can be tailored to their specific circumstances.

XII. Miscellaneous

Section 104 imposes liability on an arbitrator or mediator (or their employees and agents) in the discharge of their functions "only if it is proved that the act was done or omitted to be done dishonestly". For this purpose, the expression "mediator" means a person who is appointed as mediator under s.32.

B. Application of the Ordinance to Some Basic Questions

What is the proper approach to applying the Model Law (as enacted by the Ordinance) to questions which might arise in an arbitration?

The adoption of the Model Law by a growing number of international jurisdictions (including Hong Kong) facilitates the development of a common law of arbitrations. The increased availability of Model Law case reports of different jurisdictions over the internet makes it easier for everyone involved in the arbitration industry to identify "trends" in this developing common law of arbitrations.

Arbitrators, lawyers and judges, in particular, will have to be aware of Model Law case precedents in other states, not just their own. That will ensure that, as much as possible, the Model Law is uniformly interpreted and applied in all jurisdictions.

On the other hand, if arbitrators and judges take too narrow a view of the Model Law, construing it purely in light of domestic conditions and institutions, a sharply conflicting jurisprudence will inevitably develop in different jurisdictions.

Such an outcome is obviously undesirable and should be avoided as much as possible.

However, one cannot be categorical. There may be local conditions which justify occasional deviations from a uniform approach to the interpretation of the Model Law. Awareness of what is going on in other states will always need to be coupled with a sensitivity as to whether Model Law decisions in one jurisdiction should be followed (in whole, part, or not at all) in light of special conditions prevailing in another jurisdiction.

In this section, I briefly analyse 3 questions which commonly arise in connection with arbitrations, not just in Hong Kong, but elsewhere also. The 3 issues have themselves been highlighted in vol.77 (2011) of the journal *Arbitration*[9] as having sparked much debate in Australia, with different Courts there taking different approaches on occasion.

The 3 issues are:

(1) Whether parties can agree that the Model Law is not to apply to their arbitration;

(2) Whether it is possible to set aside an award on the ground of manifest error;

(3) Whether it is possible to set aside an award for not being sufficiently reasoned.

This book focuses on imparting a practical understanding of the arbitral process. Consequently, I will not consider the case law on the 3 issues in depth. Instead, I will merely suggest how, in light of the Ordinance and case law elsewhere, the Hong Kong Court might deal with the 3 issues. I hope that such an exercise will lead to a better appreciation of how the Model Law works.

I. Issue 1: Can parties opt out of the Model Law?

Section 47 of the Ordinance enacts Model Law Art.19 (Determination of Rules of Procedure). This provides that "the parties are free to agree on the procedure to be followed by the arbitral tribunal in conducting the proceedings". But this freedom is not absolute. It is expressly stated by Art.19 to be "subject to the provisions of this [Model] Law".

Section 47 and its qualifying proviso therefore have 2 consequences.

First, in many instances, the Model Law states that the parties are free to agree on a particular matter.[10] To that extent, the parties are at liberty to agree on the procedure to be followed in their arbitration. That would be the case even where the rules agreed by the parties are different from those which the Model Law says are to apply in the absence of the parties' agreement.

Second, the parties are not free to agree anything and everything. Where specific procedural rules deviate from what is stated to be mandatory under the Model Law, the mandatory provisions of the Model Law will override any agreement to the contrary by the parties.

In short, it is not possible to opt out of the Model Law entirely as arbitrations taking place in Hong Kong are regulated by local law.

Note that the procedural rules agreed by the parties can supplement the Model Law (where the Model Law expressly or impliedly gives the parties freedom to agree on specific matters). But the Model Law can also supplement the parties' chosen procedural rules where those rules are silent on a matter. Of course, the Model Law will override the parties' wishes where, on a true construction of the Ordinance, the Model Law imposes a mandatory rule from which derogation is not possible.[11]

II. Issue 2: Can an award be set aside for "manifest error"?

Under the Ordinance, there are 4 scenarios to consider.

First, suppose that the parties have not incorporated any of the opt-in provisions in Schedule 2. In that case, recourse against the award would only be possible under s.81 (importing Model Law Art.34).

The complaining party will have to establish that, in consequence of the manifest error, the award falls foul of one of the situations listed in Art.34 (2). Unless the complaining party can do this, then s.81(3) stresses that "the Court does not have jurisdiction to set aside or remit an arbitral award on the ground of errors of fact or law on the face of the award". Thus, mere "manifest error" without more would not be sufficient to support an application to set aside an award.

Of the limited grounds in Art.34 for setting aside an award, only 2 would appear to be potentially applicable where manifest error is being alleged.

Those are Art.34(1)(a)(iii) (award contains "matters beyond the scope of the submission to arbitration") and Art.34(2)(b)(ii) (award "in conflict with the public policy of [the] State").

Art.34(1)(a)(iii) does not strike one as having a realistic prospect of success. A submission to arbitration carries the risk of an arbitrator getting the law wrong, even badly wrong. Where then there is a manifest error on the face of the award (in the sense of some plain or obvious error apparent without much (if any) further consideration), such an outcome cannot constitute "a matter beyond the scope of the submission". On the contrary, the outcome of an error of law by the arbitrator is a known risk.

Case law as to when the Court can refuse enforcement of an award on the ground of "public policy" suggests that Art.34(2)(b)(ii) is equally unpromising.

My own decision in *A v. R* [12] holds that "public policy" is a narrow ground. I reached this conclusion after looking at decisions in England, Singapore and Hong Kong.[13] Those cases stress that the "public policy" ground typically entails "reprehensible or unconscionable conduct" or a result which would "shock the conscience" or "be clearly injurious to the public good". "Public policy" should only be invoked where an award would be "wholly offensive to the ordinary reasonable and fully informed member of the public" or where the award "violates the [enforcing] forum's most basic notions of morality and justice".

Therefore, the Court would not allow recourse purely on the basis of a manifest error on the face of an award. There is nothing morally or otherwise reprehensible in an award being manifestly wrong. As noted in *A v. R*, the Court has to be alert to the misuse of the public policy ground as an excuse to re-open matters which have been (or ought to have been) determined in an arbitration. Such an approach would be consonant with the 2 cardinal principles of the Model Law identified in Section A of this chapter.

Thus, in this first scenario, there is no basis for challenge under the Model Law solely on the ground of manifest error.

A second scenario is where the parties have opted for Sch.2 s.5 (allowing appeal on a question of law). In that case, there may be a basis for challenging the award, but not on the mere allegation of a manifest error. One has to show that there is some (not necessarily immediately manifest) error of law. There would be no recourse if what is alleged is only a misunderstanding of the facts.

A third scenario is where the parties have opted for Sch.2, ss.5 and 6 together. Section 6 requires a party to obtain leave to appeal from the Court before being allowed to challenge an award on a question of law pursuant to s.5.

Leave will only be granted under s.6 if certain criteria are met. These are:

> (1) "that the decision of the question will substantially affect the rights of one or more of the parties";
>
> (2) "that the question is one which the arbitral tribunal was asked to decide"; and,

(3) "that, on the basis of the findings of fact in the award:

    (i) the decision of the arbitral tribunal on the question is obviously wrong; or,

    (ii) the question is one of general importance and the decision of the arbitral tribunal is at least open to serious doubt".

This is similar to the test in *Swire Properties v. Secretary for Justice*[14] which was applied to determine whether leave to appeal against a domestic award should be granted under the old Ordinance. The Hong Kong Court is likely to apply the test in s.6 of the new Ordinance in the same manner that it previously applied the *Swire Properties test*.

That does not mean that leave to appeal will be granted in every case where there is a "manifest error". It will only be in cases where the error will "substantially affect" the parties' rights that leave will be granted.

In some jurisdictions, judges have distinguished between a "manifest error" and something which is "plainly or clearly wrong". The expressions "obviously wrong" or "open to serious doubt" in s.6 seem closer to the sense of "plainly or clearly wrong" rather than to "manifest error". It might be suggested therefore that s.6 imports a different test from "manifest error".

But, in practice, it is hard to distinguish between the different shades of meaning implicit in expressions such as "manifest", "plainly" or "clearly". I suspect that the Hong Kong Court will take a robust approach. It will then decide whether to grant leave based only on the degree to which a substantial error is apparent on a quick examination of the award without consideration of protracted argument.

A fourth scenario arises where the parties opt for Sch.2, s.4. This enables an award to be challenged on the ground of "serious irregularity". That last phrase is defined to mean:

> "an irregularity of one or more of the following kinds which the Court considers has caused or will cause substantial injustice to the applicant:
>
> (a) failure by the arbitral tribunal to comply with section 46 [requiring an arbitral tribunal to be independent, fair, impartial, expeditious and proportionate and to treat the parties "with equality"];
>
> (b) the arbitral tribunal exceeding its powers (otherwise than by exceeding its jurisdiction);
>
> (c) failure by the arbitral tribunal to conduct the arbitral proceedings in accordance with the procedure agreed by the parties;
>
> (d) failure by the arbitral tribunal to deal with all the issues that were put to it;
>
> (e) any arbitral or other institution or person vested by the parties with powers in relation to the arbitral proceedings or the award exceeding its powers;
>
> (f) failure by the arbitral tribunal to give, under Section 69, an interpretation of the award the effect of which is uncertain or ambiguous;
>
> (g) the award being obtained by fraud, or the award or the way in which it was procured being contrary to public policy;
>
> (h) failure to comply with the requirements as to the form of the award;

> (i) any irregularity in the conduct of the arbitral proceedings, or in the award which is admitted by the arbitral tribunal or by any arbitral or other institution or person vested by the parties with powers in relation to the arbitral proceedings or the award."

None of the limbs of s.4 seem promising as far as recourse for manifest error is concerned. An "error" may be "manifest" but the mistake may not be a sufficiently "serious irregularity" within the terms of s.4.

The best candidates for a challenge on the ground of manifest error would seem to be sub-sections 4(b), (c), (d), (g) and (h). But each is fraught with difficulty.

On s.4(b), it is difficult to see how a tribunal can exceed its powers by making a mistake in law, whether or not the mistake is obvious. This is because the possibility of a tribunal getting the law wrong is a problem inherent in arbitration.

On s.4(c), the tribunal will presumably have conducted the arbitration in accordance with agreed procedures. It simply erred by coming to a wrong conclusion on a point of law.

On s.4(d), the manifest error would presumably have been made in connection with an issue actually dealt with by the tribunal.

On s.4(g), it is hard to see how a tribunal making a mistake of law (whether or not obvious) automatically means that the award was "procured" in a manner contrary to public policy. There is also the difficulty of the narrow meaning of "public policy" discussed above.

On s.4(h), it is hard to see how a mistake of law necessarily implies that an award is non-compliant in form.

I therefore doubt that Sch.2, s.4 would permit recourse against an award due for manifest error of law.

In summary, in practical terms, except where the parties opt for Sch.2 s.5, there will be no real scope for recourse against an award for manifest error under the new Ordinance. Such an outcome under Hong Kong law would be in line with the trend in Model Law jurisdictions for Courts to respect the decisions of arbitrators even where they go wrong.

III. Issue 3: Can an award be set aside for insufficient reasoning?

Section 67 (enacting Model Law Art 31) requires that an award "shall state the reasons upon which it is based, unless the parties have agreed that no reasons are to be given".

This prompts the questions: (1) what are adequate reasons and (2) how does one deal with an award that is not adequately reasoned?

Guidance on the first question may be found in the decision of the Supreme Court of Victoria in *Thoroughvision Pty Ltd v. Sky Channel Pty Ltd and Tabcorp Holdings Ltd*.[15] There Croft J stressed the need for proportionality as far as the giving of reasons was concerned. He said (at para. 55):

> "It is well established that reasons need show only that the arbitrator grasped the main contentions advanced by the parties, and communicated to the parties, in broad terms, the reasons for the conclusions reached. The reasoning process must be exposed so that the reader of the award can understand how and why the conclusion was reached. It is clear that reasons need not be elaborate or lengthy, provided that these requirements are met. ...

> [A]n arbitrator must address each issued raised for
> decision within the scope of the arbitration agreement.
> However it does not follow ... that the nature and extent
> of reasons is not to be fashioned by reference to the
> nature of the matters in dispute and, proportionately,
> having regard to the complexity of the issues, the
> importance, monetary or otherwise, of the arbitration
> proceedings and the nature of the arbitral proceedings,
> expeditious or otherwise, as agreed between the parties."

In support, Croft J cited *Gordian Runoff*.[16] Allsop P there pointed out
(at paras. 213-222) that there was a fundamental difference between
using the Court and using arbitration as a mechanism of dispute
resolution. Consequently, it would be wrong to expect an award
to be as closely reasoned as a Court judgment in all cases. Allsop P
expressed the difference thus (at para. 216):

> "The Court is an arm of the state; its judgment is an
> act of state authority, subject generally in a common
> law context to the right of appeal available to parties.
> The arbitration award is the result of a private
> consensual mechanism intended to be shorn of the costs,
> complexities and technicalities often cited (rightly or
> wrongly, it matters not) as the indicia and disadvantages
> of curial decision making."

I think that the Hong Kong Court would follow the analyses of Croft
J and Allsop P as to the standard expected of arbitrators when they
give reasons. The analyses of Crofts J and Allsop P seem compelling
in practical terms.[17]

On the question how a challenge to an award can be made where
no (or inadequate) reasons are given, the Hong Kong Court might
allow recourse under the public policy ground in Model Law
Art.34(2)(b)(ii). Given the object of the Ordinance is "to facilitate the
fair ... resolution of disputes", it cannot be consistent with public

policy to allow an insufficiently reasoned award to stand.

If only as a matter of fairness, a loser is entitled to know why one has lost. Where an award gives inadequate reasons, the loser will not be able to understand why. The loser would harbour a justifiable sense of grievance as the award will appear arbitrary. In that circumstance, to allow the award to stand would not be conducive to fundamental notions of justice. It should not be regarded as an inherent risk of arbitration that a tribunal will give no (or no adequate) reasons for its award.

The Court, however, may hesitate to set aside an award altogether because it has not been sufficiently reasoned. Under Art.34(4), the Court has the option to suspend any setting aside proceedings "in order to give the arbitral tribunal an opportunity to resume the arbitral proceedings or to take such other action as in the arbitral tribunal's opinion will eliminate the grounds for setting aside". The Court may exercise this power "where appropriate and so requested by a party".

This approach would be consonant with s.69 of the Ordinance (enacting Model Law Art.33). Art.33 empowers the tribunal at the request of the parties (made within 30 days of the award or within such other period of time as the parties might agree) to give an interpretation of its award.

Thus, where it regards the setting aside of an entire award as too draconian a step to take, the Court may invite the party in whose favour the award was made to agree to the award being remitted back to the tribunal, so that the latter can clarify (interpret) any too cryptic reasoning. Note that, in contrast to Art.33 which sets a time limit within which the parties may ask the tribunal to interpret its award, Art.34(4) does not seem to stipulate a period within which the Court is allowed to ask the tribunal to clarify its award.

C. Summary

This chapter has given a framework overview of the arbitration process in Hong Kong by reference to the new Ordinance. From that survey, the following are key concepts to bear in mind:

1. The objective of the Ordinance is to facilitate the fair and speedy resolution of disputes by arbitration without unnecessary expense.

2. As much as possible, the parties to an arbitration agreement should be free to agree on how any dispute between them should be resolved.

3. The Court should interfere as little as possible with the parties' agreement to arbitrate and, if the Court interferes, it can only do so within the bounds permitted by the Ordinance.

4. The Ordinance only applies to arbitration agreements in writing, but what constitutes "writing" is very broadly defined.

5. The law treats an agreement to arbitrate as "autonomous", that is, as existing separately from the rest of a contract in which such agreement appears.

6. Under the "competence-competence" principle, a tribunal is competent to rule on whether or not it has jurisdiction to arbitrate a given dispute.

7. However, where the tribunal rules that it has jurisdiction, that ruling may be challenged before the Court which will have the ultimate say on the scope of the tribunal's competence.

8. In conducting an arbitration, an arbitrator must be

independent, fair and impartial.

9. An arbitration tribunal is not bound to follow the strict rules of evidence in the conduct of its proceedings.

10. An award must state reasons.

11. There are limited avenues for appealing to the Court against an award.

12. An award may be enforced by converting it into an order of the Court.

13. It is not possible to opt out of the Model Law completely.

14. There is little real scope for recourse against an award on the ground of manifest error alone.

15. An award may be set aside for insufficiency of reasoning, although there is the possibility of the Court remitting the award back to the tribunal for clarification of its reasons.

16. In construing the Model Law, arbitrators should have regard to cases relating to the Model Law decided in other jurisdictions.

1. Unless otherwise stated, references to sections are to be read as references to sections in the new Ordinance. References to articles are to be read as references to articles in the Model Law. The text of the Ordinance may be obtained from www.legislation.gov.hk/eng/index.htm.

2. [2010] 3 HKLRD 611 (Stone J).

3. I discuss the extent to which this is possible in Section B below.

4 If this is the draughtsman's rationale for the provision, I have doubts as to its validity. It is true that in litigation the parties cannot, by waiver or agreement, confer upon the Court a jurisdiction which it does not have under the law. But that principle may not apply to arbitrations. This is because the scope of an arbitration (including the extent of an arbitrator's jurisdiction) hinges entirely on the parties' agreement. The parties may not be able to confer on an arbitrator powers which the Ordinance disallows. An attempt by parties to confer such impermissible powers is not, however, a matter of enlarging an arbitrator's jurisdiction. It is merely a matter of the law prohibiting a tribunal from doing what the parties authorise it to do. It is thus unclear to me why a party cannot by inaction be treated as having accepted (that is, as having waived the right to object to) an irregularity, even if as a matter of law such irregularity should never have occurred in the arbitration.

5 (1865) 5 HL Cas 811.

6. Option II differs from Option I only in that this additional sentence has been omitted from Option II.

7. Med-arb, in which the same person or tribunal acts both as mediator and arbitrator, is popular in Mainland China. But such practice is not common in Hong Kong, where many feel that the potential for conflict of interest is too great. I discuss this problem in Chapter 5.

8. Contrast Model Law Art.18 which requires that each party be given "a full opportunity of presenting [a] case". I doubt that there is much (if any) practical difference between the 2 wordings.

9. See, especially, the following articles: McComish et al, "Understanding Australia's New Domestic Arbitration Regime: A Comparison of the Australian State Commercial Arbitration Acts and the New Model Commercial Arbitration Bill" at 7 ff; Megens et al, "Emerging Trends in Judicial Approach to International Arbitration in Australia: The Winds of Change", at 33 ff; and Rudge et al, "More Than an Empty Gesture: The Reversal of *Eisenwerk*", at 43 ff. My analysis of the Hong Kong position relies heavily on the insights which I have gained from the foregoing articles and the cases there discussed.

10. See, for instance, Arts.3(1); 10(1); 11(1) and (2); 13(1) (but subject to 13(3)); 17B(1); 20(1); 21; 22; 23; 24; 25; 26; 28(3); 33(1).

11. Examples of Model Law articles that do not appear to allow deviation are Arts.4 (Model Law To Have Force of Law); 7 (Definition and Form of Arbitration Agreement); 16 (Competence of Arbitral Tribunal to Rule on Its Jurisdiction); 28 (Rules Applicable to Substance of Dispute); 31 (Form and Contents of Award).

12. HCCT No.54 of 2008 (30 April 2009).

13. See *Hebei Import & Export Corp. v. Polytek Engineering Co Ltd* (1999) 2 HKCFAR 111 (at 118D-E); *Profilati Italia SrL v. PaineWebber Inc*. [2001] 1 Lloyds Rep 715 (Moore-Bick J); *Soh Beng Tee & Co Pte Ltd v. Fairmount Development Pte Ltd* [2007] SGCA 28 (Rajah JA); and *Asuransi Jasa Indonesia (Persero) v. Dexia Bank* [2006] SGCA 41 (Chan Sek Kong CJ).

14. [2003] 2 HKLRD 986 (CFA).

15. [2010] VSC 139. For a detailed discussion of *Thoroughvision, Gordian Runoff* and other cases, see Megens et al, *ibid*., at pp.34-37.

16. [2010] NSWCA 57 (Spiegelman CJ, Allsop P and Macfarlan JA).

17. Megens et al., *op. cit*., comment (at para. 37): "Unfortunately *Thoroughvision*, being a first instance decision, cannot bind intermediate appellate courts in other states and territories. It is high time that Australia's High Court clarified this area." See also *R v. F* HCCT No.32 of 2011, 3 August 2012 (Au J), paras. 36-37.

Chapter 2

A Detailed Look at the Arbitration Process

Chapter 2 fleshes out the overview of arbitration in the preceding chapter. This is done by examining the arbitration process from appointment of a tribunal to publication of an award. The discussion highlights matters which a would-be arbitrator should bear in mind. It also suggests ways of resolving problems which conventionally arise in arbitrations.

This chapter has 5 main sections. Section A describes how an arbitration is started. Section B deals with a tribunal's powers to grant interim measures pending trial. Section C considers the effective case management of arbitrations. Section D looks at the trial. Section E deals with awards.

A. Getting Started

I. Request for arbitration

The process typically starts with the claimant writing to the respondent to request that a dispute be referred to arbitration.[1] The arbitration will then start on the day when the respondent receives the written request.

By s.49(2) a request must be in writing.

Detailed rules specifying when a written communication is deemed to have been received are found in s.10.[2] Essentially, a request is received on the day when it is delivered.

In the absence of any agreement to the contrary, a request is treated as having been "delivered" if it is delivered to the addressee personally or if it is delivered to his or her place of business, habitual residence or mailing address. If none of the latter addresses can be discovered despite reasonable inquiry, the request may be sent to the respondent's last-known place of business, habitual residence or mailing address by registered letter or any other means which provides a record of the delivery attempt. The request is then deemed to have been delivered on the day it was sent to the relevant last-known place.

But s.10 allows for the possibility of a request being sent instantaneously by e-mail or other electronic means (that is, "by any means by which information can be recorded and transmitted to the addressee"). Where there is a record of the receipt by the respondent of (say) an e-mail request for arbitration, the communication will be treated as having been received (and the arbitration as having commenced) on the day the e-mail was sent.

II. Appointment of tribunal

Once the arbitration has been commenced, the claimant and the respondent should appoint a tribunal. They are free to agree on how many arbitrators (1, 2, 3 or more) are to be appointed and on the procedure for their appointment. However, it is not a good idea to appoint a tribunal comprising an even number (2, 4, 6 etc.) of arbitrators as this could lead to deadlock if the tribunal is divided on an issue.

A common mechanism employed for the appointment of a tribunal is for each party to nominate an arbitrator and for the 2 arbitrators so nominated to appoint a third person to serve as chairman or umpire.

The role of the third arbitrator appointed by this procedure will depend on the agreement of the parties or (on occasion) on the agreement of the 2 arbitrators nominated by the parties.[3] For instance, the third arbitrator might be allowed to participate in the deliberations of the tribunal in exactly the same manner as the other 2 arbitrators. Or, the third arbitrator may only sit as umpire. In such case, although the third arbitrator has the relevant papers and attends hearings, he or she will only participate if the other 2 arbitrators are unable to reach a decision on some or all issues in contention.

A drawback of this procedure is that it produces a tribunal of 3 persons. That will be expensive. Further, it will be harder to coordinate the diaries of a 3-person tribunal with the diaries of the parties and their representatives. It may be difficult to find conveniently available early dates for hearings.

It is thus not every dispute that will merit the logistical difficulties and expenses of a 3-person tribunal. The parties should seriously consider whether such a tribunal is necessary for their dispute and, if not, should attempt to agree on a single person as arbitrator.

At times the parties will have specified the procedure for the appointment of a tribunal, as well as the number of persons to be appointed, in an arbitration agreement entered into before their dispute arose. In that case, the parties need only follow their agreed procedure.

But at other times the parties will merely have agreed that they are to settle their disputes "by arbitration". Thereafter, the parties may be unable to agree on anything, including how many arbitrators there should be or how a tribunal should be appointed. Alternatively, even though the parties may have settled upon a procedure for appointing an agreed number of arbitrators, that procedure may not be operative for some reason (such as the authorised appointment body ceasing to exist).

Where any of these last scenarios occur, the Ordinance provides that a party may ask the Court or the HKIAC to appoint the requisite tribunal. [4] In such situation, the Court or the HKIAC shall have regard to the "any qualifications required of the arbitrator by the agreement of the parties" and "to such considerations as are likely to secure the appointment of an independent and impartial arbitrator".

III. Challenges to appointment

When a person is approached by a party or its lawyers to act as an arbitrator, the person will wish to obtain an idea of the nature of the dispute between the parties. The person will normally also want to see the arbitration agreement. Armed with that information, the person can satisfy one's self that he or she is qualified to act and (arguably at least) would have jurisdiction under the terms of the arbitration agreement.

The would-be arbitrator should also assess whether there are "any circumstances likely to give rise to justifiable doubts as to ... impartiality or independence".[5]

In Hong Kong, the Court applies the test set out in *Porter v. Magill* [6] in evaluating whether there may be an appearance of bias ("apparent bias"). That test asks whether a fair-minded observer knowing all relevant facts would apprehend "a real possibility of bias" on the part of the person purporting to act as arbitrator. Where there is "apparent bias" as defined by the test, the Court will likely conclude that there are circumstances giving rise "to justifiable doubts as to ... impartiality or independence" and allow a challenge by a party to the arbitrator's appointment.

Thus, if there is any real possibility of a conflict of interest, a person should decline to act as arbitrator. At the very least, the person should draw the parties' attention to matters which might render him or her unsuitable to sit in the particular case.

Once a tribunal has been constituted, a party has 15 days within which to challenge the appointment of an arbitrator.[7] The challenge will typically be on the ground of real or apparent bias. The tribunal will rule on the challenge. If the tribunal rules against the challenge, the unsuccessful party has 30 days in which to appeal to the Court or the HKIAC. But, pending the outcome of the appeal, the tribunal may proceed with the arbitration and even make an award.

IV. Terms of engagement

When approached to act as arbitrator, a person will need to agree terms of engagement with the parties. For example, the would-be arbitrator would certainly wish to negotiate a fee structure for his or her remuneration.

Remuneration might be calculated on the basis of an hourly rate (subject to a cap?) or a percentage of the amount in dispute. There may also be terms for payment of a deposit (refundable or non-refundable?) and the payment of fees by instalments at defined intervals as the arbitration progresses. The arbitrator may also wish to identify what (if any) disbursements are to be borne by the parties.

The agreement may also deal with possible contingencies. For instance, what is to happen if the parties do not proceed with the arbitration within a reasonable period of time? If the Court remits an award back for further consideration or clarification, should anything be chargeable for the longer engagement of the arbitrator? If for some reason (such as illness), the arbitrator is unable to continue with an ongoing arbitration, what happens?

Note that s.62 empowers the Court to declare, where an arbitrator's mandate has been terminated by a successful challenge to appointment or as a result of the failure or inability to act, that an arbitrator should not receive the whole or part of any agreed fees or expenses.

Some arbitrators have extremely detailed terms of engagement. But a novice who is unsure of the market for one's services as an arbitrator may be better advised to produce something more modest. The more complex one's terms (including generous provisions for non-refundable booking fees and staged payments), the greater the risk that a newcomer will price one's self out of a competitive arbitration market. It may be that, when one is starting out, the simplest of terms (an hourly rate with a cap and possibly a small commitment fee) may have to suffice.

V. Seat of arbitration

Early on in the determination of their dispute, the parties need to decide on the place (also known as "the seat") of arbitration, if they have not already done so in the arbitration agreement. One has to pay some attention to the choice of a seat. The place of arbitration may have ramifications on the conduct of the arbitration. For example, if Hong Kong is the seat of arbitration, the proceedings will be subject to the Model Law as promulgated by the Ordinance.

Different seats will have their own arbitration statutes. There will inevitably be variations from place to place as to how an arbitration is to be conducted. From the parties' viewpoint, the laws of one seat may pose greater or fewer inconveniences than the provisions of some other seat. The laws of a given jurisdiction may thus have a bearing on the efficient and cost-effective resolution of a dispute.

But, whatever the seat of arbitration, the tribunal may meet at such other place or places as it considers appropriate.[8]

VI. Preliminary directions

Once appointed, the tribunal will have to determine the languages to be used in the arbitral proceedings. The parties may agree this or the arbitrators will have to decide themselves.[9] It will also have to be decided whether documents in the arbitration are to be translated into one or more of the selected languages.

It will be useful (and normal) at the outset, shortly after being appointed, for the tribunal to give directions for the conduct of an arbitration. The directions may be given in the course of an actual or telephone conference among the tribunal and the parties. Or, more simply, the directions might be issued following receipt of short written submissions from the parties on the appropriate manner of proceeding.

What might Directions No.1 look like?

I have so far said little about pleadings.[10] It is possible that, by the time the tribunal is appointed, the parties will already have exchanged pleadings. Those pleadings will have defined the issues requiring determination by the tribunal. Where pleadings exist, the arbitrators should obviously study them at the outset to obtain a better idea of the parties' differences. The tribunal can then consider how those differences might most expeditiously be resolved.[11]

But it often happens that no formal pleadings will have been filed by the time the tribunal is appointed. At best, there may only be a brief statement from the claimant of the broad nature of its grievance and there may be a general statement from the respondent of the broad nature of its defence. In such case, the arbitration would benefit from the parties filing more precise statements of claim or defence to which are attached copies of the documents upon which the parties wish to rely in support of their cases.

Directions No.1 would in that situation set out a timetable for the filing of more formal pleadings.

Paragraph 1 of Directions No.1 might require that a Points of Claim (to which is attached the documents upon which the claimant seeks to rely) is to be filed within (say) 28 days.

Paragraph 2 might then require a Points of Defence and a Points of Counterclaim (if any) are to be filed within (say) 28 days thereafter. The respondent is likewise to exhibit the documents upon which it seeks to rely to this defence and counterclaim.

Paragraph 3 might be a direction that the claimant file a Points of Reply to the Defence and (where required) a Points of Defence to Counterclaim within (say) 14 days thereafter. Again the claimant is to exhibit to its pleading, the documents upon which it relies.

Paragraph 4 might direct that the respondent file within (say) 14 days thereafter, its Points of Rejoinder (if there is such need) and (insofar as necessary) a Points of Reply to the Defence to Counterclaim. Again relevant documents are to be attached to the pleadings.

It is usual to treat the pleadings as closed at the latest once the time in paragraph 4 has lapsed. By way of confirmation, a paragraph 5 to Directions No.1 might stipulate that the pleadings are deemed to be closed after (say) the period in paragraph 4 has expired. Paragraph 5 might also require the parties to arrange a short conference with the tribunal upon the close of pleadings so that further directions on the conduct of the arbitration may be given.

The effect of the Direction No.1 just sketched out will be to enable the arbitrators and the parties to work out what exactly the differences among the parties are supposed to be. The main issues requiring resolution can be identified.

The pleadings filed by each side will enable all concerned to determine what facts are admitted and what matters are in dispute. The documents attached by each side to their pleadings will give all concerned some idea of the relative strengths, on paper at least, of a party's case.

From its study of the pleadings and the attached evidential documents, the tribunal should be in a position to determine soon after appointment how the rest of the arbitration is to proceed.[12] For instance, should the arbitration proceed on documents and written submissions alone or will there be need for oral hearings and examination of witnesses? Should there be further discovery of documents by one side or other? Will there be expert evidence as well as evidence from witnesses of fact? What is the soonest date when the trial of the dispute can take place and approximately how many days might be needed to try the matter?

The tribunal can invite comments from the parties on how they think the arbitration should proceed to trial. Having received those comments (either as a result of a short conference or through written commissions), the tribunal can issue its Directions No.2 covering the conduct of the arbitration from close of pleadings to the start of trial.

What would Directions No.2 look like?

Paragraph 1 might direct that, within (say) 28 days, each side file statements summarising the evidence of each witness of fact to be called at trial. Those statements are to stand as the evidence-in-chief of the relevant witnesses.

The paragraph might also give directions on whether there is to be cross-examination, or whether the arbitrators are to decide on the basis of documents alone including untested witness statements.

Paragraph 2 might deal with expert witnesses (if required).

It could provide that, within (say) 14 days from the issue of Directions No.2, the parties are to agree what expertise (accountancy, foreign law, quantity-surveying, engineering, etc.) is required for the trial and how many experts of a particular discipline each side may call. Normally, the parties should only be allowed one expert each per discipline.

The parties should also be required to agree the specific questions which the experts of a particular discipline are to answer in their report. The questions should be in "yes or no" form or in multiple-choice format (that is, restricting the experts to a choice from among options a, b, c, d or "none of the above" as their answer to the question).

This last direction will greatly assist the tribunal. Frequently, parties instruct their experts to venture an opinion on some only loosely defined matter. The result is that each side produces reports which deal with different matters and there is only a tenuous overlap in the coverage of the 2 reports. In writing its award, the tribunal is left to pick up the pieces. It will be hard-pressed to match up what one expert says on an issue with what another opines on that topic.

By insisting that the parties only put forward agreed questions for the experts to answer, the tribunal will be setting the equivalent of a "true or false" or multiple-choice examination for itself. In its award, the tribunal need only choose from among one or other expert's answers and reasons.

Without Prejudice Reports, in which the experts answer the questions posed, are to be exchanged by the parties within (say) 28 days after the statements of factual witnesses have been exchanged. Thereafter, each side's experts are to meet within (say) 14 days to work out Points of Agreement and Disagreement among them.

Within (say) 7 days after meeting, the experts are to put out a Joint Report identifying the questions upon which they are agreed on an answer and the questions upon which they are unable to agree an answer.

Within (say) 7 days after the Joint Report, each expert is to produce a Final Reports (on a "with prejudice" basis), in which the expert sets out one's answers to the questions upon which agreement could not be reached. In the Final Reports, each expert should also explain why one's answer is to be preferred to the other expert's answer.

Paragraph 3 might deal with any specific discovery that is required.

In ordinary litigation within common law jurisdictions (such as Hong Kong), there is an obligation to make general discovery. This means that a party is required to disclose all documents in one's possession, custody or control which are "relevant" to a dispute. A document is "relevant" if it supports the other side's case; if it undermines one's own case; or if it might reasonably be considered as capable of leading to a train of inquiry which would result in supporting the other side's case or undermining one's own case. The last limb of the relevance test may be called "the train of inquiry criterion".

In contrast to common law procedure, arbitrations tend to follow the practice prevalent in civil law jurisdictions of having no general discovery, but only specific discovery. In consequence, each party attaches to its pleading all documentary evidence upon which it proposes to rely. If a party A believes that the other party B has in its possession, custody or control of an important document which has not been exhibited, A can apply to the tribunal for B to make specific discovery of that document. The tribunal will decide whether to order that B produce the document.

The tribunal will only so order if A can demonstrate that the document is "relevant" in the sense mentioned above; that justice would best be served by ordering production; and that production of the document will lead to a significant saving of time and cost in the trial of the dispute.

It may be that, early on, a party requires further particulars of the other side's pleadings, in order to have a better idea of the case which the party has to answer at trial. If the tribunal agrees, a paragraph 4 could direct that one side or other provide better particulars of its case within so many days.

Paragraph 5 might direct that the trial of the dispute is to be heard by the arbitrators at a given venue on specific dates. This is a controversial suggestion. Some arbitrators may not wish to appoint trial dates so early on. But experience suggests that fixing trial dates as soon as pleadings are closed is an effective means of getting the parties to focus on the timely preparation of their cases.

Arbitrators need to be firm. If the tribunal makes it clear (and adheres to the principle) that trial dates once fixed will only be adjourned in exceptional circumstances, the parties will have little option but to proceed with all appropriate dispatch.

Paragraph 5 could be supplemented by directions on whether there are to be physical bundles containing the pleadings, witness statements, expert reports and documentary evidence for the purposes of the trial, or whether all materials are to be accessible in electronic format alone. In either case, there will need to be directions on how and when the physical or electronic bundles are to be prepared and delivered.

There may also need to be directions on the filing by the parties of opening statements or skeleton submissions for the trial.

All relevant materials should be with the tribunal in good time to enable a thorough preparation for the trial. The more familiar the tribunal is with the trial bundle, the more efficiently the substantive hearing can be conducted.

With Directions Nos.1 and 2, there should be a sufficient blueprint to bring an arbitration to trial. The parties may from time to time still need further directions for the conduct of the arbitration. But it is hoped that applications will be kept to a minimum in order to keep down the expenses of the arbitration to a proportionate level.

B. Interim Measures Pending Trial

I. Public concern over interim measures

Chapter 1 referred to a tribunal's powers to grant interim measures under both ss.35 [13] and 56. It was pointed out that, although there is apparent overlap between the 2 provisions, s.35 clearly confers wider powers than s.56.

The power to enact interim measures under s.35 is new. The old Ordinance only gave arbitrators the powers in s.56. The powers under s.35 being therefore unfamiliar, some have expressed worry over the possibility of those powers being abused. The unease has been such that the *South China Morning Post* ran a front page article on the matter.[14]

The article reported that judges and lawyers had reservations about the power to order interim measures conferred by the Ordinance. The concern was that anyone, lawyer or lay person could, when sitting as arbitrator, issue *Mareva* injunctions or *Anton Piller* orders.

A *Mareva* injunction is an order freezing a person's assets (including bank deposits and real property) pending trial of a dispute. The order is made to prevent an unscrupulous defendant from hiding assets in a different jurisdiction, thereby making it difficult for a successful plaintiff to enforce against the defendant.

An *Anton Piller* order enables a plaintiff to search a person's premises to obtain incriminating evidence.

Marevas and *Anton Pillers* are typically sought from a Court or tribunal *ex parte*, that is, without forewarning being given to the other side. The fear is that a party who learns of an impending application will immediately transfer away assets or destroy incriminating evidence.

Marevas and *Anton Pillers* are draconian orders. They interfere with a person's rights by preventing the use of one's property or by requiring that one allow strangers to enter and search one's premises. The Court only grants the orders where a party can demonstrate that (in the case of *Marevas*) there is a real risk of dissipation of assets by a defendant or (in the case of *Anton Pillers*) there is a real risk that a defendant will destroy evidence.

The Post was reporting a fear among some that the "nuclear weapons" of civil procedure (as *Marevas* and *Anton Pillers* are sometimes called) were now in everyone's hands. So (it was suggested) a party to an arbitration might find one's bank account suddenly frozen or one's premises searched at the say-so of any person purporting to act as arbitrator.

The scenario just painted might, if it were true, be frightening. But the question is whether it is a correct evaluation of the consequences of enacting s.35. I do not think that it is.

It is right that, when delivering the lectures on which this book is based, I myself referred to unease as a judge at the thought of a novice or inexperienced arbitrator being able to grant *Marevas* or *Anton Pillers*. But I qualified my unease at the same time.

I stressed that, far from being a real source of concern, once properly analysed, the power to grant interim measures opens up exciting possibilities for arbitration to become the premier mode for effective resolution of commercial disputes. The new Ordinance should not be regarded as a source of pessimism, but instead as an occasion for optimism about arbitration.

To achieve the promise of the Ordinance will require work. It will require a shift in the way we think about the relationship between arbitration and the Courts. That shift will require the cooperation of parties, arbitrators, and judges to make arbitration work as a means of expeditious and inexpensive dispute resolution. We must stop thinking of arbitration as a self-contained mode of dispute resolution, but instead think of arbitration as a process involving arbitrators working together with the Courts.

I will say more about this necessary change of thinking in Chapter 4. Here I shall focus on conveying an idea of the possibilities which the new provisions on interim measures have opened up.

The obvious convenient starting point is s.35 itself.[15] It enables arbitrators, by way of interim measures, to order a party A to do the following:

(1) To maintain or restore the status quo pending determination of the dispute;

(2) To take action that would prevent, or refrain from taking action that is likely to cause, current or imminent harm or prejudice to the arbitral process itself;

(3) To provide a means of preserving assets out of which a subsequent award may be satisfied; or,

(4) To preserve evidence that may be relevant and material to the resolution of the dispute.

There are 4 points to note about the power conferred by s.35(1).

The first point is that the power is expressly made subject to the agreement of the parties. This means that the parties may (expressly or by implication) limit, in whole or part, the powers conferred by s.35(1) on a tribunal.

The second point is that interim measures may be granted "in the form of an award or in another form". Section 35(2) makes clear that an interim measure may be in a form (for instance, an order that A take certain steps) other than an award. But s.35(3) states that where a tribunal has granted an interim measure, it may on the application of a party make an award to the same effect as the interim measures order.[16]

One might wonder what difference it makes whether an interim measure is granted as an order or an award–probably little difference in substance, but there may be procedural consequences.

For instance, note s.67 (ML 31) on the form and content of an award. That requires that, unless the parties agree otherwise, an award "shall state the reason upon which it is based". If the interim measures are in the form of an order (as opposed to an award), there may be no need to state in writing what one's reasons are for the grant of the interim measures.

Interim measures are typically given to maintain a balance of convenience or status quo pending the outcome of an arbitration. At this stage, the tribunal will not have made any findings of fact and can only take a provisional view of the merits of a dispute following a cursory examination of the evidence.

A party may wish to have an award in writing for the purpose of appealing against an interim measure to the Court or enforcing the measure as an order of the Court. Apart from those situations, there is likely to be little utility to anyone in an award which only states that the tribunal is granting an interim measure, because in all the circumstances that is what the tribunal believes will best preserve the status quo pending trial.

This does not mean that reasons can be omitted, however, when granting an interim measure in the form of an order rather than an award. As a matter of good form, a tribunal should at least strive to give short oral reasons to explain whatever directions or orders it makes, even where no written award has been sought.

The third point is that interim measures granted under s.35(1) will in effect be directions that a party act, or refrain from acting, in a particular way. The orders are enforceable against a party because, by the arbitration agreement, it has contracted to be bound by the orders of the tribunal. That is all.

Assume that an arbitrator grants a *Mareva* as an interim measure. The arbitrator orders B not to withdraw or dispose of funds in a bank, in order to preserve assets from which a subsequent award against B may be satisfied.

There would be little to be gained if A (the other party to the arbitration) were to present a copy of the tribunal's order to B's bank. That is because B's bank is not a party to the arbitration agreement between A and B. There would be no compelling legal reason for B's bank to obey the tribunal's order, which is not a Court order.[17] The tribunal's order would not carry with it the sanction of being held in contempt of Court if its terms were disobeyed.

If B were to withdraw funds from B's bank, B would be in breach of the arbitration agreement. B may accordingly open itself up to consequential adverse orders by the tribunal for disobeying the latter's interim measure. But, unless the tribunal's interim measure has first been converted into a Court order bearing the sanction of contempt for disobedience, B (if sufficiently determined and thick-skinned) could flaunt the tribunal's orders. B would, in effect, be daring A to sue B in Court for breach of contract.

The fourth point (as pointed out in Chapter 1) is the cryptic reference in s.35(2) to s.56. Section 35(2) states: "An interim measure referred to in Art.17 of the UNCITRAL Model Law is to be construed as including an injunction, but not including an order under s.56." What does that mean?

Section 56 confers a list of "general powers exercisable by an arbitral tribunal". Those powers are also subject to a contrary agreement by the parties. By s.56(1), a tribunal has the power:

(1) To order security for costs;

(2) To order discovery or interrogatories;

(3) To direct that evidence be given by affidavit;

(4) To order the inspection, photographing, preservation, custody, detention or sale of property which is relevant to the arbitration proceedings; and

(5) To direct samples to be taken or experiments to be carried out on relevant property.

Section 56(8) confers other powers, including the power to administer oaths; to examine witnesses; and to direct the attendance of witnesses to give evidence or produce documents.

Section 56 seems to be less intrusive than s.35 in that s.56 essentially concerns procedural matters to facilitate the hearing of an arbitration. For instance, in contrast to s.35, s.56 does not enable arbitrators to order the equivalent of *Marevas*.

But s.56(8) does include what, at first glance, may appear to be a highly intrusive power. On its face, the provision empowers a tribunal to order persons who are not party to an arbitration agreement to appear before the tribunal to give evidence or produce documents.

On closer analysis, the power to summon a person to appear before a tribunal lacks teeth. Again, on a conservative reading of the Ordinance, unless the tribunal's order is converted into a Court order, there would be no sanction if a person (who is summoned to appear before a tribunal and produce documents) refuses to attend. Contrast a subpoena – that is an order of the Court compelling a witness to appear to give evidence, on pain of punishment (Latin, *poena*) if one fails to obey. The order of a tribunal lacks that threat of punishment by the Court and so could not be the equivalent of a subpoena.

But there is still an apparent overlap between ss.35 and 56. For example, the power under s.35 to order a party to preserve evidence or to refrain from taking a step which might prejudice arbitration proceedings is wide enough to encompass the power under s.56(1) to order a party to preserve relevant property pending the resolution of arbitration proceedings in relation to that property.

Why should there be an overlap? Is there meant to be an overlap? Or, is any overlap more apparent than real?

I suggest that what s.35(2) means is that, injunctions apart, if a power can be construed as falling within the terms of s.56, it should not be treated as an interim measure capable of being ordered under s.35. Thus, except where injunctions are concerned, the powers under ss.35 and 56 are to be regarded as mutually exclusive. For example, the power under s.56 to order the preservation pending trial of relevant property (property which is the subject matter of arbitration proceedings) should not be treated as an interim measure under s.35.

Any overlap between ss.35 and 56 would only be in relation to injunctions. I suspect that injunctions (which are usually negative orders requiring a party not to do something (as opposed to positive orders requiring a party to do something)) were excepted by s.35(2) because some interim measures listed in s.56 may be characterised as orders to refrain from acting in a particular way.

One might ask why the Ordinance should enact such a seemingly cumbersome distinction between an intrusive power to grant interim measures in relation to a respondent's assets or property under s.35 and procedural powers to facilitate the hearing of an arbitration under s.56?

The answer to the question is not obvious. Having reflected on the matter, my proposed answer is that what I have just described as a "seemingly cumbersome distinction" is by no means so. The distinction between ss.35 and 56 is merely one of several ways in which the Ordinance seeks to make arbitration proceedings as flexible as possible in responding to the needs of different users of arbitration.

There are many types of arbitrations. Some may not require knowledge of the law, but may instead need specialist knowledge or expertise in order to resolve a technical dispute. The latter arbitrations would not normally require a tribunal with the power to grant *Marevas* or *Anton Pillers*.

Other arbitrations may involve the resolution of labour or family disputes. These disputes may benefit from a tribunal having all of the powers under s.56, but only some (not all) of the powers under s.35.

Still other arbitrations may be wholly commercial disputes where it would be convenient if the tribunal could exercise all the powers conferred by ss.35 and 56.

There is a whole gamut of possibility.

What the Ordinance does is to offer ready-made ("off-the-peg") packages from among which different would-be users of arbitration services can "pick and choose" to suit their requirements and taste.

Some may prefer the less intrusive measures of s.56 to the interim reliefs available under s.35.

Others may prefer their arbitrator to wield the powers in both sections. That is the default position under the new Ordinance.

Yet other users might choose a mix of some of the powers in s.35 and some of those in s.56, rather than adopting either section wholesale. This last option requires more careful attention by the parties and their legal advisers when drafting an arbitration agreement. The parties will have to address their minds to coming up with a consistent package of powers which enables their chosen tribunal to accomplish that which the parties want it to do.

An important innovation of the Ordinance then is to allow parties to tailor the bundle of powers which they are to confer upon their tribunal to that which is most suited to their needs. To make use of this flexibility, however, the parties and their advisers have to focus from the outset on how much power they wish to grant to a tribunal. The parties will have to balance between their mutual need for interim protection and their personal desire to retain as much control as possible over their assets.

Flexibility having been deliberately built into the new Ordinance in relation to interim measures, parties should take advantage of that and work out the most suitable balance for their circumstances.

That leaves the question whether interim measures ordered by a tribunal under ss.35 or 56 will have a coercive effect on persons other than the parties to an agreement. Plainly, judicial support will be necessary to give teeth to any system of interim measures.

But how should the Court provide support? The 2 cardinal principles introduced in Chapter 1 should serve as guidelines. Section 3(2)(b) stipulates that "the Court should interfere in the arbitration of a dispute only as expressly provided in this Ordinance". The principle is reinforced by s.12[18] : "In matters governed by this law, the Court should not intervene except where so provided in this law."

Complexity arises from the fact that, as well as being able to convert a tribunal's interim measure into an order of Court, the Court also has the power to grant interim measures in aid of arbitration.

A party can apply to the Court for an interim measure. Section 21[19] confirms that "it is not incompatible with an arbitration agreement for a party to request, before or during the proceedings, from a Court an interim measure of protection and for a Court to grant such measure".

Section 45(4) (disapplying ML 17J) does give the Court a discretion to refuse an interim measure where "the interim measure sought is currently the subject of arbitration proceedings" and "the Court considers it more appropriate for the interim measure sought to be dealt with by the arbitral tribunal".

But, on a literal reading of s.45(4), nothing prevents a party from directly applying to the Court for an interim measure instead of first asking an arbitral tribunal. This is because an application for an interim measure, having been initially sought from the Court, would arguably not be "the subject of arbitral proceedings" and s.45(4) should therefore not apply.

Section 60(4) enables the Court to decline to make an order for (say) the preservation of relevant property if "the matter" is currently the subject of arbitration proceedings and the Court considers it more appropriate for the tribunal to deal with "the matter".

But again what happens if "the matter of preserving related property" is first brought to the Court? That would seem to be possible and the Court might well deal with the question as the first forum seized with the matter. Note, however, that under s.60(5) a Court order for preservation of relevant property may provide for its automatic cessation when a tribunal makes an order for its cessation.

All this implies that, unless the Court is careful in working out how to deal with interim measure applications, we could easily end up with parallel proceedings for interim measures: one before the Court and the other before the tribunal. That would be undesirable, since costs will certainly be duplicated and much time wasted on mere interlocutory skirmishing. Unfortunately, the Ordinance having only been recently enacted, it remains unclear what procedures the Court will follow in relation to the enforcement of interim measures.

Let us examine 2 scenarios to see what can quickly go wrong.

In Scenario I, party A applies *ex parte* to the Court for a *Mareva* without first bringing the matter before an appointed tribunal. This type of application was possible under the old Ordinance and still seems possible under the new Ordinance. Should the Court now decline to intervene on the principle that the matter is best left to the tribunal?

Assume the Court decides to grant an *ex parte Mareva* against the other party B. Under the practice followed with the old Ordinance, such decision would lead to the Court giving directions for the filing of evidence for an *inter partes* hearing where both parties appear before the Court to argue whether there should be a *Mareva* pending trial by the tribunal.

Should that practice still be followed? If the whole process of arguing about the interim measure is to proceed before the Court, that will take time. What happens to the arbitration in the meanwhile? There is a danger that nothing will happen. Instead the parties will be focusing all their energies on the coming *inter partes* interlocutory hearing before the Court. The Court's well-intentioned intervention at this early stage may jeopardise the resort to arbitration as a speedy means of resolving the parties' substantive dispute.

Suppose that, in retaliation to A's Court application, B asks the arbitration tribunal for an order under s.35 that A refrain from enforcing the Court's *Mareva* in whole or in part, or for an order that A apply to the Court for the discharge of the *Mareva*. What happens then? We would be in a situation of tactical manoeuvring, where each party plays off one forum against the other or each party seeks to enjoin the other from applying to one forum or another for relief. Costs escalate and tempers flare, even before anyone has begun to assess the merits of the parties' substantive dispute.

In Scenario II, A applies for a *Mareva* from the arbitration tribunal under s.35. The tribunal grants the *Mareva* after an *inter partes* hearing and, at the request of A which wishes to enforce the interim measure as a Court order, makes the interim measure in the form of an award. A then applies to the Court for the award to be made into an order of the Court. What procedure does the Court follow?

One can apply for the award to be enforced as an order of the Court under Part 10 of the Ordinance. Under the old Ordinance, analogous applications would be determined *ex parte* in the first instance on documents alone. The procedure was for the Court then to make an order *nisi* on the *ex parte* application. The order so obtained expressly provided that it would be enforceable unless (Latin, *nisi*) B applied to set it aside within (say) 28 days. If B applied to set aside, the order would remain suspended until the determination of B's application.

Assume the old procedure continues to apply. If B applies to set aside A's order, the Court will give directions for the filing of affidavit evidence and set a date for the substantive hearing of B's setting aside application.

In the meantime, what is the status of the tribunal's *Mareva*? It remains enforceable solely as a matter of contract between A and B. Until converted into an enforceable Court order, the tribunal's *Mareva* would not affect third parties (including B's bank). Presumably, the Court could grant a temporary order restraining B from doing anything to render the tribunal's order ineffective.

But the point is, if the old procedures continue to apply, once again, before we realise it, there will be 2 forums dealing with the same question of interim measures: the tribunal and the Court.

The Ordinance gives A another option to facilitate a more general enforcement of the tribunal's *Mareva*. A can apply to enforce the tribunal's interim measure order as a Court order by seeking leave under s.61. That being a new provision, it remains to be seen what procedure the Court will follow on an application under it. Obviously, there is still a risk of duplicate proceedings if one is not careful.

The problems I have sketched out are not insurmountable. Neither is the duplication of proceedings (involving a needless waste of time and cost) inevitable. For example, in Scenario II, the Court may take the view that, where an interim measure has been fully argued *inter partes* before a tribunal, the Court will refuse to allow the validity of the interim measure to be re-litigated before it on the ground of *res judicata*.[20]

What is required to solve the problem is (among other things) for the Court (sooner rather than later) to clarify precisely what general procedures and principles it will follow with applications for interim measures. A Practice Direction on the matter would be welcome.

Just as importantly, arbitrators have to be sensitive to the symbiosis between their orders for interim measures and equivalent or related orders of the Court. Unless arbitrators are alert to the complications which can arise, we will rapidly degenerate into a situation where the left and right hands are not acting in coordinated fashion.

C. Case Management

It will be apparent that much work is required to prepare an arbitration for trial. I shall refer to the process of getting an arbitration ready for trial as "case management".

In all but the simplest of cases, there are likely to be several interlocutory hearings between the appointment of a tribunal and the trial of a dispute. Those hearings may be the result of applications by the parties or they may be instigated by the tribunal on its own motion. In the course of those hearings, the tribunal will typically be making orders which serve one or more of the following functions: [21]

1. To establish (or decline) jurisdiction to hear a case;

2. To order security or other relief pending trial of a dispute;

3. To crystallise the issues to be investigated at trial by requiring further particulars of a party's case or by giving leave for specific types of evidence (such as expert evidence) to be adduced;

4. To strike out all or parts of the other side's case on the ground that such parts are unreasonable, frivolous, vexatious or an abuse of process; and

5. To obtain evidence in the possession of a party to the arbitration or in the possession of a person not party to the arbitration.

In this section, I will describe common interim orders which the tribunal might make by reference to the 5 functions which I have just identified. I will suggest what a tribunal might wish to think about when making such orders. I will conclude with some general comments about case management.

I. Category (1): Orders to establish or decline jurisdiction

Challenges to jurisdiction will conventionally be made at the start of an arbitration, probably almost as soon as a tribunal is appointed. This is because, if a party waits too long before mounting a challenge, it risks being treated as having waived the right to object to the dispute being resolved by the tribunal. If (for example) one actively participates in an arbitration without protesting jurisdiction, one may be treated as having accepted the tribunal's competence to decide a dispute.

This is only common sense.

A party should not blow hot and cold. It should not be allowed to "wait and see" if the arbitration is going in its favour before objecting to jurisdiction. It would be blatantly unfair if a party were able to pursue such a tactic. If a tribunal were to accept a delayed challenge, substantial time and money already spent in resolving the dispute by arbitration would be wasted.

The two types of application that are often made are: (a) a challenge to jurisdiction based on actual or apparent bias, and (b) a challenge to jurisdiction based on the alleged absence of an effective arbitration agreement.

Challenges on the basis of real or apparent bias have been mentioned above.

As for the second challenge, I have mentioned "competence-competence". An arbitrator may rule on one's own jurisdiction, but that determination cannot be conclusive. The Court has the final say.

Consider the situation where a plaintiff attempts to litigate a dispute in Court and the defendant applies to stay the plaintiff to arbitration.

In many instances, the Court will be able to construe an alleged arbitration clause to determine whether or not it covers a dispute. The Court can decide whether or not to grant a stay depending on its construction of the agreement.

But suppose that it is unclear on the facts whether an arbitration agreement has been incorporated into a contract between the parties. Or, suppose that the documentary evidence of the supposed arbitration agreement is challenged as inaccurate or incorrect in light of certain facts. Then who is to assess whether or not the facts render an alleged arbitration agreement null, void or inoperative?

In practice, the Court will likely confine itself to assessing whether, on the evidence adduced by the party alleging the existence of an arbitration agreement, there is an arguable case that a dispute is covered by that agreement. If the Court feels on a brief examination of the evidence that there is an arguable case, it will probably not decide the matter definitively, but will instead stay the action and leave the question of jurisdiction to be determined in the first instance by the arbitrator. This approach would *prima facie* be consistent with the principle of minimum interference by the Court in matters potentially subject to arbitration.

It will then be for the tribunal to decide if it does have jurisdiction. Of course, if one or other party is unhappy with the tribunal's decision on jurisdiction, that party may later come back to the Court for a definitive ruling.

I have misgivings, however, about whether the practice just mentioned should be followed in all cases by the Court. I doubt that there can be a neat rule of practice on how to deal with questions of jurisdiction raised in applications to stay Court proceedings. Flexibility is needed.

Accordingly, the Court's approach should (I suggest) depend on what is expedient in a particular situation. For example, the issue may be merely one of construing an agreement to determine whether, on largely undisputed facts, a matter falls within an arbitration agreement. There would be little point in leaving the question of jurisdiction to be provisionally determined by an arbitrator. Should not the Court, in the interests of saving time and cost, construe the agreement one way or other in the course of hearing the stay application and decide the issue of jurisdiction definitively?

In contrast, it may be necessary to conduct a full-blown inquiry (including examination of witnesses) into the facts behind an alleged agreement to arbitrate before one can discern the parties' objective intentions. There may in that case be an advantage in granting a stay of Court proceedings to enable an arbitrator to determine the relevant facts and rule on his or her own jurisdiction. As always, if a party is not satisfied with the arbitrator's conclusion, the party may apply to the Court.

But this last solution will not obviate all difficulties.

Assume that a party unsuccessfully maintains before an arbitrator that the latter lacks jurisdiction. On challenge to the Court, the party might query whether the arbitrator had jurisdiction even to determine the facts on which the arbitrator rested his or her conclusion of jurisdiction. The party may forcefully submit that, under the principle of competence-competence, the tribunal's findings of fact cannot be final and conclusive as far as the Court is concerned.

It is unclear under the present law whether the Court is bound in all cases to conduct its own inquiry of fact before arriving at its own determination on jurisdiction. If the Court has to do so, there would obviously be considerable duplication of effort and cost.

My suggestion is that the Court should be robust. Where there is an agreed note or transcript of the evidence given before the tribunal on the question of jurisdiction, the Court might merely refer to such evidence in drawing its own conclusion on the issue. The Court (I suggest) should, to the extent possible, treat the application to set aside the tribunal's finding on jurisdiction as a re-hearing analogous to an appeal from the decision of a first instance judge to the Court of Appeal.

An appeal to the Court of Appeal is supposed to be a complete re-hearing. But the Court of Appeal only reviews the evidence (including witness statements and transcripts) actually adduced before the first instance judge. The Court of Appeal does not usually re-hear witnesses or allow fresh evidence. Everything merely proceeds on the basis of documents (including witness statements and transcripts) augmented by submissions from counsel for the parties.

However, it will not be every case where there is an agreed or reliable transcript of the evidence adduced in an arbitration. In that case, there may be little alternative. The Court may unfortunately have to re-hear the whole issue of jurisdiction with examination of live witnesses where necessary.

A problem which commonly leads to a jurisdictional challenge in the Hong Kong Courts occurs where a Main Contractor and a Sub-Contractor enter into a Sub-Contract on a "back-to-back basis" with the Main Contract between the Employer and Main Contractor. The question is whether the Sub-Contract incorporates an arbitration clause in the Main Contract which only refers to the Employer and Main Contractor submitting their future disputes to arbitration. In other words, does the expression "back-to-back" in the Sub-Contract mean that the words "Employer" and "Main Contractor" in the Main Contract's arbitration clause should be read as referring to disputes between the "Main Contractor" and "Sub-Contractor" respectively?

Hudson's Building and Engineering Contracts [22] §18-032 states:

> "It will frequently happen that the parties may refer to a document which cannot be used to fit the parties' own contractual relationship or description without some necessary modifications. In the case of an arbitration clause in a main contract, for example, it may or may not be worded so as to be applicable to sub-contracting parties without modification of at least some parts of the clause. In the analogous field of marine contracts of affreightment, a substantial case law has built up as a result of the practice whereby bills of lading incorporate by reference the terms of the principal charterparty. Relatively rigid rules of interpretation have been developed by the English Commercial Court in bill of lading cases, to the effect that where the terms of the charterparty's arbitration clause are not applicable

without some modification of its provisions to suit the bill of lading relationship or transaction. A general incorporating reference to the charterparty without some more specific reference to the arbitration clause itself will not suffice. However, it would be wrong, it is submitted, for any such rigid rule to apply in the quite different commercial relationship between construction contracts and sub-contracts, although [a] recent case in the Court of Appeal [*Aughton Ltd. (formerly Aughton Group Ltd.) v. M. F. Kent Services Ltd.* (1991) 57 BLR 1] shows a difference of opinion on the point."

More recently, the 2004 Supplement to Hudson refers (at pp.299-300) to an inclination by the English Courts to reject the requirement of a specific reference by a Sub-Contract to an arbitration clause in (say) a Main Contract. The Courts instead look for "an arbitration intention" by construing the relevant documents "as a whole". *Hudson* concludes:

"The majority view in all jurisdictions, therefore, appears to be against any rigid or artificial 'specific reference' test of an incorporating provision (it is submitted rightly), since the commercial reasons behind parties' references to the provisions of other contracts or other standard forms can vary very considerably in construction cases and their draftmanship is unlikely to pay slavish regard to previous judicial precedents, unlike marine insurance policies covering risks incurred under bills of lading."

My personal view is that *Hudson* is right in suggesting that there can be no rigid rule. I would, however, go further and argue that, as a matter of principle, there should not be a difference between general approaches in shipping and construction contract cases.

It must always be a matter of objectively construing a relevant contract to determine the intention of the parties. Each case will depend on its own facts and the best that one can do is to lay down a rule of thumb. I think that *Hudson* implicitly itself accepts this at §3-049 when it states: "The intention to incorporate must be sufficiently clear and the provisions sought to be incorporated sufficiently certain".[23]

I doubt that a provision that a sub-contract has been entered on a "back-to-back" basis is, without more, sufficiently unambiguous to incorporate an arbitration clause in the Main Contract which is expressly stated to be between Employer and Main Contractor. In my view, something more is required to demonstrate that a Main Contractor and Sub-Contractor meant to import an obligation to refer their disputes to arbitration. In the absence of that "something more", the natural inference (I believe) would be that only the Main Contractor's obligations in relation to construction work are being assumed on a "back-to-back basis" by the Sub-Contractor.

It is sometimes argued that a particular dispute is outside the scope of an arbitration agreement. It is then submitted that a stay should only be granted in respect of part of an action and that claims relating to disputes which are outside the scope of an arbitration clause should be allowed to proceed in Court.

The fact that some disputes between 2 parties in respect of a single project may fall within the scope of an arbitration agreement, while other disputes may not, can lead to procedurally "messy" situations. There is a danger that (where common facts are involved in both sets of disputes) the Court and a tribunal will make contradictory findings. Set-offs and cross-claims are especially problematic for this reason.

Assume that a Main Contractor claims damages in Court against a Sub-Contractor for breach of a Sub-Contract A not subject to arbitration. By way of defence and counterclaim, the Sub-Contractor pleads that it is not liable by reason of a right of set-off. The Sub-

Contractor alleges that the set-off arises out of a liquidated debt due from the Main Contractor under a Sub-Contract B. B is subject to an arbitration agreement.

Can the Main Contractor insist on a judge staying the trial of the Sub-Contractor's alleged right of set-off and any associated counterclaim to arbitration? Or, can the Sub-Contractor at least maintain the alleged set-off under B as a defence (even if not as a counterclaim) in the Court proceedings?

If the former solution is adopted, it could be argued that, solely as a matter of procedure, the Sub-Contractor is deprived of a defence of set-off that in the ordinary course of litigation it should be entitled to raise against the Main Contractor. If the latter solution is adopted, there is a danger that the Court and a tribunal will come to different conclusions. The Court, for instance, may find that there is a defence of set-off. But when adjudicating the Sub-Contractor's counterclaim, a tribunal may reject the Sub-Contractor's case entirely.

The analysis of set-off claims proposed in the 2001 Companion to *Mustill & Boyd on Commercial Arbitration* (at p.142) is (I respectfully suggest) confusing:

> "The modern tendency is to classify set-offs as either transactional (which encompasses common law abatement and equitable set-off...) or independent ... [I]t has been held that transactional set-off gives rise to a true defence, whereas transactional set-off [*sic*] does not. In the case of transactional set-off, a cross-claim which was arbitrable could not be pleaded as a set-off in an action on a claim which was not arbitrable, if the cross-claim was subject to a mandatory stay under section 1 of the 1979 Act. The reason is that the statutes of set-off from which independent set-off derives require the claim and cross-claim to be tried by the same court. The court has, however, power to prevent injustice to the defendant

to the action by staying the proceedings or execution pending the determination of the cross-claim. The position with regard to transactional set-off is less clear. There is authority in a case which was not subject to a mandatory stay that the court would itself decide on the merits of the cross-claim: *Gilbert-Ash (Northern) Ltd. v. Modern (Engineering (Bristol) Ltd.* [1974] AC 689. But this hardly seems appropriate in a case where legislation giving effect to the New York Convention requires the court to grant a stay. See generally on this topic *Aetna Refining and Marketing Inc. v. Exmar NV* [1994] 1 WLR 1634, and *Glencore Grain Ltd. v. Argos Trading Co. Ltd.* [1999] 2 Lloyds Rep 410."

This is not the place to venture deeply into the problem of set-offs and cross-claims. Again I doubt that there is an elegant solution to the practical difficulties posed. The problem is best tackled at the earliest possible stage by lawyers drafting contracts which foresee the possibility of consolidating related claims between the parties into a single arbitration. But often little thought is given to this possibility until too late.

Once a dispute arises the parties are unlikely to be cooperative, so that each insists on a different forum to obtain tactical ascendancy or inflict maximum inconvenience on the other. Arbitrators and the Court will have to be alert to the problems arising in set-off claims (common in construction cases) in order to fashion practical solutions between them which are cost-effective and expeditious.

Yet another question which crops up is whether an arbitration agreement warrants the stay of litigation in Court, if a defendant has no arguable defence.

Typically, an application by a defendant for a stay is countered with a summons by the plaintiff for summary judgment. Should the plaintiff be allowed to show that the defendant has no defence? The argument would be that, if there is no arguable case, the arbitration agreement is "null and void, inoperative or incapable of being performed" in the sense that, once properly analysed, there can be no serious dispute to the plaintiff's claim.

The Court follows a pragmatic practice.

Unless the defendant has unambiguously admitted the plaintiff's claim, there must at least be a dispute between the parties as to whether there is an arguable defence to a claim. Consequently, given an agreement to refer all disputes arising between the parties to arbitration, it should be within a tribunal's jurisdiction to determine the dispute whether the defendant has an arguable case.

Thus, the Court will stay the matter to arbitration in the absence of a clear admission of liability by the defendant. The Court should in this case decline to determine whether summary judgment should be granted and leave that question to the tribunal.

II. Category (2): Orders for security or other relief pending trial

Three sorts of applications are normally made within this category. The first is an application by a claimant for a *Mareva*. The second is an application by a respondent that a claimant put up security for the costs of an arbitration. The third is an application for an injunction to prevent a person from doing some act (or (in rare instances) to require a person to do some act) pending trial.

I have already considered aspects of the first type of application in Section B. Such application is normally initiated *ex parte*.[24] That means that a party will usually apply without forewarning the other side. This is so as not to tip off the respondent and give it an opportunity to transfer its assets out of the jurisdiction before the application is made. If the respondent could make such a transfer, the purpose of the Mareva would be frustrated.

Because the application is initially made unilaterally, the claimant has a duty of full and frank disclosure.[25] The claimant must inform the tribunal of all relevant facts which might reasonably be regarded as bearing on whether or not the tribunal should make an order. The duty of frank disclosure also requires the claimant to point out possible weaknesses in its case. The claimant will then have to explain why those weaknesses do not rule out the grant of relief.

A *Mareva* may (not must) be granted if the tribunal is satisfied that 2 conditions are satisfied.[26] In essence, the 2 conditions involve a balancing exercise.

Condition 1 is that the applicant has "a reasonable possibility of succeeding on the merits of the claim".

Condition 2 is that:

> "Harm not adequately reparable by an award of damages is likely to result if the measure is not ordered, and such harm substantially outweighs the harm that is likely to result to the party against whom the measure is directed if the measure is granted."

When an *ex parte* application is made for a *Mareva*, the tribunal will form a view as to whether the 2 conditions are met. If so satisfied, the tribunal may grant a preliminary order to the effect that, pending an *inter partes* hearing where the respondent will have a chance to object to the claimant's application, the respondent should do nothing to frustrate the interim measure being requested (for example, by disposing of assets).

A preliminary order having been made, the tribunal must immediately notify the respondent of what has transpired. [27] It should also give the respondent a chance to object to the proposed *Mareva* "at the earliest practicable time".

Unless converted into an interim measure, the preliminary order will automatically lapse after 20 days. Within that 20 day limit, the tribunal must give the respondent an opportunity to be heard. Having been given notice and afforded the opportunity to be heard, the respondent may or may not wish to make submissions against the grant of the *Mareva*.

The tribunal should obviously consider any objections made by the respondent, before the tribunal decides whether to grant a *Mareva* as an interim measure. If the respondent does not do anything despite having been given a reasonable chance to object, the tribunal can proceed to consider whether to grant a *Mareva* solely on the materials adduced by the claimant.

In practice, *Marevas* are granted if an applicant has a reasonably arguable claim and the tribunal believes that there is a real risk that a respondent will dissipate its assets. Applications for *Marevas* thus frequently fail before the Court, because a claimant is unable to establish a real risk of dissipation.

Further, an injunction (including a *Mareva*) is a form of equitable relief. As a matter of principle, equity will not assist a person who "sleeps" on his or her rights. Thus, if a party inexplicably delays in applying for an injunction, the Court may in its discretion refuse to grant the relief.

A claimant will on occasion assert that there is a "real risk" of dissipation of assets merely on the basis of evidence that a respondent has been selling its property. A tribunal must be wary of granting a *Mareva* if such sale is the only evidence relied upon.

Few will have, in ready cash, the amounts necessary to finance the litigation of a substantial dispute, whether before the Court or a tribunal. Litigation is not such a daily occurrence in most people's lives that at any given moment one will have the liquidity to fund a major ongoing dispute. Faced with the prospect of a dispute which may go to arbitration or litigation or both, a respondent may naturally decide to liquidate assets to raise the financing necessary to conduct its case.

It would be ironic then if, in liquidating assets to deal with litigation, the respondent should be deemed by the Court to be showing a "real risk" of dissipation of assets. By granting a *Mareva* merely because a respondent has been selling off property, a tribunal may be giving a claimant an unfair tactical advantage. On the barest evidence, the claimant would be freezing a respondent's assets, thereby inflicting maximum pressure and inconvenience on the respondent's conduct of an effective defence. A tribunal has to guard against being used in this way by claimants.

Claimants may realise that their "evidence" of dissipation is weak. In that circumstance, a few might attempt to give a prejudicial slant to the respondent's failure to pay an alleged debt or discharge an alleged obligation. It will be said that, in refusing to pay or perform, the respondent has shown a "low standard of commercial morality" which justifies the tribunal imposing a freezing order.

Again a tribunal should be sceptical. In many cases where a respondent's "low commercial morality" is prayed in aid of a *Mareva* application, a claimant is saying nothing more than that it has entered into a bad commercial deal from its point-of-view.

In most cases, the mere fact that a respondent has not paid up is not likely to be proof of much, as the respondent may not be paying up for what it believes (rightly or wrongly) to be a good reason. Whether or not there is a valid reason for the respondent's failure to pay will usually have to be the subject of a trial. It will be rare where, without cogent evidence, a tribunal comes to a view at only an interlocutory hearing that the respondent's non-performance alone exemplifies a "low commercial morality".

Applications for a *Mareva* typically also fail before the Court because of delay by a claimant in making an application. The same principle should hold true in arbitrations.

A claimant unilaterally asks for a *Mareva* to be imposed because, in the absence of a freezing injunction, assets (the claimant alleges) will be dissipated. If a claimant delays in making such application, the respondent will presumably have had ample time (if so minded) to transfer its assets elsewhere. Accordingly, where there has been inexplicable delay by a claimant, there would be little justification for a *Mareva*. The claimant will either be too late (in that monies would already have been dissipated) or, if the respondent has not already transferred its monies out despite having had the chance, the respondent can hardly be said to have an intention to dissipate assets.

In practice, the Court distinguishes between 2 situations. One is where a *Mareva* is sought to freeze assets belonging to a respondent. The other is where a *Mareva* is sought to freeze assets which are held in the name of a respondent, but which the claimant contends belong to the claimant beneficially. In the latter case, the Court may be prepared to grant a *Mareva* despite delay. The Court does this because there is an arguable case that the disputed assets belong to the claimant and one should not be penalised for a delay in claiming what belongs to one.

At the end of the day, a *Mareva* will usually only be justified where a claimant can adduce strong *prima facie* evidence of fraud or dishonesty on the part of a respondent. That will be rare in run-of-the-mill commercial situations.

The second type of application is one where a respondent asks that a claimant put up security for the respondent's costs. An order for security is routinely granted where there is cogent evidence that a claimant lacks assets with which to satisfy any adverse costs order at the end of an arbitration.

But a respondent may seek an inflated amount of security from the claimant. The strategy there would be to deter a claimant from pursuing even a meritorious claim in the domestic jurisdiction. Arbitrators should scrutinise a bill of costs robustly, with a sceptical eye at alleged "necessary" expenses, before ordering a particular amount.

The converse situation where a claimant seeks security against a defendant is rare. This is because it should normally be unfair to force a respondent to put up money for having to defend itself. A respondent should always be entitled to defend itself, whether or not it has funds to do so.

The only exception may be where the respondent's defence is so palpably bad or "shadowy" that it amounts to little more than a waste of time. A tribunal may be reluctant to strike out such case outright. But it may require some form of security to be put up as a condition of being allowed to proceed.

There is one more situation of which a tribunal should be aware. That is where the tribunal deals with both a claim and a counterclaim and the latter is merely the reverse of the other. In other words, a claimant claims that a respondent is in breach and thus liable to do X, while a respondent counterclaims that in actuality the claimant is in breach and liable to do Y.

In that situation, there will not be much point in the tribunal ordering the claimant to put up security for costs in favour of the respondent. That is because the normal sanction for a failure to put up any security ordered would be to bar a claimant from pursuing its claim. But such sanction would not work here, since (whatever happens) the counterclaim will have to be tried and the counterclaim is simply the other side of the claim.

The trial of the counterclaim will proceed and the same matters as the tribunal would have had to consider in relation to the claim, would be determined under the counterclaim.

The third type of interim application commonly made is for an injunction to maintain a defined state of affairs pending trial.

This will usually entail a claimant seeking to prevent a respondent from committing an act. The respondent is ordered to refrain from doing something. That is a negative injunction.

On occasion, the claimant may ask that a respondent be ordered to do something. That is a positive injunction. Since the grant of a positive injunction will often require a respondent to spend time and money to perform the act ordered, this type of interim measure is normally refused. A tribunal should only make the order where it is satisfied that a claimant's case is likely to succeed at the end of the day.

The tribunal may order an injunction if the balancing exercise (as described in the context of *Marevas*) favours the grant of relief.

An interlocutory injunction may initially be sought *ex parte* where notifying the respondent of the application in advance will likely frustrate the purpose of the interim measure. In that case, the tribunal will follow the preliminary order procedure outlined above.

III. Category (3): Orders to clarify issues

A standard application in this category is one requesting further or better particulars of a vague claim. The application is routinely granted to enable the requesting party to understand the other side's case.

On occasion, a party applies for the other side to answer innumerable minutely detailed questions about a pleading. This is often a tactical ploy. The thinking of the requesting party would be to delay the progress of a case by forcing the other party to use up its resources in answering the questions.

It may also be that the party seeking particulars is not asking questions in order to know the other side's case (which may already be sufficiently clear). Instead, a party attempts by seeking particulars to win a case through requests which no one could reasonably be expected to answer. Arbitrators therefore should ensure that particulars are only ordered where they are genuinely necessary to understand a party's case. A tribunal should not allow requests for particulars to become instruments of oppression.

Another application (perhaps less common) is to raise interrogatories. These are questions addressed by one party A to the other party B or (if B is a corporation) to a responsible officer of B. The questions are to be answered on oath. Interrogatories are raised where information is necessary to enable A to prepare its case for trial.

A tribunal, however, should also guard against oppressive interrogatories. A may pose detailed questions in order to tie up B's energies and hinder B's preparations for trial. If so, the tribunal should refuse the interrogatories. The questions cannot be for the purpose of enabling A to know B's case and to help A to prepare accordingly. Moreover, to the extent that some questions may be relevant, A can usually always ask those questions of B's witnesses at trial. That should be the normal order of things. Thus, once more, unless the questions are plainly necessary in order to enable A to understand B's case and prepare adequately for trial, the tribunal should not require B to answer the questions in advance of trial.

I have dealt with directions for experts in Section A. The issues which the experts are to address should be identified and agreed upon by the parties in advance of experts producing any report. This will ensure that both sides' experts deal with the same issues and do not act at cross-purposes.

A party may apply for there to be trial of a preliminary issue X. The motivation for this procedure would be that, by deciding X early, time and money will be saved. If the tribunal decides X in favour of one party A, it will be unnecessary to proceed further. The tribunal's decision on X will be conclusive. It will only be if the tribunal decides X as contended by the other side that a trial of the remaining issues will be necessary.

An arbitration should usually decide all issues at one trial. But there may be substantial savings in time and cost by hiving off specific matters as preliminary issues. If this course is to be adopted, it will be important to ensure that the preliminary issue X which the tribunal is to determine is precisely identified and drafted. Ideally, the issue should be phrased as a "yes or no" or multiple-choice question.

The tribunal must also have a high degree of conviction that a resolution of the preliminary issue in one way will likely preclude the need for further trial. One does not want to find one's self in the position where, the tribunal having decided the preliminary issue in a manner which one party had previously argued would be conclusive, the other party, or sometimes both parties, then say that in actuality the decision has not really obviated the need for a trial.

IV. Category (4): Orders to strike out all or part of a party's case

In applications for a strike out, the respondent will usually contend that the claim should be dismissed in whole or part on one or other of 2 broad grounds.

The first ground is that the Points of Claim (or parts of it) do not disclose a reasonable cause of action against the respondent. Typically, in this sort of application, the tribunal declines to examine evidence. Instead, it proceeds by assuming that the facts pleaded in the Points of Claim (or in the part impugned) are true. The tribunal asks itself: If the facts pleaded were found at trial to be true, would the respondent arguably be liable to the claimant? If yes, the respondent's strike out application is dismissed. If no, the claimant's strike out application is allowed.

The second ground is that the facts alleged in the Points of Claim are scandalous, frivolous, vexatious or otherwise an abuse of process. A respondent will only succeed here if the tribunal finds that the claimant's allegations are patently untrue or irrelevant. That will normally be hard to establish without a trial.

In principle, pleadings should only be struck out where a party can establish without protracted argument that they disclose no reasonable cause of action or are obviously untrue or irrelevant. If complicated and protracted argument is required, then it will usually be a better, more cost-effective strategy to go to trial. That is because in the latter case hearing and determining the strike out application will not save time and money. It may take the arbitral procedure almost as long to determine the strike out. That could make the arbitration more (not less) expensive, especially if the tribunal refuses the application.

A tribunal should be wary of assessing the rights or wrongs of one side's case after only a cursory examination of a fraction of the evidence. Where important facts are hotly disputed, a tribunal will usually prefer to see and hear witnesses being cross-examined before drawing conclusions.

Where a claimant believes that the respondent's defence is unsustainable, the claimant will not usually apply to strike out the respondent's Points of Defence. But it will instead seek summary judgment. The claimant will contend that a respondent's pleading discloses no arguable defence.

The validity of a claimant's case inevitably depends on whether the facts it has pleaded are or are not true. That will usually require a trial to determine. So how does a claimant persuade the tribunal to grant summary judgment without recourse to trial? In effect, the claimant has to show, solely on the basis of undisputed facts or uncontroverted evidence, that the respondent can have no viable defence.

A respondent should normally be entitled to have its evidence (weak though that may be) considered at trial. It should normally also be given a chance to test the evidence of the claimant's witnesses in cross-examination. Save in the clearest of cases, it will be unfair to give judgment against a respondent even on very strong evidence.

But that does not mean that a respondent is permitted to be vague about its case. A respondent is required to condescend to particulars of its defence. It is not allowed merely to say that its defence might be this or that, depending on what comes up at trial. The respondent must identify all principal facts and matters upon which it relies. It must then explain how those facts and matters (if established at trial) would amount in law to a defence. If it cannot do that, a tribunal could properly conclude without recourse to trial that it has no reasonably arguable case and grant summary judgment.

Although the power to strike out or grant summary judgment should be sparingly used, it can be a powerful tool in narrowing down the issues to be tried. Thus, if it appears that parts of a pleading are hopeless such that certain allegations must fail, the tribunal should have no hesitation in striking out those matters from a Points of Claim or a Points of Defence at the interlocutory stage.

It occasionally happens that a tribunal is asked by party A to strike out parts of a witness statement adduced by party B. The application will typically be made where it is contended that a witness statement introduces scandalous or irrelevant material. It will be said that such material has been included by B purely to embarrass A. It will be argued that the material, if allowed to remain in a statement, will have to be answered by further witness statements from A, thereby causing the proceedings to be unduly prolonged.

In dealing with such application, arbitrators have to be careful about spending too much time at an interlocutory stage in deciding whether the impugned statements are or are not irrelevant. If a hearing of the strike out application is going to be long, there may be little difference between considering the matter at an interlocutory stage and dealing with the matter in the course of trial.

As a rule of thumb, if it would take time to assess the probative value of the parts of the statement sought to be struck out, it will often be better in terms of time and cost to allow the material to remain for the moment without prejudice to the same being declared inadmissible or irrelevant at trial.

At an early stage, the tribunal may have an insufficient appreciation of the key facts or contentions of each side. It may not therefore be in a position confidently to assess the relevance or irrelevance of parts of witness statements. The lesser of two evils may be to allow the other party to adduce a short additional statement which is solely directed at rebutting the allegedly scandalous material under challenge. This may add to the costs of the arbitration. But on balance it will be fairer to the other side. One should be wary of prematurely barring a party from adducing evidence which might later turn out to be highly pertinent.

V. Category (5): Applications to obtain evidence

The typical applications which a tribunal will face are applications for specific discovery; applications for the preservation of evidence said to be in the possession of a party; and applications for a person who is not a party to the arbitration to give evidence or produce documents.

I have referred to discovery and the test of relevance. Arbitrators must be satisfied before ordering discovery against a party not only that the documents sought are in the possession or control of the party, but also that the documents are necessary for the fair trial of the dispute and the saving of time and costs.

A party should explain why a document is relevant to a dispute. It should not be allowed to "fish" for a case by seeking massive discovery of documents which are only likely to be of peripheral assistance to the trial.

Unless kept under strict control, discovery may easily be abused. The electronic documentation (such as e-mails) which even a small organisation will have stored up in its computers and servers will be significant. The cost of a general process of discovery (including weeding out irrelevant material) can be prohibitive.

The huge cost may be unavoidable in major cases. But arbitrators should be alert to the need to keep the costs of discovery to a manageable level by discussing with the parties, as soon as possible, just what may be required for the fair conduct of the proceedings. As much as possible, discovery should be restricted to specific documents which are absolutely necessary for the determination of the issues in a dispute.

The tribunal may consider modifying the test of relevance. Discovery, for instance, can be limited to documents which will either advance the other side's case or detract from one's own. That would leave out the train of inquiry criterion of the standard test for relevance. Resort to this more limited test will radically reduce the amount and cost of discovery involved in a case.

Moreover, if discovery is to be ordered, the tribunal should lean towards the disclosure of specific documents rather than vaguely described classes of documents. The tribunal should discourage parties from seeking discovery of allegedly "specific" classes of documents which are in actuality impractically wide descriptions of slews of documents.

For example, a request for discovery may be couched in terms such as "all documents which evidence X". That description is too wide to be incorporated into an order. How can a person sensibly decide whether a given document is or is not "evidence" of X? It is for the tribunal to decide whether a document is evidence of something. The tribunal should instead insist on a document being specifically identified, such as "Bill of Lading No.1 dated 1 April 2012" or "the minutes of the board meeting on 25 December 2011".

A tribunal has the power to order parties to preserve evidence or to conduct experiments which may assist the tribunal in resolving a dispute. An *Anton Piller*, for example, is an order which requires a respondent to allow the claimant and its representatives to enter premises with a view to collecting and gathering up possibly incriminating evidence. Such power may be highly intrusive. Since an *Anton Piller* encroaches upon a person's right to privacy, a tribunal should only make such order with good reason and on the basis of cogent *prima* facie evidence.

A tribunal can order persons to attend before it to give evidence as witnesses or produce relevant documents in their possession. This is again an intrusive power. It should be used sparingly and with sensitivity for the circumstances and convenience of the individual being summoned to appear before the tribunal.

An intended witness should have adequate notice of any hearing at which he or she is supposed to appear. If the witness is to bring along documents, those should be identified with specificity and limited to what is truly necessary for the fair trial of the dispute. The power should not be used to enable a party to "fish" for whole bundles of evidence, e-mails or whatever in the hope that something useful may turn up.

VI. General approach

The foregoing sub-sections have provided a catalogue of the more common types of interlocutory applications which a tribunal is likely to encounter. The catalogue is not meant to be exhaustive. It is instead intended to give a better feel for the case management process and to stress important principles to bear in mind when dealing with a particular application.

I have thus far pointed out what arbitrators might be looking out for in specific types of applications. But one might still ask what should a tribunal's general attitude to interlocutory applications be.

Arbitrators must "use procedures that are appropriate to the particular case, avoiding unnecessary delay or expense, so as to provide a fair means for resolving the dispute".[28] An arbitrator therefore has to manage a case (including interlocutory applications in the period leading up to trial) so that the case progresses expeditiously towards its fair resolution. One should not get bogged down in interlocutory applications such that one never gets to trial or at least does not get there within a reasonable time.

It is impossible to list the attributes of good case management exhaustively. To a certain extent, it is an art rather than a science and, while experience helps, as in many things in life some persons will inevitably be better at it than others. Nonetheless, there are some key traits which all arbitrators should keep in mind.

First, in whatever one does, an arbitrator must be fair. In the course of a dispute, we have seen how one party or other may attempt through procedural manoeuvring to obtain a tactical advantage over the other. An arbitrator must guard against having the tribunal's directions and orders used to gain an unfair ascendancy over the other.

Second, good case management requires that a tribunal keep an eye on the clock as well as on the costs being incurred by everyone concerned.

Arbitrators will have to insist that the parties stick to the stipulated timetable. This may entail arbitrators politely and succinctly, but firmly, querying whether the benefits to be gained from a course of action being proposed or pursued by a party are such as to justify the time and expense which the action might require. Where an arbitrator is unconvinced by a party's justification of a course of conduct, the arbitrator should not hesitate to direct and explain why some other action will be followed instead.

Case management conferences and other hearings with the parties should be kept to a minimum to save cost. Conferences should have an agenda and that agenda should be covered within the time scheduled. As many outstanding applications as possible should be consolidated together and dealt with in a single conference. It would not be conducive to the saving of time and cost for each application to be heard separately on its own.

Hearing dates (including trial dates), once fixed, should only be adjourned in exceptional circumstances. A party has to give cogent reasons for a failure to be ready on time. It should not be a good reason that a party or its legal team failed to spot some line of argument until just before trial.

It will not be conducive to justice for a case to drag on. It is often said by way of an excuse for delay that the other side can always be compensated in costs and interest at the end of the day.

But delay is not merely a matter of compensating the other side with interest or costs. There is anxiety that comes with litigation. There is also the problem of maintaining sufficient cash flow to fund litigation over a long period of time. The payment of interest or costs at the end of the day when an award is finally published may not compensate for the substantial inconvenience caused by these factors.

With delay, the meritorious claimant will be unduly prevented from enjoying whatever it may be entitled to receive, while an innocent respondent will have a cloud of litigation anxiety hanging over one for longer than necessary.

To ensure compliance and minimise delay, arbitrators should not hesitate to make self-executing peremptory orders. Those are orders which impose an automatic sanction for non-compliance. The expectation is that an appropriate sanction will cause a party to obey an order or direction of the tribunal within the specified time frame.

Of course, it must be clear what sanction is being imposed. It must also be clear what conduct or default will trigger the sanction and when. The peremptory order might thus be in the form: "Unless party X does Y by time T on date D, then consequence C will automatically ensue."

However, any automatic sanction must be proportionate. It must bear a logical relationship with the default being penalized.

Thus, for example, where a party fails to provide particulars of certain paragraphs of its pleading, the sanction may be that the relevant paragraphs are struck out. That would prevent the party in default from arguing a case based on the vague paragraphs. The sanction should not be that the party's whole pleading is struck out and the party's case is dismissed. That would be over the top, particularly where the particulars sought are only of a few paragraphs.

Where a party fails to make discovery of a particular document, the sanction may be that the tribunal will be entitled to draw adverse inferences against the defaulting party in connection with the document.

Where a party has had more than a reasonable opportunity to put in factual witness statements or expert evidence but has failed to do so, the sanction may be that the party is barred from calling witnesses of fact or experts in support of its case.

Where a party has failed to put up security despite being given more than a reasonable opportunity to do so, the tribunal may consider the sanction of striking out the party's case as a whole and proceeding to make an award.

Where a party has unreasonably delayed in progressing a case, arbitrators should not shrink from making an award dismissing that party's claim and making an order prohibiting the latter from commencing further arbitral proceedings in connection with the claim.

The sanction of dismissing an application for unreasonable delay is authorised by s.59. That section requires that a claimant "must" pursue a claim "without unreasonable delay". The section describes a delay as "unreasonable" where "it gives rise, or is likely to give rise, to a substantial risk that the issues in the claim will not be resolved fairly" or ""it has caused, or is likely to cause, serious prejudice to any other party".

Third, arbitrators should be proactive. They must actively work out with the parties what a forthcoming trial is actually going to be about. The arbitration should be issue-driven, in the sense that it is all about resolving disputes in respect of particular issues or questions. That means insisting that, as early as possible, the parties agree on the main issues to be determined at trial. In the course of preparing a case, that preliminary list of issues can be refined by the parties if necessary with the assistance of the tribunal.

Arbitrators, however, should bear in mind that every one of their interventions has the potential to cause a trial to be delayed as the parties attempt to deal with whatever the tribunal has said. One must be careful not to be overly proactive.

One should not unnecessarily interfere with the parties' preparations. The parties and their lawyers live with the case on an almost daily basis. A tribunal should accord their decisions on how a case should be run with a wide margin of deference. A tribunal should be wary of insisting that a case be conducted in some way which neither party has advocated.

In order to be effectively proactive, one has to be prepared. That means that one needs to have read up and have reflected upon the papers in advance of a scheduled hearing. The days are long gone when an adjudicator can come to a hearing "cold" and expect to be instructed from scratch by the parties, or their lawyers, on the facts and law relevant to a case.

Thorough preparation by an arbitrator will be rewarded with enormous savings in time. One can move more confidently through the matters to be discussed. Where a party's submissions are not understood or are unhelpful, one will be able to ask relevant questions that get straight to the heart of a dispute. By the same token, one will be on firm ground when one tells a party to move on to some other point, either because the tribunal fully understands the subject currently being discussed, or because the tribunal believes that there is not much substance in the current subject.

Fourth, arbitrators should be robustly practical. They should not be overly technical. They should not feel bound to adhere, for example, to all of the formal rules of evidence used in Court.

One of the virtues of arbitration is its informality. That informality will rapidly be lost if a tribunal mimics the formalities of Court civil procedure. The undesirable consequence of such conduct might be that arbitration becomes just as (if not more) technical and costly than normal litigation within the High Court's Commercial List. Arbitration will not then be competitive with commercial litigation.

D. Trial

I. Preliminary matters

A trial may be based solely on documents (including witness statements), albeit supplemented by oral or written submissions from the parties or their legal representatives. But, in more complicated cases, the tribunal will almost certainly prefer not just to consider untested witness statements, but would also wish to hear the witnesses cross-examined. This section deals with the latter sort of trial.

Evidence for the trial will consequently come in 2 forms: (1) documents (including final expert reports) and (2) oral testimony (including expert testimony).

The documents will normally be compiled in bundles which are made available to the tribunal. At some point in the preparation stage, the tribunal will have given directions as to what documents or extracts of documents should be included in the bundle.

Those directions would have given guidance on how the documents are to be arranged. For example, should the documents be arranged chronologically, by type, by subject or in some other way? There will usually be a separate bundle containing pleadings and the tribunal's orders and directions. Where materials have been attached to the pleadings, will both the pleadings and documents bundles include copies of the attachments? Or, should the attachments be inserted in their appropriate place within the documents bundle and an annotation merely be written into a pleading to refer the tribunal to the page in the documents bundle where an attachment is to be found?

The documents (or extracts from documents) in the bundles should be restricted to the minimum necessary for the purposes of presenting each side's case. There is no point, for example, in including the entirety of a bulky document in the bundle if only short sections of the document will be mentioned at trial. Similarly, there is no point in including reams of invoices, receipts, accounts and other tables, if it is only intended to draw a few aspects of those materials to the tribunal's attention. In particular, no one will have the time to go through every one of numerous invoices or receipts. To the extent necessary, the invoices or receipts may be summarised on one or two sheets of paper and only a few samples included in the trial bundle.

There is a tendency to include everything which has been disclosed by one party or the other in the documents bundle without any attempt at discriminating between what is relevant and what is not. Such a practice is unhelpful. As part of its preparation, the tribunal will be reading through the document bundles before trial, it will be a waste of their time if they have to read innumerable irrelevant materials which have been inserted into the bundle for no other reason than that they were disclosed by a party.

There is much talk currently about paperless arbitration trials. Those envisage that pleadings and documents will all be scanned into electronic format, stored in computer databases or in cyberspace, and accessed through notepads or laptops during the trial.

The possibility of a paperless trial is not a cure-all. Such possibility will certainly save on paper, which is a scarce resource. But it will not obviate the need to give guidance as to which documents are to go into an electronic or virtual bundle. Unless clear directions are given by a tribunal, there is the danger that the parties will merely scan everything into a virtual bundle. This will mean that the tribunal still has to go through a lot of useless material when reviewing the virtual bundle in its preparation for trial.

Trial will normally unfold in 4 stages. First, the parties will present opening statements, starting with the claimant. Second, each party will call its witnesses of fact for examination, starting with the claimant's witnesses. Third, each party will call its experts for examination, starting with the claimant's experts. Fourth, each party will present its closing submissions, starting with the respondent.

II. Opening statements

Openings may be oral, in writing or in a combination of speech and writing.

But in whatever form they take, openings should identify the main issues which the tribunal is to determine in its award. The openings might first summarise in a background section the key undisputed facts and evidence. Then the openings can set out the parties' contentions in relation to the main issues, briefly indicating the weaknesses of the other party's case on an issue.

To save time and cost, I suggest that oral opening statements be dispensed with. Instead, the parties or their representatives should be encouraged (or even directed) to lodge written openings within (say) 2 weeks of the start of trial. This would enable the tribunal to understand the parties' respective contentions in the course of preparing for trial. The written submissions can be used as reading guides to the document bundles used at trial.

I recommend that there be no pre-conditions imposed on the length or style of written openings. They may be in skeletal bullet-point format or they may be in full sentences and paragraphs.

Some arbitrators, being pressed for time, direct that skeleton openings of no more than x pages of double-space text with margins of at least width y be filed. Such requirements are set because otherwise parties (it is feared) may lodge lengthy openings which will take hours to read through and digest.

I am not in favour of putting an arbitrary limitation. There should be a balance between orality and writing. If an oral opening is to be dispensed with, the parties should be allowed to submit written submissions of whatever style and length they believe appropriate to get their points across to the tribunal. If the parties' written openings are to be confined to bullet points, then they should be entitled to flesh out those points orally at the start of trial.

As a rule of thumb, if oral submissions are to be limited in duration or done away with altogether, the parties should be able (if they wish) to lodge much fuller written submissions.

III. Examination of witnesses of fact

The witnesses of each side (starting with those of the claimant) are called in turn to be examined on their statements. A witness is first examined in chief by the party A calling him or her to give evidence. The witness is then cross-examined by the other side B. A witness's examination concludes with his or her re-examination by A.

Witnesses are normally examined under oath. Section 56 caters for this practice by conferring a power on arbitrators (unless otherwise agreed by the parties) to administer oaths.

As a general rule, a party may not ask leading questions when it examines its witnesses. A leading question is one which suggests its answer ("You did X, did you not?" or "Was it the case that you decided to do X because you wanted to achieve Y?"). However, when examining the other side's witness, a party may (and typically will only) ask leading questions.

I suggest that, to save time and cost, a witness's statement stand as his or her evidence-in-chief. That means that, apart from a few "top-up" questions to clarify or correct obscurities in a witness statement, a party's examination-in-chief of its own witness should take no more than a few minutes. That will mean that a witness should expect to be cross-examined by the other side almost as soon as he or she is called.

Arbitrators should be especially vigilant in the course of a witness's cross-examination. This is a stage of proceedings where much time and expense can be wasted through the parties or their lawyers asking meaningless, irrelevant, repetitive, or vague questions of witnesses. Where the point behind a party's line of inquiry remains obscure after some questions have been put to the witness, I suggest that the tribunal ask the party to state the rationale for its line of inquiry. If the party is unable to do so or if the tribunal is not satisfied that the rationale given is valid, it should politely insist that the party move on to another topic.

There is a well-known rule of evidence known as the rule in *Browne v. Dunn*.[29] That requires a party to put the key points of one's case as to what did or did not happen at a relevant event, to any witness who was involved with that specific event.

Thus, for example, if one's case is that the witness's evidence as to what happened at the event is completely wrong, one has to put that point to the witness. The reason is that fairness requires that a witness be given an opportunity to respond to criticisms of that witness's evidence. If (for instance) a witness is to be accused of lying, the witness should be given a chance in cross-examination to respond to that serious accusation and to defend one's self against it.

If a party fails to put its case to a witness as required by the rule in *Browne v. Dunn*, the party will be barred from querying the witness's evidence in closing submission.

In litigation, the result of an overly pedantic application of the rule is that, at some point in their cross-examination, typically at the end of each topic of inquiry, counsel will routinely fire off numerous propositions at the witness for the latter merely to state whether he or she agrees with each proposition being put. That will be done, despite the fact that it will usually already be plain from the witness's cross-examination that he or she disagrees with every proposition. An unthinking application of *Brown v. Dunn* can easily lead then to time being wasted in the witness merely confirming the obvious.

In contrast, an arbitration is free to take a more relaxed approach in the interest of a more efficient trial. One can, for example, adopt the touchstone of "fairness" as a basis for cross-examination. One might then modify the rule to something like this: [30]

(1) A party will not have to put every material proposition of its case to a relevant witness, if the witness's attitude to the proposition is plain from the course of that witness's cross-examination.

(2) Even though a material proposition has not been expressly put to a witness, a party will not be barred from criticising that witness's evidence, if in all circumstances the witness may be considered to have been afforded a reasonable opportunity to respond to the gist of the criticisms.

Re-examination will be restricted to the clarification of matters arising out of cross-examination.

Leading questions are not allowed in re-examination. But a common technique to get around this restriction is to begin by reminding a witness of what the latter said in cross-examination in response to a question. The witness's attention is then drawn to documents which (typically) evidence something different from what the witness has said. The examiner then asks, in light of the witness having refreshed his or her memory by sight of documents, whether the witness would like to clarify the answer previously given in cross-examination.

The whole exercise is in effect one massive leading question, attempting to get the witness to qualify a possibly inconvenient answer made in cross-examination by suggesting what the answer should be. Any response made by the witness as a result of the exercise is unlikely to have much probative value, since the response would largely have been prompted by the documents just shown.

This practice in re-examination may be tolerated if not carried to excess. But it can be abused by an examiner taking the witness over a protracted period through numerous documents "to refresh the witness's memory" and then essentially asking the witness to repeat what has just been drawn to his or her attention in a document as a "clarification" of the previous answer. A tribunal should be sceptical of the practice and, where necessary, take steps to curb it, so that time is not expended on an exercise of little evidential value.

IV. Examination of expert witnesses

In commercial cases especially, it is routine for experts to be examined after the factual evidence has been heard. This will enable experts to fine tune their opinions in light of the new matters which have emerged from witnesses of fact.

The process follows the same procedure as that described above in relation to factual witnesses. One refinement, however, is that the tribunal may prefer to group together evidence from experts of a particular discipline, where the evidence of more than one set of expert disciplines is involved. This may be achieved in 2 ways.

One way would be to hear the claimant's expert in discipline X, followed by the respondent's expert in that discipline. Following the examination of the experts in X, the tribunal could then hear the parties' experts in discipline Y and so on.

The other way has been colourfully called the "hot-tubbing" of experts. The tribunal can essentially conduct a conference among all the experts in X. The parties and the tribunal would then be free to discuss specific issues with those experts and attempt to achieve some consensus. If no consensus can be attained, the tribunal will have to decide on the basis of the evidence which has come out in the conference.

Having finished with the experts in X, one can move on to a conference with all the experts in Y and so on.

"Hot-tubbing" was controversial when it was first introduced in some Courts a decade or so ago. But it has become the norm in many jurisdictions (especially New South Wales) for dealing with expert evidence in an expeditious manner. Of course, it will involve substantial preparation (as well as the use of conference-conducting skills) by the tribunal if it is to run smoothly.

V. Closing submissions

The old-fashioned way of proceeding was for the respondent to start with oral closing submissions immediately after the last witness was examined. That remains an option.

But the tribunal may prefer to give the parties a couple of days' adjournment for the preparation of written closing statements. Those can be submitted to the tribunal a day or so before a final oral hearing.

This last approach has the advantage of furnishing the tribunal with a written record of the parties' points. That should make it easier for the tribunal to summarise the parties' arguments in its award. Further, having read the written closings, the tribunal can raise whatever questions it has on obscure matters at the final oral hearing.

Given that the parties are allowed to submit closing written statements in whatever length or style they deem appropriate, the oral hearing can be restricted to clarifying points or responding to unexpected matters raised by one party or another in their written closings.

The closing submissions should mirror the parties' opening statements. The parties should return to the issues specifically identified at the opening for the tribunal's determination. The parties should see whether those issues can be refined, narrowed or eliminated altogether. They should then try to answer the balance of remaining issues by systematically identifying the other side's arguments on an issue and succinctly explaining why those arguments are wrong. They should also specify the specific relief which they wish the tribunal to order at the end of the day.

The identification and narrowing of outstanding issues by the parties is especially important as the issues will provide a framework for the tribunal's reasoned award.

E. The Award

An award may be made at any time.[31] A tribunal can also make more than one award at different times and on different aspects of a dispute.[32]

There is no particular form which an award must follow. Nonetheless, it is usual for an award to come in 2 parts.

The first is a formal part which will typically identify the arbitration agreement and state that a dispute has arisen been the parties. It will then give a narrative of the appointment of the tribunal and the hearings following such appointment. There will be a record of the pleadings filed and the orders and directions made by the tribunal. The chronology will culminate with a statement that the trial of the parties' dispute was heard on certain identified dates.

The formal part concludes with a statement that, having heard and examined the evidence and having considered the parties' pleadings and submissions, the tribunal makes its order. The order is set out. The detailed reasons for the order are stated to be contained in the second part, which is to be treated as an integral part of the award.

I recommend that this second part, which will contain the tribunal's reasons, follow a set template. That template would comprise the following:[33]

(1) An "Introduction" section where the tribunal identifies the main issues which it is supposed to determine;

(2) A "Background" section where the tribunal summarises undisputed matters of fact and law which it will be necessary for the reader to know in order to fully understand the tribunal's reasons for deciding each issue as it has done;

(3) A "Discussion" section where the tribunal takes each issue identified in the Introduction and makes a determination on that issue. The tribunal does so by taking each point made by the losing party on the relevant issue and briefly explaining why the point is invalid;

(4) A "Conclusion" section where the tribunal summarises what it has decided and sets out the precise terms of the order which it is making in consequence.

The rationale for having 2 components to the award is that the more formal first part can be exhibited as part of a public document (such as a Court order converting an award into a judgment of the Court). The second part containing the tribunal's detailed reasons can remain confidential.

Under s.61 an award has to be in writing and signed by the arbitrators. The award must state the date when it is made, as well as identify the place of arbitration. Reasons must be given as part of an award.

Arbitral proceedings are terminated by a "final award".[34] So in rendering an award, a tribunal should ensure that it does not inadvertently render itself *functus*.[35]

A tribunal becomes *functus* when the arbitration is terminated. This means, as a matter of law, that the tribunal ceases to have jurisdiction to determine any further question in relation to the dispute. The only exception is where there is a need to correct or interpret the award under s.69.[36]

There will often be outstanding matters for the tribunal to deal with, even after publication of its award following trial. Thus, for instance, there may be questions involving the incidence or taxation (quantification) of the costs of the arbitration. Where an award is in relation to a preliminary issue, it may be that further matters will have to be determined by the tribunal as a result of its decision on the preliminary issue.

Thus, it is common for awards following trial to be called "First Partial Final Award" or similar terminology, in order to signal that the arbitration is not yet completely over and the tribunal is not to be treated as *functus*.

An award may grant "any remedy or relief that could have been ordered by the Court" in civil proceedings.[37] Unless the parties agree otherwise, the tribunal can order that a party perform a contract (that is, the tribunal can grant an order of specific performance). But, regardless of the parties' agreement on the matter, a tribunal does not have the power to grant specific performance of a contract relating to land or any interest in land.

A tribunal can award costs to one party or another.[38] In so doing, the tribunal shall have regard to any written settlement offer by one party to another.

In practice, a tribunal is not informed of a settlement offer until it makes its award. That way the tribunal may make its award without being influenced by the terms of a settlement offer. The tribunal may make a provisional order as to costs in its award. That costs order can then be modified where the tribunal is later told of an earlier settlement offer which has not been bettered by the tribunal's award.

Another method is for the parties to hand the arbitrator a sealed envelope which is not to be opened until the arbitrator has made a determination on the substantive merits of the dispute. The sealed envelope will usually contain the terms of any settlement offer and the arbitrator can then take those into account in making an award of costs.

Unless the parties agree that costs are to be taxed (quantified) by the Court, the tribunal must assess the amount of any costs awarded. [39]

The tribunal shall deliver a copy of its award to each party once the latter is made.[40] But the tribunal may withhold delivery where it has not been paid its fees and expenses in full.[41] In certain circumstances where a party believes that the arbitrator's fees are too high, that party may apply to the Court for a direction that a lesser amount be payable.[42]

F. Summary

This chapter has followed the process of an arbitration from the appointment of arbitrators to the making of an award. It has attempted to give an idea of the common sorts of problems which a tribunal will face over that process. It has also suggested possible ways of dealing with typical applications and questions which might arise. It has highlighted matters about which a tribunal should be wary or sensitive.

Key concepts to bear in mind include the following:

1. Arbitrations will typically be started by a claimant writing to a respondent with a request that a dispute be referred to arbitration.

2. It is usual to appoint an odd (as opposed to even) number of arbitrators in order to avoid deadlock on an issue. But the more arbitrators there are, the more costly proceedings will be. It will also be more difficult to coordinate the diaries of a 3-person tribunal. Thus, parties should seriously consider whether more than one arbitrator is necessary for the resolution of a dispute. In many cases, a sole arbitrator may be appropriate.

3. At the time of appointment, a would-be arbitrator should satisfy one's self that he or she is qualified to act in the case and, in particular, that there is no real or apparent risk of a conflict of interest. The would-be arbitrator should also satisfy one's self that it is at least arguable that the arbitration agreement confers jurisdiction on the intended tribunal to deal with the relevant dispute.

4. Directions Nos.1 and 2 should provide a sufficient blueprint for the preparation of an arbitration up

to trial. The Directions will typically have to do with pleadings (including further and better particulars of pleadings), factual witness statements, expert evidence, specific discovery beyond the documents attached to the pleadings, and the setting of trial dates.

5. The tribunal has the power to grant interim measures under ss.35 and 56. The powers conferred by the 2 provisions apparently overlap. But, save where injunctions are involved, s.56 essentially only concerns procedural matters to facilitate the hearing of an arbitration.

6. Arbitrators must be sensitive to the interplay between their orders for interim measures and equivalent orders of the Court. Unless everyone is alert to the complications which can arise, the parties may rapidly find themselves wasting time and cost fighting duplicate battles on purely interlocutory matters before the Court and a tribunal.

7. In preparation for trial, arbitrators may have to manage applications to establish jurisdiction; to order security or other relief pending trial; to clarify issues; to strike out all or parts of a party's case; and to obtain further evidence. A tribunal should deal with such applications proactively, but fairly. It will have to balance the benefits to be obtained by granting an interlocutory order, against the disadvantages to be incurred by such action. It will also have to be firm about ensuring timely compliance with its directions and ensuring that costs are kept to a proportionate level.

8. Similar concerns as to fairness, time and cost should motivate the tribunal in the course of a trial.

9. Following trial, a tribunal will make its written award.

That award will need to have reasons for the order made to resolve the parties' dispute. Once a Final Award is published, the tribunal becomes *functus*.

10. tribunal must provide a copy of its award to the parties. But it may withhold a copy when it has not been fully paid its fees and expenses.

11. From beginning to end of the arbitration process, the tribunal should be concerned to identify and narrow down the real issues in dispute between the parties.

---

1. See s.49 (ML (= "Model Law Art.") 21).

2. ML 3.

3. See s.31.

4. See s.24 (ML 11).

5. See s.25 (ML 12).

6. [2002] AC 358 (HL).

7. See s.26 (ML 13).

8. See s.48 (ML 20).

9. See s.50 (ML 22).

10. See s.51 (ML 23) on pleadings generally.

11. In this case, the tribunal could issue as its Directions No.1 the matters suggested below for Directions No.2.

12. See s.52 (ML 24).

13. ML 17. Section 56 does not correspond to any article in the Model Law.

14. See *SCMP* 19 March 2012, "Rise in arbitrators' powers queried".

15. ML 17.

16. Where a party applies for a *Mareva* or other interim measure *ex parte*, the tribunal may make a "preliminary order" pending a hearing at which the other side can present its objections to the interim measure. A "preliminary order" is an order "directing a party not to frustrate the purpose of the interim measure requested" (s.37 (ML 17B(1))). The preliminary order will expire after 20 days unless, having given notice to and heard the objections of the other side, the tribunal grants an interim measure adopting or modifying the preliminary order. ML 17C(5) (enacted by s.38) specifies that a "preliminary order shall be binding on the parties but shall not be subject to enforcement by a Court. Such a preliminary order does not constitute an award". However, an interim measure based on a preliminary order may be granted in the form of an award at the request of one of the parties. The award might then be converted by the applicant into an order of the Court for the purposes of enforcement pursuant to Part 10 of the Ordinance.

17. Under the common law doctrine of privity, only parties to a contract are bound by its terms.

18. ML 5.

19. ML 9.

20. This is the principle that once a matter has been argued before a competent forum, the Court will not allow a party to re-argue the same matter before a judge.

21. These correspond with the 5 functions of interlocutory applications identified in Chapter 2 of my *Reflections on Civil Procedure under Civil Justice Reform*.

22. London: 1995 (11th ed.).

23. See now Atkin Chambers, Hudson's Building and Engineering Contracts (London, 12th ed.), at 3-055, to similar effect: "[M]erely because the document is referred to for one purpose, and may be incorporated to that extent, it does not dollow that the whole of the document will be incorporated. Moreover, the intention to incorporate must be sufficiently clear and the provisions sought to be incorporated sufficiently certain."

24. See s.37 (ML 17B).

25. See s.41 (ML 17F).

26. See s.36 (ML 17A).

27. See s.38 (ML 17C).

28. See s.46 (ML 18).

29. (1894) 6 R 67.

30. Warren Chan SC has coined the wonderful expression "the deemed put" to encapsulate this modified approach to *Brown v. Dunn*.

31. See s.72.

32. See s.71.

33. Here I follow the insights of Professor James Raymond on the components of a good judgment. See jamescrzymond.com for further details.

34. See s.68 (ML 32).

35. A legal term derived from the past participle of the Latin verb *fungi*. The expression literally means "having performed [one's task]".

36. ML 33.

37. See s.70.

38. See s.74.

39. See ss.74(5)-(9) and 75. The arbitrator, when assessing costs, "must only allow costs that are reasonable having regard to all the circumstances". Unless agreed otherwise by the parties, the arbitrator may "allow costs incurred in the preparation of the arbitral proceedings prior to the commencement of the arbitration".

40. See s.67(4).

41. See s.77(1).

42. See ss.77(2)-(4) and 78.

Chapter 3
A Look At Arbitration Rules

The parties may agree that their arbitration is to be conducted in accordance with the rules of a specified arbitral organisation. The Model Law does not prevent adoption of such rules. Rules so adopted will supplement the provisions of the Model Law as enacted by the Ordinance.

This section summarises the main provisions of 5 sets of arbitral rules commonly adopted in Asian arbitrations. The rules examined are the Administered Arbitration Rules of the HKIAC; the Arbitration Rules of the Singapore International Arbitration Centre (SIAC); the Terms of the London Maritime Arbitrators Association (LMAA); the Arbitration Rules of the International Chamber of Commerce (ICC); and the Arbitration Rules of the China International Economic and Trade Arbitration Commission (CIETAC).

Despite some differences, there are numerous similarities among the 5 sets of 105 rules. These similarities are summarised at the end of this chapter.

A. HKIAC Administered Arbitration Rules [1]

The Rules came into effect on 1 September 2008.

I. General rules

The parties can adopt the Rules in an arbitration agreement entered into before a dispute arises. They can also adopt the Rules by an *ad hoc* agreement, made after a dispute has arisen, to submit their differences to arbitration.

The parties can agree that the Rules are to apply to their arbitration purely as procedural rules (that is, without administration by the HKIAC) or they can agree that the HKIAC is to administer their arbitration in accordance with the Rules. [2] If the parties opt for the latter course, the HKIAC will supervise their arbitration (including assisting the parties to appoint a tribunal) so as to ensure the timely progress of the arbitration.

Article 2 provides rules for calculating time and notice periods. When circumstances require, the HKIAC Secretariat may extend the time periods stipulated in the Rules.

Who interprets the Rules? According to Art.3, the tribunal does that "insofar as [the Rules] relate to its powers and duties" in a given arbitration. Otherwise, the HKIAC interprets the scope of the Rules.

II. Commencement of arbitration [3]

The claimant submits a Notice of Arbitration to the HKIAC. The arbitration commences on the date when the HKIAC receives the Notice. Where a Notice is submitted in hard copy (as opposed to electronic format), there should be as many copies submitted as there are parties, plus an extra copy for the HKIAC.

A Notice[4] must include a demand that a dispute be referred to arbitration; the names and contact details of the parties and their counsel; a copy of the arbitration agreement; a reference to the contractual provision or other document in relation to which the dispute has arisen; a general description of the claim; a description of the relief or remedy sought; and a proposal on the number of arbitrators to be appointed.

The Notice must be accompanied by a registration fee as set out in the HKIAC's current Schedule of Fees and Costs of Arbitration.

The HKIAC Secretariat will forward a copy of the Notice to the respondent. The respondent is to submit an Answer to Notice within 30 days. The Answer should include the following: a statement as to whether jurisdiction is challenged; comments on the Notice; a statement as to whether the respondent accepts the relief or remedy sought by the claimant; a statement as to whether the respondent agrees to the number of arbitrators proposed.

The HKIAC will send copies of the respondent's Answer to the claimant. It will also provide a copy of the Notice and Answer to the members of the tribunal.

Throughout the proceedings, the parties may be represented by persons of their choice (who may not necessarily be lawyers).[5]

III. Arbitrators and the arbitral tribunal [6]

If the parties cannot agree on the number of arbitrators, the Council of the HKIAC will decide the number. It will do so by taking into account the amount at stake, the complexity of the arbitration, the nationalities of the parties, trade customs, the availability of potential arbitrators, and the urgency of the matter. The parties will be invited to comment before the Council decides.

Where a sole arbitrator has been agreed by the parties or decided by the Council, the appointment will be made within 30 days. If a tribunal of 3 arbitrators is required, Art.8 sets out the procedure for appointing the tribunal. Essentially, each party nominates an arbitrator and the 2 persons nominated designate a presiding arbitrator. If the process of appointing the third arbitrator takes too long, the Council appoints the presiding arbitrator.

Before deciding the number of arbitrators or appointing an arbitrator, the Council must consult at least 3 members of the HKIAC's Appointment Advisory Board. The Board's advice is not binding and shall be kept confidential from the parties. All appointments (whether of a sole arbitrator or a 3-person tribunal) need to be confirmed by the Council.

Article 11.1 requires that arbitrators "shall be and remain at all times impartial and independent of the parties". A nominated person must disclose any circumstances known to him or her which may cast doubt on that person's suitability to sit as arbitrator over a given dispute. Further, a party may challenge an arbitrator's suitability within 15 days of the latter's appointment or after that party "became aware or ought reasonably to have become aware" of an impediment.

Article 11.2 provides that, where the parties are of different nationalities, a person having the same nationality as any party is not to be appointed as sole or presiding arbitrator, unless the parties agree.

Challenges to the appointment of a person as arbitrator are determined by the Council. If the challenge succeeds, the arbitrator is replaced. The arbitration resumes from the point when the previous arbitrator ceased to perform his or her functions, unless the parties agree otherwise.

IV. Arbitral proceedings[7]

Article 14.1 provides that a tribunal "shall adopt suitable procedures for the conduct of the arbitration, in order to avoid unnecessary delay or expenses". But the obligation is qualified. The tribunal must also see to it that such procedures as it adopts "ensure equal treatment of the parties and afford the parties a reasonable opportunity to be heard and to present their case".

Article 14.7 imposes a corresponding obligation on the parties who "shall do everything necessary to ensure the fair and efficient conduct of the proceedings".

Thus, an arbitration is not supposed to be a matter of one party arguing every point that it can think of (whether bad or indifferent) in order to prolong a dispute or wear out the other side. The parties and their representatives are duty-bound to assist the tribunal to achieve the speedy and just resolution of a case.

With these strictures in mind, a provisional timetable is to be prepared by the tribunal at an early stage, following consultation with the parties.[8] The timetable is copied to the HKIAC Secretariat.

There are to be no unilateral communications with arbitrator. Article 14.4 requires that all documents or information supplied to the tribunal by a party shall at the same time be communicated to the other party.

The tribunal may appoint a secretary (if needed) after consultation with the parties. [9]

On the application of a party, the tribunal may join one or more persons to the arbitration.[10] But the applying party and the persons to be added as parties must agree in writing to the joinder.

Article 15 provides for Hong Kong to be the seat of arbitration, unless the 9parties agree otherwise. But the tribunal may meet or hear witnesses and submissions "at any place it deems appropriate, having regard to the circumstances of the arbitration". Art.15.4 stipulates that the award shall be deemed to have been made at the seat of arbitration.

Where pleadings have not been exchanged prior to its appointment, the tribunal can give directions for the filing of the same. There should normally be a Statement of Claim (stating the parties, the facts, the issues to be tried and the relief sought) with supporting documents annexed to it. In response, there is to be a Statement of Defence (including any counterclaim and the factual and legal bases of a challenge to jurisdiction) with supporting documents annexed.

Amendments may be made to the pleadings, but only subject to permission from the tribunal. The tribunal will decide whether to allow amendments having regard to delay or prejudice and to the scope of the arbitration agreement. Fees may be adjusted in light of any amendments.

Article 20 deals with jurisdiction.

Article 20.1 preserves the "competence-competence" principle. The tribunal may rule on its jurisdiction. Article 20.2 preserves the principle of the autonomy of an arbitration clause from the rest of a contract. Article 20.3 provides that, if possible, a plea of no jurisdiction should be raised in the respondent's Answer. Otherwise, the challenge must be raised no later than in the Statement of Defence or, if the claimant is objecting to the tribunal's jurisdiction to entertain a counterclaim, in the claimant's Reply to Counterclaim.

The tribunal is to decide whether further pleadings (that is, beyond the Statement of Claim and the Statement of Defence) are required.[11]

Article 22 stipulates that the periods of time for communication of pleadings should not exceed 45 days. But the tribunal may extend that time, if appropriate.

Article 23 regulates the evidence to be adduced at trial.

By Article 23.1 each party "shall have the burden of proving the facts relied on to support its claim or defence". The tribunal may require each party to provide a summary of the documents and evidence upon which it proposes to rely.

The tribunal may give directions on factual and expert witnesses, including determining how (if at all) witnesses are to be examined.[12] Parties may interview their witnesses.

The tribunal may appoint its own experts to assist on specific issues.[13]

Hearings are to be private, unless the parties agree otherwise.

Article 23.10 empowers a tribunal to "determine the admissibility, relevance, materiality and weight" of any evidence presented, "including whether or not to apply strict rules of evidence".

Interim measures are dealt with in Art.24. The measures may be granted in the form of an "Interim Award".

The tribunal may make peremptory orders where a party acts in default of its directions "without showing sufficient cause for such failure".[14]

The tribunal may declare proceedings closed where it is "satisfied that the parties have had a reasonable opportunity to present their cases".[15]

Where a party knows or ought reasonably to have known that provisions of the Rules have not been followed, it should object promptly.[16] If it proceeds with the arbitration without objecting, it may be deemed to have waived strict compliance with the Rules.

V. The award[17]

Where there are 3 arbitrators, decision is by a majority.[18]

The tribunal has the power to make interim, interlocutory or partial awards and to award costs that are not final.[19]

An award shall be in writing.[20] It will be final and binding on the parties who are to be treated as having undertaken to carry it out without delay.

An award "shall state the reasons upon which it is based". It should be signed by the arbitrators and state the date and place where it is made. It shall also bear the seal of the HKIAC.

The tribunal's decision shall be in accordance with rules of law agreed by parties or the law with which a dispute has closest connection.[21] The tribunal may decide as *amiable compositeur or ex aequo et bono* [22] only if the parties have so authorised it to do so. But at all times the tribunal must decide in accordance with terms of the parties' contract and applicable trade usages.

Article 32 sets out the procedure to be followed where the parties have agreed to settle an arbitration before an award has been made.

Articles 33-35 respectively deal with the interpretation of an award, the correction of an award, and the making of an additional award at the request of a party.

Article 36 sets out how the tribunal's fees and the costs of the arbitration are to be calculated by reference to a Schedule of Fees and Costs appended to the Rules. There are also rules on deposits to be made by the parties in respect of the fees and costs payable (Art.37).

VI. Other provisions [23]

Unless agreed otherwise, the expedited procedure in Art.38.2 is to be followed where the amounts claimed and counterclaimed together do not exceed US$250,000.

There are detailed provisions in Art.39 on preserving the confidentiality of the parties.

There are provisions excluding liability for the HKIAC in Art.40.

B. SIAC Arbitration Rules [24]

SIAC was established in 1991. It is a non-profit, non-governmental organisation based in Singapore. According to its publicity materials, it provides "neutral arbitration services to the global business community". [25]

The most current Rules came into effect on 1 July 2010.

If the parties agree to refer a dispute to SIAC, then the arbitration will be conducted and administered in accordance with its Rules.[26] But if the Rules conflict with the mandatory provisions of any applicable law, then the latter will prevail.

Detailed rules for the calculation of notice and time periods are in Art.2. Any notice, communication or proposal should be in writing. Notices are deemed to have been received on the day delivered.

Arbitrations are commenced by the claimant filing a Notice of Arbitration with SIAC's Registrar. The Notice should include the matters set out in Art.3.

The respondent is to file a Response within 14 days from the receipt of the Notice of Arbitration. The Response should contain the details set out in Art.4.

Before a tribunal is appointed, a party may apply for the arbitration to be conducted using SIAC's Expedited Procedure.[27] That is possible where the amount of claim, counterclaim and set-off do not exceed S$5 million in total; where the parties agree; or where there is "exceptional urgency".

There will be a sole arbitrator, unless the parties have agreed otherwise or the Registrar directs that there should be 3 arbitrators in light of the complexity or other circumstances of the dispute.[28] Nominations for arbitrator by the parties have to be approved by SIAC's Chairman.

Arbitrators "shall be and remain at all times independent, and shall not act as advocate for a party".[29] In approving an appointment, the Chairman must consider whether a person has "sufficient availability to determine the case in a prompt and efficient manner appropriate to the nature of the arbitration".

A proposed arbitrator should as soon as possible disclose "any circumstance that may give rise to justifiable doubts as to his impartiality or independence".[30] If a circumstance arises in the course of an arbitration which may cast doubt on an arbitrator's impartiality or independence, it should be disclosed immediately to the parties, the other arbitrators, and the Registrar.

Challenges to an arbitrator's suitability should be made within 14 days after receipt of the arbitrator's appointment.[31] Challenges will be determined by a committee (known as "the Committee of the Board") comprising at least 2 directors appointed by the Chairman from SIAC's board.

The tribunal "shall conduct the arbitration in such manner as it considers appropriate, after consulting with the parties". [32] However, in its conduct of the proceedings, the tribunal must "ensure the fair, expeditious, economical and final determination of the dispute". To this end, it "may ... direct the order of proceedings, bifurcate proceedings, exclude cumulative or irrelevant testimony or other evidence and direct the parties to focus their presentations on issues the decision of which could dispose of all or part of the case". The presiding arbitrator of a 3-person tribunal may make procedural rulings alone, but subject to revision by tribunal.

Where necessary, the tribunal shall give directions for the filing of a Statement of Claim, a Statement of Defence, and other pleadings.[33] All such submissions should be accompanied by supporting documents. The tribunal may also give such directions as it deems appropriate where there has been non-compliance with its directions for filing pleadings.

Article 18 allows the parties to agree on the seat of arbitration. In the absence of agreement, Singapore will be the seat unless the tribunal determines somewhere else in light of all the circumstances of the case. Regardless of the seat, hearings may take place at any location.

The tribunal shall determine the language of the arbitration.[34] It may also determine which documents shall be translated into that language.

The parties may be represented by legal practitioners or any other representatives during the arbitration.[35]

Provisions on the conduct of hearings, the appearance of factual and expert witnesses, and the use of tribunal-appointed experts may be found in Arts.21, 22 and 23 respectively. They are similar to the equivalent provisions in the HKIAC's Rules.

Article 24 confers additional powers on a tribunal to the extent that they are not in derogation of any mandatory law applicable to the arbitration. The powers include the power to rectify contracts and to determine any claim for legal professional or other privilege. An interesting additional power is the ability under Art.24j to direct that a party "ensure that any award which may be made in the arbitral proceedings is not rendered ineffectual by the dissipation of assets by a party".

Article 25 deals with "competence-competence" and the principle of the autonomy of the arbitration clause from the rest of a contract. Where the jurisdiction to go to arbitration is challenged before a tribunal is appointed, the Committee of the Board shall first determine whether there is a *prima facie* case that the dispute is subject to arbitration. If the Committee is not so satisfied, the arbitral proceedings shall be terminated.

Article 26 enables the tribunal to grant interlocutory injunctions and other interim relief. The tribunal may require security for any measure granted. Where a tribunal has not yet been constituted, a party may apply to an Emergency Arbitrator appointed following the procedures set out in Schedule 1 of the Rules.

The tribunal shall apply the rules of law designated by the parties.[36] In the absence of such designation, the tribunal shall apply such law as it deems appropriate. It shall only decide as *amiable compositeur* or ex *aequo et bono* if expressly authorised by the parties.

The arbitration proceedings are closed when the tribunal is satisfied that "the parties have no further relevant and material evidence to produce or submission to make".[37] A draft award is submitted to the Registrar within 45 days of the close of proceedings. The Registrar "may ... suggest modifications as to the form of the award". The Registrar "without affecting the Tribunal's liberty of decision, may also draw its attention to points of substance". No award may be issued by the tribunal to the parties unless the Registrar has approved its form.

Article 28.9 provides that "the parties undertake to carry out the award immediately and without delay". The provision further stipulates that the parties "irrevocably waive their rights to any form of appeal, review or recourse to any state court or other judicial authority, insofar as such waiver may be validly made". The award is final and binding from the date when it is made.

Article 29 deals with the correction of awards and the making of additional awards.

Provisions relating to fees, costs and deposits are in Art.30. It is also worth noting Art.33 whereby the tribunal may order that all or part of the legal fees or costs of a party (apart from the costs of the arbitration) be paid by another party.

There is an exclusion of liability for SIAC in Art.34. Confidentiality is preserved by Art.35.

Under general provisions in Art.36, a residual power is vested in the Chairman, Registrar and tribunal to fill in lacunae in the Rules. But, when so acting, they must "ensure the fair, expeditious and economical conclusion of the arbitration and the enforceability of the award". From time to time, the Registrar may issue Practice Notes to facilitate the administration of arbitrations under the Rules.

C. LMAA Terms [38]

The LMAA was established in 1960, when a number of London Baltic Exchange brokers who had previously been acting as arbitrators decided to come together as an association. Today the LMAA consists of Full and Supporting Members.

In contrast to the HKIAC, SIAC and ICC, the LMAA does not administer arbitrations. Arbitrations are conducted under the LMAA Terms as procedural rules.

The current LMAA Terms came into effect on 1 January 2012.

The purpose of the Terms is "to obtain the fair resolution of maritime and other disputes by an impartial tribunal without unnecessary delay or expense". [39] Arbitrators are "under a duty to act fairly and impartially between the parties and an original arbitrator is in no sense to be considered as the representative of his appointor".

Section 14 of the English Arbitration Act 1996 (the Act) determines the date when arbitral proceedings are deemed to have commenced. [40]

The Terms apply when the parties so agree. [41] The parties are deemed to have so agreed (unless they say otherwise) when a dispute is referred to a sole arbitrator who is a Full Member or when the arbitrators appointed by each party are Full Members.

Absent agreement by the parties to the contrary, if the Terms apply, English law is to be the law applicable to the arbitration agreement and the seat of arbitration will be England. [42]

Proceedings are governed by the Act. [43] But if the seat of arbitration is outside England and Wales, the Terms shall apply "save to the extent that any mandatory provisions of the law applicable to the arbitration agreement otherwise provide".

If the arbitration agreement does not provide for the number of arbitrators, there are to be 3. The procedure for appointing the 3-person tribunal is set out in para. 8. In short, the parties each appoint an arbitrator and the 2 persons nominated appoint the third arbitrator. The latter will be the chairman unless otherwise agreed.

There are provisions in para. 9 for the appointment of an umpire if the tribunal is supposed to consist of 2 arbitrators and an umpire. The umpire is provided with the papers in the arbitration and takes part in hearings. But the umpire does not decide matters unless the 2 original arbitrators are unable to agree. In that case, the umpire will replace the 2 arbitrators and act as sole arbitrator.

The tribunal's jurisdiction extends to "determining all disputes arising under or in connection with the transaction the subject of the reference".[44] It is for the tribunal to decide when and how the dispute is handled in the course of the arbitration.

The tribunal decides all procedural and evidential matters, including the extent to which there is to be oral or written evidence and submissions.[45] But the parties should try to agree whether an arbitration is to be on documents alone or whether there is to be an oral hearing.

The tribunal has the powers set out in the Act. In addition, it has the specific powers in para. 14. These specific powers are "to be exercised in a suitable case so as to avoid unnecessary delay or expense" and "so as to provide a fair means for the resolution of the matters falling to be determined". Thus, the tribunal may direct that no expert evidence is to be called or limit the extent of expert evidence. It may consolidate 2 or more arbitrations which raise common issues of fact or law. If a claimant fails to provide security for costs, the tribunal may stay the claim in whole or part.

The tribunal can at any stage direct that there be a preliminary meeting.[46] The purpose of the meeting would be "to review the progress of the case; to reach agreement ... upon further preparation for ... the conduct of the hearing; and ... to enable the tribunal to give such directions as it thinks fit". Such meeting is compulsory in complex cases, including cases involving a hearing of more than 5 days. In exceptional cases, there may be more than one preliminary meeting.

However, all preliminary meetings should be preceded by discussion among parties to prepare an agenda.[47] Before any meeting, the tribunal should be provided with a bundle containing relevant documents; an information sheet setting out the steps already taken and steps yet to be taken by the parties; a list of proposed directions; and the agenda. The information sheets should include estimates of readiness for the trial hearing and the likely duration of the trial hearing.

Paragraph 16 deals with the situation where an arbitration is settled.

Adjournments are dealt with in para. 18. In the latter case, the tribunal will be entitled to an interim payment in respect of fees and expenses incurred.

Normally an award should be made available within 6 weeks from the close of proceedings.[48] The period should be less in matters of urgency. If an arbitration is on documents alone, the tribunal must (if asked at the time of receipt of final submissions) indicate when an award will be available.

An award should be reasoned.[49] But the parties may agree to dispense with reasons. Under s.69 of the Act, such agreement will preclude the English Court from hearing an appeal on any question of law arising from the award. Even where the parties agree to dispense with reasons, the tribunal will issue (together with the award) a document outlining the reasons for its decision. This confidential document is referred to as "privileged reasons".

It does not form part of the award and may not be relied upon in proceedings relating to the award.

The tribunal shall notify the parties in writing that an award has been made.[50] The tribunal will then be entitled to the full payment of its fees before the award is delivered. If the award is not collected within a month of publication, the tribunal may order any party to pay for and collect the award within 14 days.

There is provision for the correction of an award and the making of an additional award in para. 25.

The tribunal may publish its award if neither party objects.[51] The award will be redacted before publication in order to preserve the parties' anonymity.

Where the tribunal has reserved costs, a party may apply within 3 months of the award (or such longer period as the tribunal permits) for the matter to be determined.[52]

On matters not covered by the Terms, a tribunal shall act in accordance with the tenor of the Terms.[53]

The Terms include 4 Schedules.

Schedule 1 deals with fees, in particular the payment of a standard appointment fee; the payment of interim fees; the right of an arbitrator to resign for non-payment of fees; the payment of booking fees for the substantive hearing of the arbitration; the provision of security for the costs of an award; the accounting of advance payments; and the payment of accommodation costs.

Schedule 2 sets out the normal procedure followed in LMAA arbitrations. Paragraph 11 of Schedule 2 provides for the completion of a Questionnaire within 14 days of the close of pleadings. The answers to the Questionnaire will inform the tribunal of the main issues which it has to determine, the evidence which is likely to be called, and the directions which each party is likely to seek.

Schedule 3 is the Questionnaire.

Schedule 4 gives an idea of what might be regarded as a reasonable time (estimated from the parties' expected readiness date) by which a substantive hearing should take place. Paragraph 3 of the Schedule stipulates that a "sole arbitrator who is unable to offer a date within the relevant time-scale will offer to retire". Paragraph 4 deals with the situation where a tribunal is unable to sit for a substantive hearing within the relevant time-scale.

D. ICC Arbitration Rules[54]

The ICC was established in 1919 as a non-profit organisation based in Paris. It consists of National Committees and Groups, trade organizations and companies. It has as its object the promotion of global trade and commerce.

The ICC has a World Council and an Executive Board. In 1923 it established the International Court of Arbitration as an independent arbitration body attached to the ICC. The Court administers arbitrations conducted under the ICC Rules.

The current ICC Rules came into effect on 1 January 2012.

Time limits are reckoned and notifications effected as set out in Art.3.

An arbitration is started by a claimant filing a Request for Arbitration with the ICC Secretariat.[55] The arbitration commences from the date when the Secretariat receives the Request.

The Request shall contain the information listed in Art.4(3). It should be accompanied by the requisite filing fee. The Secretariat may impose a time limit for a claimant to comply with the requirements for filing a Request. If the claimant fails to comply within that time, the file shall be closed.

Within 30 days of its receipt of the Request from the Secretariat, the respondent must submit an Answer. The latter should contain the matters set out in Art.5(1). An extension of time is possible. The Answer may include a counterclaim. If there is a counterclaim, the claimant must submit a reply within 30 days of receiving the same.

Challenges to a tribunal's jurisdiction are determined by the tribunal.[56] But the ICC's Secretary-General may refer a challenge to the Court. The Court will then consider whether there is a *prima facie* case for jurisdiction. If the Court believes that there is, the Court will remit the matter to the tribunal for decision.

There are provisions for the joinder of additional parties, the treatment of claims among multiple parties or claims arising out of different contracts, and the consolidation of arbitrations in Arts.7, 8, 9 and 10.

Arbitrators "must be and remain impartial and independent of the parties involved in the arbitration".[57]

The parties may agree upon the number of arbitrators.[58] If they are unable to do so, the Court will appoint a sole arbitrator unless it takes the view that the dispute warrants the appointment of 3 arbitrators. The parties may themselves nominate arbitrators for confirmation by the Court. If they fail to do so, the tribunal will be appointed and confirmed by the Court. The procedure for challenging an appointment as arbitrator is set out in Art.14.

Where the Court itself appoints arbitrators, it will usually act upon the proposal of a relevant ICC National Committee or Group.[59]

Article 13(5) further provides that, save in "suitable circumstances" and provided none of the parties object, a sole arbitrator or president of a tribunal "shall be of a nationality other than those of the parties".

A tribunal having been appointed, the file is transmitted to it "provided the advance on costs requested by the Secretariat at this stage has been paid".[60]

The place of arbitration will be determined by the Court unless agreed by the parties.[61] But the tribunal may conduct hearings and deliberate wherever it considers appropriate.

In the absence of agreement by the parties, the tribunal shall determine the law applicable to a dispute.[62] The tribunal may only decide as *amiable compositeur* or *ex aequo et bono* if the parties agree.

Article 22 requires that a tribunal "make every effort to conduct the arbitration in an expeditious and cost-effective manner, having regard to the complexity and value of the dispute". The tribunal must act fairly and ensure that each party has a reasonable opportunity to be heard. In their turn, the parties are obliged to comply with any order made by tribunal.

As soon as possible after receiving the file, the tribunal is to draw up Terms of Reference (TOR) with the parties' assistance and in the parties' presence.[63] The TOR will normally include a list of issues which the tribunal is to decide. The TOR is to be submitted to the Court within 2 months of transmittal of file. After the TOR has been approved by the Court, no party "shall make new claims which fall outside the limits of the TOR unless it has been authorised to do so by the arbitral tribunal".

When drawing up the TOR or as soon as possible after that, the tribunal shall arrange a case management conference.[64] The purpose of the conference is to work out necessary procedural measures and establish a timetable for the conduct of the arbitration.

By Art.25 the tribunal "shall proceed within as short a time as possible to establish the facts of the case by all appropriate means". The tribunal is to determine what witnesses (including experts) will need to be heard or whether the arbitration can proceed solely on documents.

The proceedings will close "as soon as possible after the last hearing concerning matters to be decided ... or the filing of the last authorised submissions".[65] At that time, the tribunal will declare the proceedings closed and inform the Secretariat and the parties of the date when it expects to submit a draft award to the Court.

Article 28 gives the tribunal a power to grant interim measures. The article also provides that recourse to a judge for the grant or enforcement of an interim measure "shall not be deemed a waiver of the arbitration agreement and shall not affect the relevant powers reserved to the arbitral tribunal".

Article 29 deals with the powers of an Emergency Arbitrator appointed pursuant to Appendix V of the Rules. As with SIAC's Emergency Arbitrator, the provisions here are intended to deal with the situation where interim relief is urgently required prior to the constitution of a tribunal.

Article 30 provides that the "time limit within which the arbitral tribunal must render its final award is six months". Time starts to run from the signature or approval of the TOR. The Court may extend the time of its own initiative where necessary, or upon receipt of a reasoned request for extension from the tribunal.

An award must contain reasons. It will be deemed to be made at the place of arbitration and on the date stated in the award.[66]

Before the award is signed, the tribunal must submit it in draft to the Court for scrutiny.[67] At that point, the Court "may lay down modifications as to the form of the award". The Court may also, "without affecting the arbitral tribunal's liberty of decision … draw attention to points of substance". Once made, the parties will be notified of the terms of the award, but subject to the costs of the arbitration having been fully paid to the ICC.[68]

The award is binding on the parties.[69] They undertake to carry out the award without delay and are "deemed to have waived their right to any form of recourse insofar as such waiver can validly be made".

Article 35 covers the correction, interpretation and remission of awards.

Article 36 deals with advances to cover the costs of an arbitration. The determination of the costs of the arbitration are dealt with in Art.37.

Article 38 concerns the modification of time limits. Article 39 deals with waiver. Article 40 limits the ICC's liability. Article 41 provides that, where the Rules do not cover a particular eventuality, the Court and the tribunal shall fill in the gap "in the spirit of the Rules" and make every effort to make sure that the award is enforceable at law".

There are 5 Appendices to the Rules.

Appendix I contains the Statutes of the Court.

Appendix II sets out the Internal Rules of the Court.

Appendix III deals with the costs and fees of an arbitration. It has tables setting out the administrative fees payable and the fees payable to arbitrators by reference to the amounts in dispute in a given case.

Appendix IV is a brief catalogue of case management techniques. It may be supplemented by reference to the more comprehensive booklet *Techniques for Controlling Time and Costs in Arbitration* (ICC Publication No.843, 2007) which can be downloaded from the ICC's website.

Appendix V sets out the Emergency Arbitrator Rules.

E. CIETAC Arbitration Rules [70]

I. General provisions [71]

CIETAC (which is also known as the "Court of Arbitration of the China Chamber of International Commerce") promotes the use of arbitration to resolve international and economic trade disputes.

CIETAC administers arbitrations. For this purpose, it has a Chairman, Vice-Chairman and Secretariat. It is based in Beijing, but has sub-commissions in Shenzhen, Shanghai, Tianjin and Chongqing. The latter have their own secretariats and are authorised by CIETAC to administer arbitrations. Parties may submit their disputes to CIETAC or a subcommission.

The current Rules were adopted on 3 February 2012. They came into effect on 1 May 2012.

CIETAC accepts "cases involving economic, trade and other disputes of a contractual or non-contractual nature, based on an agreement of the parties". [72] Such cases include international or foreign-related disputes; disputes related to Hong Kong, Macau and Taiwan; and domestic disputes (including disputes between Mainland legal entities).

The parties are deemed to have agreed to arbitration according to the Rules if they agree to arbitration by CIETAC.[73] If the parties have agreed to CIETAC arbitration but subject to some modification of the Rules, their agreement prevails unless what they have agreed is inoperative under a mandatory applicable law. The parties can agree to CIETAC arbitration but pursuant to a set of rules other than those of CIETAC. In that case, CIETAC will administer the arbitration.

Article 4(4) is important as Mainland law appears to require the identification of a government-approved arbitration commission as part of an arbitration agreement. The article provides: "Where the parties agree to refer their dispute to arbitration under these Rules without providing the name of the arbitration institution, they shall be deemed to have agreed to refer the dispute to arbitration by CIETAC."

An arbitration agreement is defined as a clause in any agreement which provides for the settlement of disputes by arbitration.[74] The agreement to arbitrate must be in writing. The writing may be "contained in the tangible form of a document such as a contract, letter, telegram, telex, fax, EDI[75] or email". An arbitration agreement will be deemed to exist if it is pleaded by the claimant in its Request for Arbitration and not denied by the respondent in its Statement of Defence. The autonomy of the arbitration agreement from the rest of a contract is preserved by Art.5(4).

Where a party objects to a tribunal's jurisdiction, CIETAC may determine the challenge or it may delegate that power to the tribunal.[76] Objection to an alleged arbitration agreement must be made in writing before the first oral hearing of the tribunal or, where there is to be no oral hearing, before the submission of a first substantive defence.

The award is deemed to be made at the place of arbitration.[77] The parties may agree that place. But if they do not, the place of arbitration shall be "the domicile of CIETAC or its sub-commission/center administering the case".

Provisions for the service of documents and the calculation of time periods are in Art.8.

Article 9 requires the parties and their representatives to "proceed with the arbitration in bona fide cooperation".

Article 10 deals with waiver of the right to object on account of noncompliance with the Rules.

II. Arbitration proceedings [78]

The second chapter of the Rules is divided into 3 sections: the first dealing with "Request for Arbitration, Defense and Counterclaim" (Arts.11-21); the second with "Arbitrators and the Arbitral Tribunal" (Arts.22-32); and the third with "Hearing" (Arts.33-45).

According to Art.11, an arbitration commences on the day when the Secretariat receives a Request for Arbitration. Article 12 stipulates what documents are to form part of the Request. CIETAC will forward a properly completed Request together with a Notice of Arbitration and a list of CIETAC's Panel of Arbitrators to the respondent.

The respondent must file a Statement of Defence within 45 days from the date when it receives the Notice. The Defence needs to include the matters set out in Art.14(2). The respondent may file a counterclaim at the same time.[79]

Article 17 gives CIETAC a discretion to consolidate 2 or more arbitrations, at the request of a party and with the agreement of all the other parties. If CIETAC accepts the request for consolidation, the arbitrations are combined into the arbitration first commenced.

Article 20 provides that, in handling matters relating to arbitration, a party "may be represented by its authorized Chinese and/or foreign representative(s)". But relevant powers of attorney should be forwarded to the Secretariat by a party or its representatives.

Article 21 deals with interim measures. CIETAC will forward a party's application for imposition of conservatory measures under Mainland law to a competent Court. The tribunal may itself order interim measures at the request of a party.

Arbitrators are not to represent a party.[80] They should be "independent of the parties and treat them equally".

Unless the parties agree otherwise, a tribunal of 3 arbitrators will be appointed.[81]

Typically, arbitrators are nominated from CIETAC's Panel of Arbitrators.[82] The parties may by agreement appoint someone who is not on the Panel. But the Chairman must approve the nomination. Detailed provisions for the appointment of a sole arbitrator or 3-person tribunal are in Arts.25-27. When making an appointment, the Chairman shall have regard to the applicable law, the place and language of arbitration, the nationalities of the parties, and any other relevant factor.[83]

Article 29 stipulates that arbitrators must disclose "any facts or circumstances likely to give rise to justifiable doubts as to his/ her impartiality or independence". The procedure to be followed in challenging an arbitrator's appointment is in Art.30. Arbitrators may be replaced in accordance with Art.31 and the arbitration can continue pursuant to Art.32.

Hearings are to be conducted in accordance with Arts.33-38. In essence, a tribunal may deal with a case as it deems appropriate. Unless the parties agree otherwise, oral hearings are to take place in Beijing if the arbitration is being administered by the Secretariat there or in the domicile of a subcommission where the arbitration is being administered by a subcommission. With the approval of the Secretary-General, the arbitral tribunal may direct that oral hearings are to take place elsewhere. The tribunal may deliberate at any place or manner that it considers appropriate.

Article 36 states that hearings are to be *in camera* (that is, not open to the public). If the parties ask for a public hearing, the tribunal may decide whether to agree to the request. Where hearings are *in camera*, persons involved in the arbitration (including witnesses, experts and interpreters) "shall not disclose to any outsider any substantive or procedural matters relating to the case".

Articles 39-41 deal with evidence. A party has the burden of proving the facts on which it relies. The tribunal is authorised to conduct investigations and collect evidence on its own initiative. The tribunal may also consult experts. When it does, it may request the parties to produce materials, documents, property or goods for checking, inspection, or appraisal by an expert. The parties are obliged to comply with the request.

Article 45 allows the tribunal to act as conciliator (mediator) between the parties. It can do so if the parties so wish or agree. If conciliation (mediation) fails, the tribunal resumes the arbitration. Article 45(9) adds that, if conciliation fails, anything said in the conciliation "shall not be invoked by either party as grounds for any claim, defence, or counterclaim in the subsequent arbitration proceedings, or any other proceedings".

III. Arbitral award [84]

An award is to be rendered within 6 months of the formation of a tribunal.[85] The Secretary-General may extend the time at the tribunal's request.

A tribunal "shall independently and impartially render a fair and reasonable arbitral award based on the facts of the case and the terms of the contract, in accordance with the law, and with reference to international practices".[86] The award must state the claims; the facts in dispute; the reasons for the award; the result of the award; the allocation of costs; and the date and place on which the award is made. The facts and reasons need not be stated, however, if the parties have so agreed. CIETAC's seal must be affixed to the award.

The award is final and binding on the parties. A party may not bring a lawsuit or ask another organisation to revise the award.

The tribunal may make a Partial Award.[87]

An award must be submitted in draft to CIETAC for scrutiny before signing by the arbitrators.[88] At that stage, CIETAC "may bring to the attention of the arbitral tribunal issues addressed in the award on the condition that the arbitral tribunal's independence in rendering the award is not affected".

The allocation of cost is dealt with in Art.50.

Articles 51 and 52 deal with the correction of an award and the making of an additional award.

The award having been made, the parties "shall automatically carry out the arbitral award within the time specified in the award".[89] Where no time is specified, the parties are to carry out the award immediately.

IV. Summary procedure[90]

Chapter IV sets out the Summary Procedure applicable in a case where the amount in dispute does not exceed RMB 2 million or (if the amount is in excess of RMB 2 million) where both parties agree to use of the Summary Procedure.

V. Special provisions for domestic arbitration cases[91]

Chapter V relates to domestic cases.

VI. Supplementary provisions [92]

Chapter VI comprises miscellaneous provisions dealing (among others) with the language of an arbitration, the charging of fees and costs in relation to an arbitration, and the interpretation of the Rules.

In the absence of agreement on language, the proceedings are to be conducted in Chinese or "any other language designated by CIETAC having regard to the circumstances of the case". [93]

The Rules are to be interpreted by CIETAC. [94]

F. Summary

This chapter has surveyed 5 commonly used sets of arbitration rules in the Asia-Pacific region. One quickly notices that the 5 sets of rules share common features. This is likely to be true of all sets of arbitration rules since there are only a limited number of permutations as to how an arbitration may proceed.

Thus, when called upon to apply an unfamiliar set of rules to a dispute, an arbitrator can rapidly become acquainted with the structure of those rules by looking for specific features which are likely to be the same (with only minor variation) in all sets of rules.

Points to bear in mind would be as follows:

1. Most rules will begin with general provisions on giving notice and reckoning time periods.

2. Most rules will provide for an arbitration to start either upon the delivery of a Notice of Arbitration to the respondent or upon the receipt of such Notice by the body administering the arbitration.

3. All rules require arbitrators to be impartial and independent. The rules will contain provisions for their appointment, including a stipulation that they disclose any circumstances which might reasonably cast doubt on their impartiality or suitability. Some rules require arbitrators to consider their availability for the purposes of hearing an arbitration substantively within a reasonable time following appointment. Most rules will set out procedures for challenging the appointment of arbitrators.

4. All rules uphold the principle of "competence-competence" and the autonomy of the arbitration clause from the rest of a contract. The rules may differ slightly on whether a tribunal straightaway determines a challenge to its jurisdiction or an administering body initially determines if there is a *prima facie* case that a dispute is subject to an arbitration agreement.

5. All rules require a tribunal to determine disputes in a manner which avoids unnecessary delay or expense, but which ensures that the parties are treated fairly and afforded a reasonable opportunity to be heard. Within that overriding principle, arbitrators may decide how an arbitration is to be conducted in terms of the filling

of pleadings, the hearing of evidence, and the making of submissions. Most rules provide that, in the absence of agreement, a tribunal is itself to decide what law is applicable for the resolution of a dispute.

6. Most rules have provisions for the determination of the place of arbitration.

7. Most rules confer powers on a tribunal to grant interim measures pending trial.

8. In complex cases, many rules contemplate the holding of at least one case management conference to identify the real issues in dispute between the parties and the procedures by which those issues may most efficiently be resolved.

9. Most rules require an award to be in writing and to be reasoned. Most rules include provisions for the correction and interpretation of an award. Some rules require that an award be made within a reasonable period after the close of proceedings.

10. Most rules provide that the parties are bound by an award and undertake to carry out the same.

11. Most rules have provisions relating to confidentiality, waiver and the limitation of an administering body's liability to the parties.

12. Most rules have provisions requiring the payment of a tribunal's fees and expenses.

13. Some sets of rules relate to "administered arbitrations" where the body issuing the rules supervises the conduct of arbitrations applying the relevant rules. Other sets of rules may simply apply as rules without administration by any one body. Still other rules may

apply either under the administration of some body or simply as rules, it being left to the parties to decide which option they wish to have for their dispute.

---

1. The Rules may be downloaded from the HKIAC's website at www.hkiac.org. In this Section, references to articles are to the HKIAC Rules. Section A sub-headings follow those of the HKIAC Rules.

2. Art.1.

3. See Arts.4 and 5.

4. Note that subsequently the tribunal may require documents which are not in the language of the arbitration to be translated. It may therefore be convenient to have foreign language materials or extracts sent with the Notice already translated.

5. See Art.5.8.

6. See Arts.6-13.

7. Arts.14-28.

8. Art.14.3.

9. Art.14.5.

10. Art.14.6.

11. Art.21.

12. Arts.23.7 and 23.9.

13. Art.25.

14. Art.26.

15. Art.27.

16. Art.28.

17. Arts.29-37.

18. Art.29.1.

19. Art.30.1.

20. Arts.30.2-30.5.

21. Art.31.

22. In essence, these expressions refer to a tribunal coming to a decision based on general principles of fairness and equity.

23. Arts.38-40.

24. The Rules may be downloaded from SIAC's website at www.siac.org.sg. In this Section, references to articles are to the SIAC Rules.

25. SIAC leaflet, "Why Choose SIAC?".

26. Art.1.

27. Art.5. The Expedited Procedure is set out in Art.5.2.

28. Art.6.

29. Arts.10.1 and 10.3.

30. Arts.10.4 and 10.5.

31. Arts.11-13.

32. Art.16.

33. Art.17.

34. Art.19.

35. Art.20.

36. Art.27.

37. Art.28.

38. These may be downloaded from the LMAA's website at www.lmaa.org.uk. In this Section, references to paragraphs are to the Terms.

39. Para. 3.

40. Para. 4.

41. Para. 5.

42. Para. 6.

43. Para. 7.

44. Para. 10.

45. Para. 12.

46. Para. 15.

47. Para. 15(c) and (d).

48. Para. 20.

49. Para. 22.

50. Para. 23 and 24.

51. Para. 26.

52. Para. 28.

53. Para. 30.

54. The Rules may be downloaded from the ICC's website at www.iccwbo.org. References in this Section to articles are to the ICC Rules.

55. Art.4.

56. Art.6.

57. Art.11.

58. Art.12.

59. Art.13.

60. Art.16.

61. Art.18.

62. Art.21.

63. Art.23.

64. Art.24.

65. Art.27.

66. Art.31.

67. Art.33.

68. Art.34.

69. Art.34(6).

70. The Rules may be downloaded from CIETAC's website at cn.cietac.org. References to articles in this Section are to CIETAC's Rules. Sub-section headings correspond with the chapter titles of the Rules.

71. Arts.1-10.

72. Art.3(1).

73. Art.4.

74. Art.5.

75. Electronic Data Interchange.

76. Art.6.

77. Art.7.

78. Arts.11-45.

79. Art.15.

80. Art.22.

81. Art.23.

82. Art.24.

83. Art.28.

84. Arts.46-53.

85. Art.46.

86. Art.47.

87. Art.48.

88. Art.49.

89. Art.53.

90. Arts.54-62.

91. Arts.63-70.

92. Arts.71-74.

93. Art.71.

94. Art.73(2).

Chapter 4

The Scrutiny Of Awards By The Court

This chapter considers the enforcement of arbitration awards by the Hong Kong Court. It will focus on applications to set aside under s.81 (ML 34) and applications to refuse enforcement pursuant to the New York Convention and ss.86, 89 and 95.

Section A describes the international scheme for recognition and enforcement of awards found in the Convention. Section B discusses the general approach to the enforcement of awards in Hong Kong and Singapore. These are considered to be among the most "arbitration-friendly" jurisdictions in the Asia-Pacific. Section B concludes with reflections on the public perception of the interplay between arbitration and the Court. Section C discusses 2 alleged problems with the enforcement of awards in Hong Kong.

A. The New York Convention[1]

The Convention on the Recognition and Enforcement of Foreign Arbitral Awards was promulgated by the United Nations in New York on 6 July 1958. As of today, it has been signed by some 146 states. The People's Republic of China is a signatory. It has extended the application of the Convention to Hong Kong and Macau. Before 1 July 1997, the Convention also applied to Hong Kong by reason of its extension to the Territory by the British colonial government.

The Convention is short. It consists of only 16 articles. The articles are expressed in general terms. It is thus left to the Courts of a contracting state to determine the ambit of an article.[2] However, since an international convention is involved, when determining how an article is to be construed, the domestic Court should have regard to jurisprudence elsewhere on the application of the Convention to specific situations.

Article 1 states that the Convention "shall apply to the recognition and enforcement of arbitral awards made in the territory of a State other than the State where the recognition and enforcement of such awards are sought".

Article 2 requires that a state "shall recognize an agreement in writing under which the parties undertake to submit to arbitration all or any differences which have arisen or which may arise between them in respect of a defined legal relationship". That "defined legal relationship" may or may not be contractual in nature, but it must be "concerning a subject matter capable of settlement by arbitration". What constitutes an "agreement in writing" is not exhaustively defined, but the expression includes "an arbitral clause in a contract or an arbitration agreement, signed by the parties or contained in an exchange of letters or telegrams".

Article 2(3) is important. It imposes an obligation on the Court of a contracting state to refer a matter to arbitration where a dispute is subject to an arbitration agreement as defined in Art.2. The Court must so act "unless it finds that the said agreement is null and void, inoperative or incapable of being performed".[3]

Article 3 stipulates that a contracting state shall recognise awards as binding and enforce them "under the conditions laid down in the following articles [of the Convention]". It should not be more difficult procedurally to enforce an award made in a Convention state than an award made within the enforcing Court's territory.

Article 4 sets out simple procedures with which an applicant must comply when seeking enforcement of an award. The applicant must submit "the duly authenticated original award or a duly certified copy thereof" and the original or a certified copy of the arbitration agreement. Where the arbitration award or agreement is not in an official language of the enforcing Court, the document must be translated.

Article 5 is the key provision of the Convention. It is worth reproducing in full. It states:

"(1) Recognition and enforcement of the award may be refused, at the request of the party against whom it is invoked, only if that party furnishes to the competent authority where the recognition and enforcement is sought, proof that:

(a) The parties to the agreement referred to in Article 2 were, under the law applicable to them, under some incapacity, or the said agreement is not valid under the law to which the parties have subjected it or, failing any indication thereon, under the law of the country where the award was made; or

(b) The party against whom the award is invoked was not given proper notice of the appointment of the arbitrator or of the arbitration proceedings or was otherwise unable to present his case; or

(c) The award deals with a difference not contemplated by or not falling within the terms of the submission to arbitration, or it contains decisions on matters beyond the scope of the submission to arbitration, provided that, if the decisions on matters submitted to arbitration can be separated from those not so submitted, that part of the award which contains decisions on matters submitted to arbitration may be recognized and enforced; or

(d) The composition of the arbitral tribunal authority or the arbitral procedure was not in accordance with the agreement of the parties, or, failing such agreement, was not in accordance with the law of the country where the arbitration took place; or

(e) The award has not yet become binding on the parties, or has been set aside or suspended by a competent authority of the country in which, or under the law of which, that award was made.

(2) Recognition and enforcement of an arbitral award may also be refused if the competent authority in the country where recognition and enforcement is sought finds that:

(a) The subject matter of the difference is not capable of settlement by arbitration under the law of that country; or

(b) The recognition or enforcement of the award

> would be contrary to the public policy of that
> country."

It should be noted that under the Convention it will not automatically follow, from proof of one or other of the grounds in Art.5, that recognition of an award will be refused. Article 5 only states that recognition and enforcement "may be refused". The enforcing Court retains a discretion whether or not to recognise and enforce an award which is vitiated by one or more of the grounds in Art.5.

It will be also noticed that the grounds for refusing recognition in Arts.5(1) and (2) are similar to the grounds for recourse against an award set out in s.81 (ML 34) and the grounds for refusing enforcement and recognition of awards in s.86 (dealing with non-Convention, non-Mainland awards); s.89 (dealing with Convention awards); and s.95 (dealing with Mainland awards). Recall, however, that under s.86(2)(c) there is an extra ground for refusing enforcement of a non-Convention, non-Mainland awards (a category including awards made in Hong Kong). That additional ground is "any other reason the Court considers it just to do so". This last basis for refusal is not in the Convention.

The Model Law follows the Convention in that establishing one or other of the grounds for refusing enforcement will not automatically lead to the rejection of an award. Again the Court retains a discretion in such circumstance whether or not to refuse recognition.

Article 6 empowers the enforcing Court to adjourn applications for enforcement pending an application to the supervising Court to set aside the relevant award.

Article 7 preserves the validity of a contracting state's multilateral or bilateral agreements relating to the recognition or enforcement of an award. Articles 8, 9, 10, 11 and 15 concern ratification of and accession to the Convention. Article 12 deals with the coming into force of the Convention, while Art.13 provides for a contracting state to renounce the Convention.

Article 14 stipulates that the Convention is to apply reciprocally. As against another contracting party, a contracting state may only rely on the Convention "to the extent that it is itself bound to apply the Convention".

Article 16 identifies the authentic texts of the Convention.

The effect of the Convention is to make an arbitral award made in one contracting state readily enforceable in another. In essence, a party A wishing to enforce the award against party B in another jurisdiction may do so by complying with the threshold evidential requirements in Art.4. Unless B can rely on one of the limited grounds in Art.5 for rejecting an award, the Court of a contracting state is bound to recognise and enforce the award in A's favour.

The flexibility of being able to enforce an award within the 146 jurisdictions party to the Convention is a major advantage of arbitration, especially when compared to the more cumbersome processes often needed to enforce the order of a domestic Court in a foreign state.

In practice, of the grounds in Art.5, the one most commonly used to resist enforcement is "public policy". A party will accordingly often suggest that recognition of an award would be contrary to the public policy for some reason or other.[4]

Until recently, there was a difficulty in enforcing Hong Kong awards in India. This was despite the fact that both India and Hong Kong (through the PRC) are parties to the Convention.

The problem was a significant drawback in relation to Hong Kong awards involving Indian parties.

The problem arose because under India's Arbitration and

Conciliation Act 1996, a state has to be notified in the Indian Official Gazette as a jurisdiction to which the Convention applies. Without such declaration, awards made in the relevant state will not be enforceable in India.

Prior to March 2012, the PRC had not been so notified. However, since 19 March 2012, the PRC has been gazetted in India as a Convention state. Consequently, since 19 March 2012 the problem of enforcing Hong Kong awards in India has been rectified. PRC awards (including Hong Kong awards) are now enforceable in India in accordance with the Convention.

This development removes what had been regarded as a major disadvantage with Hong Kong awards.

B. Enforcement of Awards

I. The "friendly" and the "unfriendly" of the arbitration market

Arbitration is a growth industry. Many states (Hong Kong included) have established arbitration centres. These jurisdictions promote themselves heavily (in competition with each other) as having the infrastructure (venues, facilities, personnel) necessary for the smooth conduct of arbitrations. They also boast of having a judiciary which enforces awards with a minimum of procedural inconvenience to parties.

In this connection, commentators are accustomed to refer to states as "arbitration friendly" or not, depending on the degree to which the Courts of that jurisdiction scrutinise awards before enforcing them. The more scrutiny there is, the less friendly the jurisdiction is said to be. On this test, Singapore and Hong Kong are frequently rated by commentators as among the most (if not the 2 best) "arbitration friendly" jurisdictions in the Asia-Pacific.

II. A need for scrutiny

But recently it has been suggested that, even in Singapore and Hong Kong, there has been a trend towards a greater judicial scrutiny of arbitral awards. This "trend" has been criticised by commentators as a retrograde step.

For instance, in "Singapore Arbitration and the Courts: *Quo Vadis*?" [5] Peter Megens has queried on the basis of 4 recent Singaporean Court decisions "whether all is well in what to many previously seemed to be arbitration's Garden of Eden?" Those 4 cases are the first instance and appellate decisions in *PT Perusahaan Gas Negara (Persero) TBK v. CRW Joint Operation* [6] and *AJT v. AJU* [7] respectively.

Persero involved an ICC arbitration pursuant to the dispute resolution terms of the FIDIC Conditions of Contract for Construction (1st ed., 1999). PGN appealed to the Singapore Court against the tribunal's Final Award. That Final Award required PGN to pay an amount which a Dispute Adjudication Board had concluded was payable to CRW. The Board had itself been convened in accordance with the FIDIC Conditions.

The tribunal made its Final Award without prejudice to PGN (if it wished) later seeking to set aside the Board's substantive decision that an amount was payable. Nonetheless, relying on Art.34(2)(a)(iii) of the Model Law (equivalent to Art.5(1)(c) of the Convention), PGN argued that the Board had exceeded its jurisdiction, because it ought to have re-opened and reviewed the Board's ruling before making a Final Award.

After detailed analyses of the FIDIC Conditions, Ang J and the Court of Appeal accepted (albeit on slightly different reasoning) that the tribunal had exceeded its jurisdiction. Both levels of Court thought that the tribunal could only make an Interim Award of the sum adjudicated by the tribunal as due to CRW. Insofar as it had purported to make a Final Award without itself looking into the correctness of the Board's decision, the judges concluded that the tribunal had not acted within the scope of its authority under the FIDIC Conditions.

AJT involved a SIAC arbitration. In its award, the tribunal concluded that there had been a valid settlement agreement between AJU and AJT to conclude the arbitration. By the settlement agreement, AJU agreed (among other things) to withdraw a complaint which it had made to the Thai police in which AJU had alleged that AJT had committed fraud and forgery.

AJU withdrew its complaint and, as a result, the Thai police ceased to investigate the matter any further. But AJT refused to terminate the arbitration in accordance with the settlement agreement.

AJT appealed to the Singapore Court to set aside the tribunal's award upholding the settlement agreement on the ground that it was contrary to public policy. According to AJT, this was because the settlement agreement "sought to stifle the prosecution of a non-compoundable offence [that is, forgery and the use of a forged document]". Further, AJT argued that the settlement agreement was illegal and unenforceable in Thailand and "bribery and/or corruption of a public authority were involved in [its] performance".

Chan J found that the settlement agreement amounted to "a stifling of the prosecution process in Thailand" and was illegal under Thai law (the law of the place of performance). It followed that, for reasons of international comity, the settlement agreement was also illegal under Singapore law (the proper law of the contract). Therefore, upholding the award based on the illegal agreement would be contrary to the public policy of Singapore. Chan J consequently set aside the award.

The Court of Appeal, however, held that Chan J erred in re-opening the tribunal's finding of fact that AJU was not required to do anything illegal under Thai law. So the settlement agreement was not an illegal contract under Thai law. Accordingly, the public policy of Singapore was not engaged in the case.

Peter Megens contrasts the Singapore cases with "the trend in Hong Kong in recent decisions ... where the trend has been staunchly pro-enforcement". [8] He discerns from *Persero* that "the Singapore Courts may be becoming more interventionist ... and may be willing to substitute their analysis, particularly in novel matters, for the reasons of respected international arbitrators". [9]

Megens concludes: [10]

> "What the Singapore courts have done in the decisions referred to in this article is to second-guess the arbitral tribunals in questions, and they have done so in circumstances where it could not be said there was a perverse or manifest error that called for correction. In adopting such a course, the Singapore courts are treading a path that is well worn by interventionist courts in jurisdictions which are not considered friendly to arbitration, and where arbitration will not flourish. It is to be hoped that Singapore will not go further down that path. The Court of Appeal decision in *AJU v. AJT* shows that, possibly, the Court of Appeal might be putting a brake on to slow what is arguably an unfortunate trend. One can only hope it goes on to execute a U-turn.
>
> It is to be hoped that judges applying any of the grounds for intervention under the Model Law Art.34 or relying on the public policy ground will bear in mind that these are not meant to be routes to a back-door appeal simpliciter."

But I do not think that the approach in Hong Kong is significantly different from the trend which Megens detects in Singapore.

Consider, by way of comparison with Singapore, 2 recent sets of

Hong Kong decisions. They are the first instance and appellate decisions in *Gao Haiyan and another v. Keeneye Holdings Ltd. and others*[11] and *Pacific China Holdings Ltd. (In Liquidation) v. Grand Pacific Holdings Ltd*[12] respectively.

Gao Haiyan concerned an award of the Xian Arbitration Commission. Before the 3-person tribunal rendered an award, the Commission's Secretary-General and one of the arbitrators attempted mediation. The mediation took place over dinner at a Xian hotel attended by the mediators and Z (described as "a person related to" the respondents in the arbitration). At the dinner, the mediators (apparently of their own initiative) suggested to Z that the respondents pay the claimants RMB 250 million to settle their dispute over the transfer of certain shares. The mediators asked Z to "do some work on [the respondents] to get them to accept this result". The mediators had not consulted the claimants about the figure of RMB 250 million and the evidence was that the claimants had actually told the tribunal that they were not prepared to settle the dispute for that amount.

The respondents rejected the mediators' proposal. The arbitration therefore proceeded. In the event, by its award, the tribunal dismissed the respondents' claim in its entirety and revoked the share transfer agreement upon which the respondents had relied. The tribunal, however, also "recommended" in its award that the claimants "shall take the initiative to pay RMB 50 million as ... economic compensation" to the respondents.

When the arbitration recommenced after the failure of the mediation, the respondents had not alleged that the tribunal was biased on account of the involvement of one arbitrator in the abortive mediation. But, following the award against it, the respondents applied to the Xian Intermediate Court to set aside the award on account of "favouritism". The Xian Court rejected the respondents' application.

The claimant sought to enforce the award in Hong Kong. The respondents applied for the Court here to refuse enforcement on the public policy ground, the award allegedly being tainted by actual or apparent bias.

Sitting as judge, I held that there was insufficient evidence of actual bias. However, I thought that what occurred in the Xian hotel gave rise to an apprehension of apparent bias. I warned that, unless care was taken, the participation of arbitrators in a mediation process (that is, med-arb) might inevitably involve a risk of apparent bias.

Further, given the public policy ground for refusing enforcement concerned Hong Kong (not Xian) public policy, I reasoned that the respondent was not estopped by the decision of the Xian Court from raising the question of bias in Hong Kong when the award was being enforced. Since a Hong Kong Court would likely refuse to enforce a Hong Kong award which was tainted by apparent bias, I concluded that it must be equally repugnant to Hong Kong public policy to enforce a foreign award which was tainted by apparent bias. A foreign award (I thought) "should normally receive no more favourable treatment ... than that accorded to a Hong Kong arbitration award by a Hong Kong Court". I accordingly allowed the respondents' application and refused enforcement of the award as a judgment of the Hong Kong Court.

The Court of Appeal disagreed. It found that, by not raising bias when the arbitration recommenced after the mediation, the respondents must be taken to have waived the right to object on account of real or apparent bias. In addition, the Court of Appeal thought that whether what happened in the Xian hotel gave rise to an apprehension of bias, "may depend also on an understanding of how mediation is normally conducted in the place where it was concluded". Thus, "due weight must be given to the decision of the Xian Court refusing to set aside the Award [on the ground of bias]".

Pacific China involved an ICC arbitration. PCH appealed against the

3-person tribunal's award on the basis of Arts.34(2)(ii) and (iv) of the Model Law (equivalent to Arts.5(1)(b) and (d) of the Convention). Essentially, it was alleged that the procedure adopted by the tribunal had unfairly prevented PCH from presenting its case. In particular, it was contended that PCH had not been given a fair chance to respond to last minute expert evidence on Taiwanese law adduced by GPH; PCH had wrongly been barred from relying on 3 Taiwanese law authorities; and PCH had wrongly been refused an opportunity to respond to certain submissions made by GPH on Hong Kong and New York law.

Saunders J held in PCH's favour in respect of all 3 procedural complaints. Because he believed that the result of the arbitration might have been different in the absence of those improprieties, he exercised his discretion to set aside the award.

The Court of Appeal disagreed. It thought that the judge should have accorded greater deference to the case management decisions of the tribunal. Further, the Court should not interfere with the arbitral process unless the conduct complained of by a party was "sufficiently serious or egregious so that one could say a party has been denied due process". The conduct criticised by PCH not having reached that level of gravity, the judge should have accorded the tribunal with "a wide discretion" and "flexibility".

On the face of things, Hong Kong would appear from the 2 judgments of its Court of Appeal to be highly "arbitration friendly". In both judgments, the appellate court resoundingly affirmed the principle of giving a wide margin of deference to the exercise of a tribunal's discretion on matters of case management. It was not for a judge (the appeal court said) to second guess a tribunal's orders. On the contrary, a judge should only intervene under ML Art.34 where there has been "serious" or "egregious" misconduct by a tribunal.

But it will be noted that the operative principles for dealing with challenges to an award which have been articulated in *Pacific China* are not really that different from the principles expressed in *AJT*.

I would go further. Not only are the principles applied by the Courts in Hong Kong and Singapore for dealing with awards similar, but I would also suggest that there is not that much difference between the methodologies (approaches) followed by the Singapore and Hong Kong Courts in handling challenges.

This is because, if a party alleges that an award should be set aside or refused recognition for some reason, judges in Singapore or Hong Kong (and for that matter anywhere else applying the Convention or Model Law) will still have to assess the validity of those allegations. The reality is that there are only a limited number of ways for a Court to deal with a challenge.

Whichever way one chooses, the Court will have to conduct some scrutiny of the circumstances of an award. In a Convention or Model Law jurisdiction, the real question is not whether there should be scrutiny, but what degree of scrutiny there should be.

There are effectively only 3 ways of assessing evidence. One can be summary and dismiss a challenge after only a cursory look at an award. One can consider affidavit evidence of facts and matters relevant to a challenge and then decide on the strength of that evidence alone without recourse to cross-examination. One can have a full-blown trial of the evidence and decide only after hearing live evidence tested in cross-examination.

What is the appropriate method where a challenge to an award is involved?

One must bear in mind that, the evidence before a Court in support of a challenge to an award may be voluminous. In *Gao Haiyan*, for example, in addition to documents, witness statements of what took place before, during and after the mediation were filed by claimant and respondent. There was an order for the deponents of the statements to attend Court for cross-examination.

One can of course answer that it is for a Court, taking into account all relevant circumstances, to choose which of the 3 ways is the most appropriate procedure for a given case. But what does this mean in practice?

The first way would rightly (I think) be regarded in most cases as too superficial. Normally, in the interests of fairness, a party should be allowed to adduce evidence in support of an allegation that (say) an award falls within one or more of the grounds listed in Art.5(1) of the Convention.

In terms of assessing evidence, the Hong Kong and Singapore Courts ordinarily follow the second approach. The judge decides whether or not to enforce an award on the basis of affidavit evidence alone, without the cross-examination of deponents. *Gao Haiyan* is a rare example insofar as directions were given there for the hearing of live evidence.

It would be impractical for the Court to limit in advance by (say) a Practice Direction the kinds of evidence which a party might put up in favour of an application to set aside or refuse enforcement of an award. The factual scenarios which might give rise to a challenge against an award are infinite. A Court could never enumerate all the permutations of fact which might conceivably lead to an award being set aside or refused recognition. It would be unwise to try.

The Court can of course urge the parties to be economical in the evidence which they present. But, if a party is minded to put forward many bundles of documents, the Court will not be able to determine whether such material is relevant without examining the same and giving the party some opportunity to be heard on the evidence.

The third way of a full-blown trial would (I believe) only be justified in exceptional cases.

At the challenge stage, the parties will usually already have gone through one trial leading up to the tribunal's award. In most cases, if the parties had to go through another trial in order to determine the validity of a challenge to the award, the additional costs and time involved in such an approach are likely to be daunting and disproportionate. It would be unfair to the party which won the arbitration to have to fight a second trial before it can even begin to enforce the award in its favour. Making the third way the procedure of choice in a majority of cases would be the death-knell of arbitration as a means of speedy and cost-effective dispute resolution.

Assume now that a Court will generally adopt the second approach as the best means of proceeding.

Even if a judge were resolutely to follow the non-interventionist principles urged by the Hong Kong Court of Appeal in *Pacific China* and the Singapore Court of Appeal in *AJT*, the judge will inevitably have to examine whatever evidence an applicant puts up in support of its contention that an award is invalid.

A Court would still have to look at what took place in the arbitration and the reasoning articulated in the award, if only to reject the applicant's contentions. Afterwards, if the applicant is not happy with a rejection of its challenge to an award at first instance, the appellate court will itself also have to look into the arbitration.

A first instance judge dealing with an application for enforcement of an award in Hong Kong, Singapore or any other Model Law jurisdiction can easily end up reviewing a substantial part of the arbitral process in detail over 1 or 2 days. The Court of Appeal in either jurisdiction may similarly require a day or so if the matter comes before it. A non-interventionist "arbitration friendly approach" therefore does not mean that a dispute over the validity of an award will be resolved in "no time at all".

The Court may eventually decide that much of the evidence is irrelevant and (say) impose a cost penalty on the party. For instance, in Hong Kong, in the absence of special circumstances, a party who unsuccessfully challenges an award must pay the other side's costs on an indemnity basis. But that would only be, after the event, once the Court has considered the party's case.

III. The time taken for scrutiny

The parties in *Persero* entered into a contract (including an arbitration agreement) in February 2006. The Board rendered its decision in about November 2008. CRW filed its Request for Arbitration in February 2009. The arbitration was heard in September 2009 and the award was made in November 2009. CRW sought to register the award with the Singapore Court in January 2010. PGN challenged the registration in February 2010.

Ang J heard the matter in April 2010 and handed down a judgment in July 2010. The appeal was heard in December 2010 and judgment was handed down in July 2011. Thus, the dispute between the parties (relating to the payment of US$17.2 million) remained unresolved for a period of at least 2.5 years. The effect of the Court of Appeal's decision was that the dispute had to go to a further arbitration in which the Board's decision would have to be reviewed substantively.

In *AJT* the arbitration began with the service of a Notice of Arbitration in August 2006. The settlement agreement was signed in February 2008. The award was issued in December 2009. AJT applied to set aside the award in early 2010. Chan J heard AJT's application in April 2010 and gave judgment in July 2010. The Court of Appeal heard the matter in late November 2010 and delivered its decision in August 2011. Thus, notwithstanding a settlement agreement, the dispute between the parties remained unresolved for some 5 years.

In *Gao Haiyan* the arbitration started in July 2009. The mediation took place in March 2010. The arbitration resumed in May 2010 and an award was made in June 2010. The Xian Court dismissed the respondents' appeal in October 2010. The Hong Kong Court made an Order *Nisi* for the enforcement of the award in August 2010. I heard the application to set aside enforcement on 30 March 2011 and handed down judgment in April 2011. The Court of Appeal heard the matter in November 2011 and delivered judgment in December 2011. Thus, the parties dispute remained unresolved for some 2.5 years after the start of arbitration.

In *Pacific China*, a Request for Arbitration was filed in March 2006. An award was issued in August 2009. Saunders J heard PCH's application to set aside the award in February 2011 and handed down judgment in June 2011. The Court of Appeal heard the matter in March 2012 and gave a decision in May 2012. The dispute was therefore ongoing for over 6 years.

The 4 cases show that a dispute might remain "live" for anywhere between 2.5 to 5 years (inclusive of court hearings and appeals) after the start of arbitration. That was the time required even within 2 of the most "arbitration-friendly" jurisdictions in Asia.

A duration of that magnitude cannot be a positive recommendation for arbitration as a "speedy" means of dispute resolution. If the 4 cases are illustrative of a normal timeline, then arbitration may not be competitive with conventional litigation within (say) the specialist Commercial or Construction Lists of the Hong Kong Court. Arbitration would not be any swifter in finally ending a dispute than going to Court.

Does this mean that the process of arbitration is unsuitable as a mechanism for efficient dispute resolution?

I do not believe so.

The 4 cases should not be taken as representative of the run-of-the-mill commercial cases which are likely to come up before arbitrators or the Court. One must accordingly be cautious about drawing general conclusions from the 4 cases.

All 4 cases involved disputes over significant amounts of money. Given the amounts at stake, a disgruntled party might have felt that it was worth it to engage in tactical manoeuvring. There would be economic incentives to engage in such conduct. This would be true even if the cases were to have been resolved by way of litigation in Court.

Not surprisingly then, in the 4 cases, there was substantial procedural wrangling. There were either related ongoing Court proceedings between the parties or there was substantial "to-ing and fro-ing" in correspondence with one party accusing the other of wrongdoing and fraud. Those complications required time to resolve.

The sad truth is that, if a party to an arbitration agreement is determined to spend time and money to prolong or multiply proceedings in order to improve its negotiating position, it will not be easy to prevent the party from so doing.

In contrast, it seems to me that, in more ordinary commercial cases where the parties wish to achieve a degree of "closure" or finality within a reasonable period of time, the Court can move things along significantly. In particular, the Court can ensure that appropriate procedures are in place to enable challenges to an award to be dealt with as promptly as possible from the time when application is made for enforcement to the time when an appellate court determines a challenge.

Appropriate procedures would include the following imperatives:

> (1) All applications relating to awards should be monitored to enable directions for the disposal of an application

to be given as soon as or shortly after the application is made.

(2) Patently hopeless challenges to an award should be weeded out at the directions stage so that such challenge proceeds no further and wastes no more time and money.

(3) Challenges are to be set down for substantive hearing at the earliest opportunity, typically for a first instance hearing within (say) 2 months of directions being given and for an appeal hearing within (say) 6 months after determination at first instance.

(4) On the premise that it is easier to give earlier dates for shorter than longer hearings, the Court may consider limiting the time for the substantive hearing (at first instance or on appeal) of run-of-the-mill challenges to between half-a-day and a day.

(5) Where on its face a challenge involves more complex issues, the Court might consider limiting substantive hearings to 2 days.

(6) To counter-balance any limits placed on hearing time, the Court could allow the parties to put in advance written submissions of whatever length they deem appropriate.

(7) To the extent possible, all hearings should be presided over by specialist judges who are fully familiar with commercial matters of the type under consideration in a challenge.

I accept that the foregoing measures may not have made too much difference in the 4 cases. But the measures should at least help to expedite the determination of more conventional challenges to an award.

IV. Refining the concept of "arbitration-friendly"

The previous sections prompt the reflection that it does not really help to speak of a jurisdiction as "arbitration-friendly" depending upon the degree to which the jurisdiction's Courts take a "hands-off" attitude to awards.

Arbitration as a dispute resolution process does not mean looking exclusively at what a tribunal does. The focus must be on the whole process, inclusive of recourse to the Court for interim measures in support of an arbitration or for setting aside (or refusing recognition) to an award. It is meaningless to talk about limiting Court interference in arbitration. The Court's involvement is itself an integral component of the arbitration dispute resolution process.

In this sense, a jurisdiction's Courts should be judged as "arbitration friendly" not so much by the extent to which they do or do not scrutinise awards. They should instead be praised (or criticised) depending on the extent to which they can be relied on to scrutinise awards carefully in accordance with the expectations of commercial persons.

By "expectations of commercial persons", I mean that a Court should not lose sight of time and cost when it scrutinises an award. Business people would not want a pedantic examination of every "jot and tittle" of an award. That would be to conduct another trial. On the other hand, neither would business people want a superficial look through an award. That would be to shirk the state's obligations under the Convention and the Model Law.

The Court has to scrutinise an award whenever a challenge is made. Whether or not the Court upholds a challenge and sets aside an award in consequence of its scrutiny is a different question. The balance on that last question is (I think) best struck by applying the guidance which the Singapore and Hong Kong Courts of Appeal have given in *AJT* and *Pacific China*. The grounds for refusing recognition in the Convention and the Model Law should be applied only in serious (as opposed to trivial) situations where a failing has had (or may have) substantial ramifications on the outcome of an award.

The Court's ultimate supervision or scrutiny stands as a guarantee of the integrity of the arbitration process. The possibility of the Court's scrutiny lends credibility to arbitration. It certifies that a tribunal has proceeded in a fair manner and, even if it may have erred in some respects, its errors are not so "egregious" as to constitute a serious miscarriage of justice (the recognition of which would be repugnant to public policy).

I am therefore not arguing that the Court should intervene at every twist or turn where it disagrees with a tribunal. That should most emphatically not be the case. All that I am suggesting is that we may have swung too far in our efforts to insulate arbitrations from Court intervention. That is to throw away the baby (namely, the possibility at all stages of asking the Court to rectify serious injustice in matters of substantive law or due process) with the bath water. It is to be embarrassed by that which arbitration should be touting as its strength.

V. The public perception of the role of the Courts

At a recent talk to Oxford students in a civil procedure seminar, I outlined the Hong Kong Court's approach to mediation.[13] I argued that, mediation being apparently successful in resolving some 70% of cases at an early stage, mediation was something which the Courts should be actively promoting as a means of reducing the prohibitive costs of ordinary litigation.

During the question and answer period, I was taken aback by a student's accusation that I was being "non-Dworkinian".[14] It was said that I was advocating the cause of mediation because for me there was "no such thing as rights anymore", but that instead there were "only negotiating positions". It was said that for me "everything was negotiable". That meant that a party could cynically ignore the rights or wrong of a particular course of action. The party (it was suggested) could deliberately breach a contract and negotiate everything afterwards in a mediation organised with the blessing of the Hong Kong Court.

Some students went so far as to suggest that the problem with mediation was that, if it was truly as successful as it claimed to be, there would be fewer civil cases going to trial. So there would be fewer pronouncements of law by the Court as a result. The law would cease to develop and somehow become "uncertain". To borrow a Marxist expression, law would "wither away" in consequence of mediation and judges would not be doing what they are supposed to be doing, namely, judging and clarifying the black spots of the law.

While I disagree with the arguments advanced (which frankly struck me as speculative and extreme), they gave me pause for thought. I have since been reflecting on the sentiment underlying them.

It seems to me that the students' points highlight a common perception that, in promoting alternative means of dispute resolution, judges are "outsourcing" their work to private bodies (such as mediators) and abdicating their responsibility of declaring right and wrong. The students were giving vent to a widespread psychological need among the public for vindication by a judgment of the Court, even if obtaining that will entail considerable anxiety, time and cost and even if there is a risk of losing. A sizeable portion of the population may prefer to have their day in Court, rather than be compelled to settle more cheaply outside of Court via mediation.

Those reflections have led me, following the seminar, to be more circumspect in the promotion of mediation. I still believe that mediation is an effective and inexpensive means of dispute resolution. But I have to accept that it will not be to everyone's taste and I am now wary of forcing mediation on the public willy-nilly.

I raise this topic here, because arbitration may be a means of squaring the circle.

On the one hand, arbitration offers a speedy and effective means of resolving a dispute insofar as arbitrations are conducted by arbitrators who are experienced in case management and specialised in the subject matter of the dispute. On the other hand, insofar as it is backed up by the possibility of recourse to the Courts to rectify serious error, arbitration may also satisfy the public's deeply felt need for a vindication of one's position by a pronouncement from the Court.

This versatility has now been reinforced through the introduction of opt-in provisions by s.99 of the Ordinance. The provisions recognise that different persons may wish the Court to be involved in an arbitration process to differing degrees. Some may want more potential for intervention by the Courts, others may want less. Both ends of that spectrum and everything in between are covered.

The opt-in provisions permit arbitration agreements to be tailored to whatever parties perceive to be the appropriate level of Court involvement in the resolution of a dispute. Thus, the parties may expressly opt to allow the Court to decide preliminary questions of law arising in the course of an arbitration (Sch.2, s.3); the parties may go further and allow challenges to an award before the Court on the ground of serious irregularity (Sch.2, s.4); and the parties may wish to have on top of all that the possibility of appeal against an award on questions of law (Sch.2, s.5) with or without a leave requirement super-added (Sch.2, s.6).

Insofar as satisfying the desire in the public mind for Court supervision over the process of dispute resolution, arbitration may thus have significant advantages. Mediation of course will have its own advantages.[15] But, in contrast to arbitration, mediation may not satisfy an innate craving among the public for a definitive statement of right.

C. Two Alleged Problems with Hong Kong Awards

The two problems which I have in mind arise from 2 relatively recent decisions of the Hong Kong Court. The first is the decision of the Court of Final Appeal in *Democratic Republic of the Congo and others v. FG Hemisphere Associates LLC*.[16] The second is the decision of Stone J at first instance in *The "HUA TIAN LONG" (No.2)*.[17]

I. FG Hemisphere

Energoinvest obtained an arbitration award against the Democratic Republic of the Congo (DRC). Energoinvest assigned the benefit of that debt to FG Hemisphere for valuable consideration.

FG Hemisphere applied to register the arbitration award in Hong Kong and enforce it as a judgment of the Court here. FG Hemisphere sought to enforce the award by garnisheeing sums said to be payable to the DRC by (among others) China Railway Group Ltd. (CR). CR is a PRC company listed on the Hong Kong Stock Exchange. The sums were payable by CR to the DRC pursuant to agreements between DRC and the PRC governments for the development of the infrastructure of the DRC in return for the right to exploit certain mineral resources in the DRC.

FG Hemisphere obtained an *ex parte* injunction against CR, prohibiting it from paying the monies to the DRC pending resolution of FG Hemisphere's case. The question before the Hong

Kong Court was thus whether the injunction should be discharged.

The DRC argued that the award was not enforceable in Hong Kong because of the doctrine of sovereign immunity. The DRC submitted that in the PRC (including Hong Kong) the principle was that a sovereign state enjoyed absolute immunity from the execution against it of a judgment or award. The DRC also maintained that it had not waived such immunity. It followed that the Hong Kong Court was bound to discharge the injunction and dismiss FG Hemisphere's claim.

FG Hemisphere contended that, under Hong Kong law, a sovereign state only enjoyed relative (not absolute) immunity. A foreign state was thus not immune where the judgment or award being executed against it arose out of purely commercial transactions which the state had entered into with third parties. FG Hemisphere argued that all transactions relevant to its enforcement proceedings were purely commercial in nature and thus enforceable against the DRC.

FG Hemisphere failed at first instance where I held that the transactions upon which its claim was based were not of a commercial nature. I concluded that, regardless of whether the doctrine of sovereign immunity was absolute or relative, FG Hemisphere could not enforce the award in Hong Kong. I discharged the injunction.

The Court of Appeal reversed my decision by a majority (Yeung JA dissenting). The majority held that, under Hong Kong law, a state only enjoyed relative immunity from suit. The majority further held that it was arguable that the relevant transactions underlying FG Hemisphere's claim were of a commercial nature. They restored the injunction.

The Court of Final Appeal held by a majority (Bokhary PJ and Mortimer NPJ dissenting) that in the PRC the doctrine of sovereign immunity was absolute in scope. As part of the PRC, Hong Kong was bound to follow that principle. The majority also found that the DRC had not waived the right to claim immunity by having participated in the arbitration. Accordingly, FG Hemisphere was not entitled to enforce the award against the DRC in Hong Kong and the injunction had to be discharged.

As a result of *FG Hemisphere*, there appears to be a concern that an award (whether made in Hong Kong or elsewhere) will be unenforceable against a PRC state enterprise in Hong Kong, even when the award indisputably arises out of a purely commercial dispute between the enterprise and a third party.

If that is the perception, then it would be wrong.

Assume that a PRC state enterprise is an entity entitled to claim sovereign immunity under public international law. That claim could not be raised in Hong Kong to resist enforcement of an arbitration award against the enterprise. That is because sovereign immunity involves a foreign country X claiming immunity from suit or enforcement in the territory of a different country Y. At least 2 countries have to be involved. A foreign country raises a claim of sovereign immunity in the Courts of another country.

That is not the situation in our example. In the latter, a PRC entity would be claiming immunity in a Court within the PRC (of which Hong Kong forms part). Only a single country (the PRC) is involved. One cannot raise a claim of sovereign immunity in the Courts of one's own country. The doctrine of sovereign immunity would simply not apply in such situation.

Contrast the position in *FG Hemisphere* where the DRC claimed immunity from suit in Hong Kong. A foreign country (the DRC) was claiming immunity from suit in the Court of another country (the PRC). Two countries were involved.

Is there anything one can do to make an award enforceable in Hong Kong against a foreign state which is entitled to claim sovereign immunity here? The problem of enforcing an award in such a situation would not be unique to Hong Kong, but would be inherent in any jurisdiction which follows the principle of absolute immunity.

The problem is perhaps best addressed at the start of an arbitration and not after an award has been made. At the beginning of an arbitration, a party concerned to obtain an enforceable award against a foreign state may apply to the tribunal for an interim measure under ML 17 (s.35).

More specifically, the party could ask the tribunal for an order that the foreign state "provide a means of preserving assets out of which a subsequent award may be satisfied". In essence, the party would be seeking security for the due performance of any award. For example, the party may request the tribunal to order that the foreign state deposit funds with a stakeholder who irrevocably undertakes to deal with the funds in accordance with the tribunal's award.

There is of course no guarantee that the tribunal will grant the interim measure requested in every case. Even if it grants the measure, there is no certainty that the foreign state will comply with the tribunal's order to put up security. But at least in the latter instance the tribunal can make a peremptory order to penalise the foreign state for its non-compliance. The peremptory order may, for instance, possibly bar the foreign state from adducing evidence or making submissions in the arbitration, unless appropriate security for an award is provided.

Note, however, that a party A seeking security along the lines just suggested, may itself be required by the tribunal to put up counter-security in event that the final award is adverse to A and in favour of the foreign state.

II. "HUA TIAN LONG"

This was an Admiralty action against a vessel belonging to the Guangzhou Salvage Bureau (GSB) of the Ministry of Communications. The plaintiffs alleged that GSB had breached a contract for the chartering of GSB's vessel. As security for its claim, the plaintiffs arrested GSB's vessel in Hong Kong.

GSB applied to set aside the arrest. It initially argued that it enjoyed sovereign immunity. But the judge (Stone J) quickly dismissed that contention, noting that "the concept has no application in the instant case, given that there is here no question of the impleading of a *foreign* sovereign state".[18]

GSB submitted in the alternative that, as a PRC state entity, GSB enjoyed an immunity from suit which was analogous to the Crown immunity enjoyed by the British Government in Hong Kong prior to 1 July 1997. GSB argued that, following the British handover of sovereignty over Hong Kong to the Central People's Government, Crown immunity did not disappear at common law. Instead, Crown immunity continued to apply to entities of the Central People's Government.

The judge accepted this alternative argument.

The crux of the debate before the judge was over the effect of s.3 of the Crown Proceedings Ordinance (Cap.300) (CPO). That provides that "a claim against the Crown ... may be enforced as of right, and without the consent of the Governor, by proceedings taken against the Crown for that purpose in accordance with the provisions of this Ordinance". The question was whether CPO s.3 abolished the doctrine of Crown immunity when the CPO came into effect in 1957.

The judge took the view that "there were two 'Crowns' in Hong Kong" prior to 1 July 1997. One was "Her Majesty's Government in the then colony" and the other was "Her Majesty's Government in the United Kingdom".

The judge reasoned that the CPO only removed the immunity of the former Crown (that is, Her Majesty's Government in Hong Kong) but not the immunity of the latter Crown (that is, Her Majesty's Government in the United Kingdom). This was because the CPO was a law passed by a colonial legislature. Only the UK Parliament had the power to curtail the immunity which the latter Crown enjoyed.

The judge concluded that, by analogy, the Central People's Government "in turn must enjoy the like Crown immunity hitherto accorded to the British Crown, as opposed to ... the 'Colonial Crown'". [19]

The plaintiff appealed to the Court of Appeal. However, the parties reached a settlement before the appeal came to be heard. There has not therefore been any pronouncement by the Court of Appeal on the continuance of Crown immunity in Hong Kong after 1 July 1997.

The common law doctrine of Crown immunity developed from the medieval concept that "the king can do no wrong". As a matter of general principle, it would seem odd that such a doctrine should now extend by analogy to a modern-day government whose authority does not rest (whether as a matter of history or ideology) on any notion of "kingship".

Nonetheless, even if one may have doubts as to the correctness of Stone J's conclusion, one cannot get around the fact that there is a judgment to the effect that PRC government entities enjoy immunity from suit in Hong Kong. Although not binding being only a first instance decision, the judgment has persuasive value as precedent.

Consequently, on the assumption that "*HUA TIAN LONG*" was rightly decided, to what extent does the judgment apply to commercial arbitrations and the enforcement of awards?

First, it should be noted that the jurisdiction of the Hong Kong Court arose because the vessel was arrested while in Hong Kong waters. Otherwise, there was little to connect the plaintiff's action with Hong Kong. The plaintiffs intended to charter the vessel for work on offshore Malaysian and Vietnamese projects. Ownership of the vessel apart, GSB does not seem to have had any presence in Hong Kong.

Second, Stone J distinguished between:

> (1) entities which are direct emanations of the Central People's Government and which are discharging state functions as such emanations; and

> (2) entities which enjoy a distinct legal personality from the Central People's Government and which undertake commercial activities independently of that Government.

The judge confined the application of Crown immunity to the first category of entity. The judge observed that an entity within the second category "from the perspective of 'Crown immunity', clearly is not part of such 'Crown'". [20]

It follows from this that a PRC state-owned corporation engaged in commercial activity in Hong Kong would not enjoy Crown immunity. The corporation would have a separate legal personality and, although its shares may be held by the state, the corporation would not be discharging state functions.

Contrast the GSB which (the judge found) is a department of the Ministry of Communications.

Through its ownership and use of the vessel (the largest floating derrick crane-barge based in Asia), the GSB discharges the state functions of marine rescue and salvage which are among the responsibilities delegated by the Central People's Government to the Ministry. Neither the GSB nor the Ministry have a separate legal personality from that of the PRC Government.

In those premises, Stone J concluded that the GSB fell within the first category of entity and enjoyed Crown immunity.

Third, Art.22 of Hong Kong's Basic Law provides: [21]

> "All offices set up in the Hong Kong Special Administrative Region by departments of the Central Government or by provinces, autonomous regions, or municipalities directly under the Central Government, and the personnel of these offices shall abide by the laws of the Region."

I read this to mean that, where an entity falling within the first category identified by Stone J has set up an office or presence in Hong Kong, then that entity is bound to abide by Hong Kong laws.

It should accordingly be possible to sue such entity in the Courts here and a plea of Crown immunity would not be available to the entity. This is because compliance with Court orders for damages or other relief in connection with the breach of commercial obligations is very much a part of the Hong Kong law which those entities are required by the Basic Law to observe.

Fourth, s.6 of the Ordinance states that the Arbitration Ordinance "shall apply to the Government and Offices of the Central People's Government in the Hong Kong Special Administrative Region".

Read together with Art.22 of the Basic Law, s.6 makes it plain that, whether or not the doctrine of Crown immunity has survived, where an entity within the first category identified by Stone J has set up an office in Hong Kong, such office must abide by the provisions of the new Arbitration Ordinance. Those provisions would include s.73 making an award "final and binding" on a party. In other words, the office should not be able to rely on Crown immunity as a basis for non-compliance with an award.

Given the foregoing, it would seem that, whatever its ambit post-July 1997, Crown immunity would have little application in arbitration matters. Where an entity of the Central People's Government has established a Hong Kong office, that office may arguably be sued pursuant to Basic Law Art.22 and s.6. Even if "*HUA TIAN LONG*" were valid in its reasoning, it would only matter (as far as arbitration is concerned) where one is dealing with a direct emanation of the PRC Government which has no established office in Hong Kong.

D. Summary

This chapter has examined how the Court upholds and enforces awards.

Points to bear in mind are as follows:

1. Awards will be enforced and recognised unless they are vitiated by one or more of the grounds set out in Art.5 of the Convention. Even then, the Court will only set aside or refuse enforcement where the failure under Art.5 is a serious or egregious one with a substantial impact on the outcome of an award.

2. Under the Convention and the Model Law, Courts will have to scrutinise awards whenever challenged. That may take time. But the Court should ensure that the necessary procedures are in place to ensure that challenges are definitively determined within as short

a time as possible.

3. One of the major advantages of arbitration is its versatility. Arbitration agreements can be tailored to the needs of particular parties. Thus, if they wish to allow for the possibility of greater supervision by the Court, parties can adopt one or more of the opt-in provisions introduced by the Ordinance.

4. *FG Hemisphere* should not normally give rise to problems in a majority of arbitration cases. It is only where one seeks to enforce an award against a foreign state in Hong Kong that one may run into difficulty in light of sovereign immunity. But a party can seek an interim measure from the tribunal at an early stage to secure the due performance by the foreign state of an award against it.

5. Neither should "*HUA TIAN LONG*" normally give rise to problems in a majority of arbitration cases. It is only where the counterparty to an arbitration agreement is a direct emanation of the PRC Government which has no presence in Hong Kong that there may be difficulty in enforcing an award here against that party in light of Crown immunity.

---

1. The Convention has 5 authentic texts (in English, French, Spanish, Russian and Chinese). It may be downloaded from newyorkconvention.org. That website gives much useful information about the Convention, including lists of cases on the Convention decided by the Courts of signatory countries. References in this Section to articles are to the Convention.

2. The Court of the seat of arbitration is often referred to as "the supervising Court", while the Court of the place where application has been made to enforce the award is referred to as "the enforcing Court".

3. See the similar provision in s.8 (ML 8).

4. See Chapter 1.B(II) for a discussion of the Court's approach to the public policy ground.

5. (2012) 78 Arbitration 26.

6. [2010] 4 SLR 672 (Ang J); [2011] 4 SLR 305 (Chao, Phang, Rajah JJA).

7. [2010] 4 SLR 649 (Chan J); [2011] 4 SLR 739 (Chan CJ, Phang and Rajah JJA).

8. *Loc. cit.*, p.35.

9. *Ibid.*, p.33.

10. *Ibid.*, p.36.

11. HCCT No.40 of 2010, 12 April 2011 (Reyes J); CACV No.79 of 2011, 2 December 2011 (Tang VP, Fok JA, Sakhrani J).

12. HCCT No.15 of 2010, 29 June 2011 (Saunders J); CACV No.136 of 2011, 9 May 2012 (Tang VP, Kwan and Fok JJA).

13. I deal with mediation more fully in the next chapter.

14. Professor Ronald Dworkin's most famous work being *Taking Rights Seriously*, I took the accusation to mean that I was a person who did not take rights seriously.

15. In the next chapter, I compare mediation and arbitration in more detail.

16. FACV Nos. 5, 6 & 7 of 2010, 8 June 2011 (Bokhary, Chan and Ribeiro PPJ; Mortimer and Mason NPPJ).

17. [2010] 3 HKLRD 611.

18. See Judgment, para. 29.

19. See Judgment, para. 88.

20. See Judgment, para. 98.

21. I am grateful to Val Chow for drawing this provision to my attention.

Chapter 5

A Glance at Mediation and the Future of Arbitration

This chapter juxtaposes mediation and arbitration as means of dispute resolution in Hong Kong. Section A introduces mediation and summarises recent case law and legislative developments in relation to mediation. Section B compares mediation with arbitration. Section C concludes with thoughts on the future of arbitration in light of the growing use of mediation in Hong Kong.

A. Mediation[1]

I. The process of mediation in light of recent Hong Kong case law

Mediation involves a neutral person helping parties to settle their disputes.

The mediation proceeds with the mediator meeting the parties together or individually as circumstances require, for the purposes of exploring options for settlement. A typical mediation involving 2 parties (A and B) might then proceed as follows:

(1) The mediator meets A and B in a general session.

(2) The mediator meets A and B individually as necessary to explore the terms they are prepared to settle their dispute.

(3) In the course of the individual meetings with A and B, the mediator obtains authority from one side or other to put forward possible terms of settlement. In the absence of that authority, the discussions between the mediator and a party are confidential. The mediator may not disclose the contents of those discussions without the express authority of a relevant party.

(4) The mediator shuttles back and forth between A and B to see whether it is possible for A and B to agree on terms of settlement.

(5) If it appears that A and B are close to settlement, the mediator can call a general session in which the details of settlement can be ironed out. Details having been worked out, the parties sign a settlement agreement.

(6) If the mediator feels that the mediation is not getting anywhere, the mediator informs the parties accordingly and terminates the mediation.

(7) The parties' lawyers may be present in general and individual sessions.

Mediation is normally regarded as being successful in about 70% of cases. An experienced mediator should also be able to tell within a day or so from the start of mediation whether there is any chance of resolving a dispute. Because of this, in many cases, a stay of Court proceedings pending the outcome of mediation should not be necessary.[2]

Mediation may, if successful, therefore be a cheaper and quicker way of resolving a dispute, when compared to litigation in Court.

Mediation has the additional advantage over Court proceedings. Parties are free to express their real concerns about a dispute to the mediator. Those concerns need not be expressed in terms of legal rights or wrongs. The mediator can help the parties to fashion a settlement on terms which are tailored to meet such concerns.

That is in contrast to a Court. The parties' subjective concerns are usually irrelevant to the Court's determination of a dispute. The Court can only decide disputes in accordance with the law. Even then, in making its dispositive order, the Court is limited in the sorts of terms which it can impose.

Thus, for instance, while a mediator can help the parties to settle on terms that involve one party apologising and paying compensation to another for some breach, the Court can only order the payment of compensation. The Court will not ordinarily be able to order a party to make an apology.

Amendments to the Hong Kong barristers' and solicitors' codes of practice mean that barristers and solicitors now have a duty to advise their clients on the appropriateness of mediation for the resolution of a case. Consequently, it would be a disciplinary offence for a barrister or solicitor to be ignorant about mediation and fail to consider whether a client should be best advised to mediate.

In *Chevalier (Construction) Co. Ltd. v. Tak Cheong Engineering Development Ltd.*[3] Lam J stressed "the importance of the lawyers explaining comprehensively and professionally all pros and cons of the litigation to their respective clients before the clients participate in a mediation". He criticised the lawyer "who paints an unrealistic rosy picture for his client". That will simply "generate unrealistic expectation on the part of the client" and the lawyer will "not [be] doing a service to [the] client".

One might wonder in which types of case mediation would be appropriate and in which it would not. It is difficult to think of a case for which mediation would not be suitable.[4]

The difference lies in the presence of a mediator. The mediator helps the parties to move beyond posturing to identifying what they want to get out of a dispute. Such "wants" need not be restricted to what the parties would obtain in a lawsuit following trial.

The "horse-trading" which the presence of a mediator facilitates works well in the settlement of commercial matters. But it also works in non-commercial matters. Mediation has been found in many jurisdictions (including Hong Kong) to be helpful in resolving disputes between couples going through a bitter divorce. Lord Woolf (former Lord Chief Justice of England and Wales and a Non-Permanent Judge of the Hong Kong Court of Final Appeal), speaking at a conference in Hong Kong in December 2008, has forcefully argued that mediation may even be used in judicial review cases.

In light of the above, it is hardly surprising that, for some time now, the Court's policy has been actively to promote resort to mediation for the resolution of disputes. The Court takes the view that a party cannot insist on tying up the Court's limited resources for substantial periods of time, if its dispute is capable of speedier and cheaper resolution through mediation.

The Court's thinking was manifested in its Practice Direction on Mediation which came into effect on 1 January 2010.

The Practice Direction had several purposes. It affirmed the principle that what takes place in a mediation must be treated as generally confidential and privileged.[5] It provided that, where a party unreasonably refuses to go to mediation, that party may be penalised with an appropriate costs order even though it eventually wins at trial. It established a protocol to be followed by a party wishing to go to mediation.

Under the protocol, A invites B in writing to refer all or part of a dispute to mediation. If B agrees, B accept A's invitation in writing. The parties then agree the details of their mediation. If B refuses, it must state in a Mediation Response why it does not wish to go to mediation.

The documents generated under the protocol are filed with the Court. The result is a paper trail which enables the Court to monitor whether a case has been resolved through mediation. If B refuses mediation and after trial A applies for a costs sanction against B for so refusing, the paper trail provides a record of B's actual reasons for rejecting mediation.

The documents filed under the protocol enable the parties to identify and agree on what constitutes a "minimum level of participation" by each party in any envisaged mediation. Provided that such "minimum level of participation" is attained by a party, no costs sanction will be imposed, even if the mediation ultimately fails.

What might be a suitable "minimum level of participation" to specify in a Mediation Notice? In *Hak Tung Alfred Tang v. Bloomberg*

LP and another [6] Registrar Lung has suggested that the standard expected minimum participation should be participation in a mediation "up to and including light of the recently promulgated Mediation Ordinance discussed below.

Surprisingly, in a number of cases, parties have had difficulty in choosing a mediator. The parties could simply not agree on a suitable person. They have then applied to the Court to break the deadlock. In *Upplan Co. Ltd. v. Li Ho Ming and another* [7] Registrar Lung set out the factors which the Court will take into account when choosing a mediator in such circumstance. The factors include the nature of the dispute, the amount involved, and the experience, fees and availability of the proposed mediators.

In an application to impose a costs sanction against a party for refusing to mediate, the burden will be on the refusing party to provide a reasonable explanation for the refusal.[8] The party suggesting mediation does not carry the burden of showing that the proposed mediation had a reasonable prospect of success.

There has been much concern about sham mediations. That is the situation where a party A agrees to go to mediation solely for the purpose of avoiding a costs sanction for unreasonably refusing to mediate. But A has no intention to cooperate in the mediation towards settling a case. A might instead (say) wish to drag out Court proceedings indefinitely in order to wear out the other side.

Typically, A will instruct its lawyers to "participate" in a mediation for a couple of hours and then to stop all negotiations on some excuse. It is currently possible in Hong Kong to find mediators willing to conduct mediations (inclusive of preparation) for about $2,500 for the first 2 hours and $500 for each succeeding hour. Thus, for a premium of $2,500, A buys insurance against a hefty costs sanction by the Court.

Does the possibility of sham mediations mean that the Practice

Direction lacks teeth and can be readily abused?

I do not think so. In the usual case, a party will be acting through lawyers. In light of their duty under to assist the Court in the resolution of disputes, it is incumbent upon the parties' lawyers to satisfy themselves that their clients are not abusing the mediation protocol by merely going through the motions.

Lawyers should not be advising their clients to go through the steps in the Practice Direction for the sake of appearance. That would not be conducive towards the resolution of a dispute. On the contrary, a sham participation only adds to overall costs without real benefit to anyone.

The Court is entitled to expect lawyers to discourage (and take no part in) blatant tactical manoeuvring on the part of their clients.

Where a litigant is in person, the abuse of the Practice Direction may be harder to police in practice. There would be no lawyer to check a party acting in person who is determined to flaunt the mediation protocol by only running through the motions. Nonetheless, the duty to assist the Court in the resolution of disputes applies equally to litigants in person. They, too, are under a strict obligation not to waste everyone's time by mere play-acting at mediation.

II. Mediation Ordinance (Ord. No.15 of 2012)

The most recent development in the practice of mediation in Hong Kong has been the passage of the Mediation Ordinance (MO) on 21 June 2012. The Ordinance will come into operation on a day to be appointed by the Secretary for Justice.

The object of the MO is "to promote, encourage and facilitate the resolution of disputes by mediation", while at the same time implementing provisions "to protect the confidential nature of mediation communications".[9]

The term "mediation" is defined in MO s.4 to mean:

> "a structured process comprising one or more sessions in which one or more impartial individuals, without adjudicating a dispute or any aspect of it, assist the parties to the dispute to do any or all of the following:
>
> (a) identify the issues in dispute;
>
> (b) explore and generate options;
>
> (c) communicate with one another;
>
> (d) reach an agreement regarding the resolution of the whole, or part, of the dispute."

The "mediator" is the "impartial individual" mentioned in the definition.

The MO applies when a mediation takes place wholly or partly in Hong Kong or when the parties' "agreement to mediate" stipulates that the MO or Hong Kong law is to apply to the mediation.[10] Further, the MO covers any "mediation communication relating to any mediation to which [the MO] applies".

An "agreement to mediate" is defined in MO s.2 as "an agreement in writing by 2 or more persons to submit a dispute between them to mediation". A note to the MO confirms that an agreement to mediate may be in electronic format.

It does not matter whether the agreement to mediate forms part of a contract or is in the form of a separate contract. Nor does it matter whether the agreement to mediate is entered into before or after a dispute arises. For there to be an "agreement to mediate" within the terms of the MO, it is irrelevant that a mediator has yet to be appointed at the time of the parties agreeing to resolve their differences by mediation.

A "mediation communication" is defined in MO s.2 to mean "(a) anything said or done; (b) any document prepared; or (c) any information provided, for the purpose of or in the course of mediation". But an agreement to mediate and a "mediated settlement agreement" (that is, an agreement by which some or all of the parties to a mediation agree to settle all or part of a dispute) do not constitute "mediation communications".

The MO applies to mediations as provided in its s.5(1) regardless of when an agreement is made (whether before, on or after the MO's commencement date) and regardless of when a mediation is conducted or completed.[11] By the same token, the MO extends to mediation communications regardless of when the relevant communication was made.

The MO applies to the Government.[12] But it does not apply to certain processes listed in Schedule 1 to the MO. The exempted processes are essentially conciliations or mediations conducted pursuant to existing statutes (such as the Labour Tribunal Ordinance (Cap.25), the Marriage Reform Ordinance (Cap.178), the Sex Discrimination Ordinance (Cap.480), the Disability Discrimination Ordinance (Cap.487) and the Race Discrimination Ordinance (Cap.602)). Arbitrators should note that med-arb conducted in accordance with s.32 of the Arbitration Ordinance is also not covered by the MO.

MO s.7 permits non-lawyers to assist or support parties to a mediation. Thus, it will not be a breach of the Legal Practitioners Ordinance (Cap.159) for a person who is neither a barrister nor a solicitor to advise or represent a party in connection with mediation.

The heart of the MO is to be found in its ss.8-10. Those deal with the confidentiality of mediation communications and the use of such communications as evidence in Court.

The basic rule is that mediation communications are confidential.

Accordingly, a person may only disclose a mediation communication in the limited circumstances specified in MO ss.8(2) and (3).

MO s.8(2) lists the situations when a person may disclose a mediation communication without first seeking leave of the Court. Those situations are as follows:

"(a) the disclosure is made with the consent of:

(i) each of the parties to the mediation;

(ii) the mediator for the mediation or, if there is more than one, each of them; and

(iii) if the mediation communication is made by a person other than a party to the mediation or a mediator – the person who made the communication;

(b) the content of the mediation communication is information that has already been made available to the public, except for information that is only in the public domain due to an unlawful disclosure;

(c) the content of the mediation communication is information that is otherwise subject to discovery in civil proceedings or to other similar procedures in which parties are required to disclose documents in their possession, custody or power;

(d) there are reasonable grounds to believe that the disclosure is necessary to prevent or minimise the danger of injury to a person or of serious harm to the well-being of a child;

(e) the disclosure is made for research, evaluation or educational purposes without revealing, or being likely to reveal, directly or indirectly, the identity of a person to whom the mediation relates;

(f) the disclosure is made for the purpose of seeking legal advice; or

(g) the disclosure is made in accordance with a requirement imposed by law."

With the Court's leave, a mediation communication may be disclosed in the 3 additional situations set out in s.8(3). Those are:

"(a) for the purpose of enforcing or challenging a mediated settlement agreement;

(b) for the purpose of establishing or disputing an allegation or complaint of professional misconduct made against a mediator or any other person who participated in the mediation in a professional capacity; or

(c) for any other purpose that the court or tribunal considers justifiable in the circumstances of the case."

Under MO s.9 mediation communications may be admitted as evidence in judicial and other proceedings (including arbitration) with the Court's leave. In the case of evidence for use in arbitral proceedings, leave must be obtained from the Court of First

Instance.[13] In considering whether to grant leave for a mediation communication to be disclosed or admitted as evidence, the Court must take account of the following:

> "(a) whether the mediation communication be, or has been, disclosed under s.8(2);
>
> (b) whether it is in the public interest or the interests of the administration of justice for the mediation communication to be disclosed or admitted in evidence;
>
> (c) any other circumstances or matters that the court or tribunal considers relevant."

It had been expected at one stage that the MO would standardise the requirements for practising as a mediator in Hong Kong. This would be with a view to mediators here eventually becoming subject to a code of conduct under the supervision and discipline of a single accrediting body. In the event, the MO has not dealt with this. That development will be a matter for subsequent debate and legislation.

B. Mediation and Arbitration Compared

In this section, I briefly compare attributes of mediation and arbitration.

First, in terms of confidentiality, both mediation and arbitration preserve confidentiality.

I have already drawn attention to the provisions of the MO preserving confidentiality. In the Arbitration Ordinance, similar provisions may be found in ss.17 and 18.

Section 17 provides that Court proceedings in relation to an arbitration are to be closed to the public. But the Court, after consulting the parties, may direct that its judgment in a matter relating to arbitration be published. Any published version of the judgment should "not reveal any matter (including the identity of any party that any party reasonably wishes to remain confidential".

Section 18 forbids any party to an arbitration from "publishing, disclosing or communicating" any information relating to an arbitration or award unless the parties agree. Section 18(2), however, allows a party unilaterally to publish, disclose or communicate details relating to an arbitration or an award in 3 situations. Those are:

"(a) if the publication, disclosure or communication is made:

   (i) to protect or pursue a legal right or interest of the party; or

   (ii) to enforce or challenge the award ...

(b) if the publication, disclosure or communication is made to any government body, regulatory body, court or tribunal and the party is obliged by law to make the publication, disclosure or communication;

(c) if the publication, disclosure or communication is made to a professional or any other adviser of the parties."

The exceptions to the general principle of confidentiality in the 2 ordinances overlap to a great extent, but are not identical. In general, the exceptions relating to arbitration appear to be fewer and narrower in scope.

Second, although sham mediations are a matter of concern, it is less likely that a party will merely make a token appearance in arbitrations. The failure to comply with the orders and directions of the tribunal may result in serious consequences for the defaulting party.

Third, there may be some case management involved in mediations. For instance, there may be a "pre-mediation" meeting before one or more substantive sessions. The "pre-mediation" meeting would have the purpose of identifying the matters to be discussed in the substantive hearing.

But, in general, the procedure adopted for substantive mediations will be open and flexible. The procedure will depend on what arises on a given day in the course of the mediator's exploration of the parties' options.

In contrast, effective case management is essential to arbitration. Proper case management leads to an early identification of the key issues to be determined by the tribunal and the means by which matters relating to those issues are to be proved by evidence. Case management ensures that the parties adhere to strict time periods, so that substantive hearings do not overrun badly in terms of time and cost.

Fourth, the Courts are reluctant to investigate what happens in mediations. In the limited circumstances identified in the MO, the Court may allow evidence of what took place in a mediation to be admitted in evidence and commented upon by the parties. But the Court will usually take a "hands-off" approach to mediation, as that process is supposed to be wholly voluntary in nature.

In contrast, in arbitration, I have suggested that the Court works in partnership with a tribunal. The Court is available to ensure that due process is followed. It may intervene on suitable occasions to rectify egregious errors of law or fact which lead to substantial injustice. The Court accords a wide deference to the decisions of a tribunal. But that does not preclude the Court from scrutinising an award rigorously whenever a challenge is made.

Fifth, settlement agreements reached by way of mediation may be enforced as orders of the Court through incorporation into what is known as a Tomlin Order.

That is an order whereby the parties agree that Court proceedings between them in an action are to be stayed indefinitely, except for the purpose of enforcing the terms of the settlement agreement (which is usually annexed to the order). If a party breaches the settlement agreement, the other side may then apply to the Court to enforce the terms of the agreement without having to start another action.

The Tomlin Order is a convenient procedural mechanism for enforcing mediation settlements in Hong Kong. But a party may have difficulty enforcing such an order in other jurisdictions.

Arbitration awards may be enforced as orders of the Court under the provisions of the Ordinance. Additionally, by reason of the Convention, awards should be readily recognised and enforced in the 146 states which are party to the latter document.

Sixth, it is possible to combine mediation and arbitration. But great care must be taken when the same person conducts both processes.

The reason is obvious. In mediation, the parties are encouraged to voice their concerns freely in individual sessions with a mediator. If the mediator is subsequently to act as arbitrator following the failure of mediation, there is an enormous potential for conflict. The arbitrator has been in unilateral communication with each of the parties.

The mediator turned arbitrator will almost certainly be privy to confidential information communicated by one or other party in the course of the abortive mediation. How then can the former mediator discharge his or her obligation of neutrality and impartiality as arbitrator?

That will only be at the price of a breach of confidentiality. The mediator turned arbitrator must disclose to one party the confidential information disclosed to him or her by the other party, if that information is material to the outcome of the arbitration.

Thus, under s.33 of the Ordinance, an arbitrator may act as mediator with the parties' consent in writing. But an arbitrator who has also acted as mediator "must, before resuming the arbitral proceedings, disclose to all other parties as much information as the arbitrator considers material to the arbitral proceedings".

One acts rhetorically: how does an arbitrator know what confidential information imparted during a mediation will be "material" to an arbitration? What is "material" may change over time as the arbitration proceeds. It will be difficult to be certain that one has made full and appropriate disclosure at any given time. The mediator turned arbitrator will always live under the shadow of apparent bias.

Med-arb is therefore difficult. For that reason, it is not popular in Hong Kong as most arbitrators here regard the inherent problems as insurmountable. Nonetheless, med-arb is commonplace in the Mainland.

C. Conclusion: The Future of Arbitration

In this book, I have argued that arbitration can be a powerful means of dispute resolution, while saving time and cost. But its effectiveness in so doing will ultimately depend on the ability of an arbitrator to be efficient while at the same time being fair. As in most things in life, some will be more skilful than others in achieving this.

There are many types of arbitration, as many as the possibilities for dispute among human beings. Some arbitrations may involve complex technicalities. Others may be simple disagreements over the fair division of a piece of property. Not every arbitration will involve a point of law, much less a point of law of difficulty.

Thus, although legal knowledge and training may be of help if one wishes to be an arbitrator, I do not believe that it is a prerequisite of good arbitrators. What is more important is for an arbitrator to keep an open mind in the course of proceedings; to allow each side a reasonable opportunity to be heard on the matters in dispute; and to attempt to understand the points which each side is making on a given issue within the reasonable time allotted to them.

All that is easy to say, but hard to achieve. It will be noticed that the skills of a good arbitrator are not skills that are limited to lawyers or other specialists. Many will have (or can cultivate within themselves) the attributes of patient attention, intellectual rigour, and sense of fairness which are the hallmarks of a good and competent arbitrator. That is why I believe that anyone (if sufficiently disciplined and determined) can become a good and competent arbitrator.

I have tried in this book to set out the key matters which I think that a person wishing to be an arbitrator should ponder. Whether the reader agrees with my views is beside the point. More important is that the reader who wishes to be an arbitrator will at least become aware of potential problems that recur time and time again in arbitrations, and can think through possible solutions for such problems in given circumstances. The purpose of this book is no more and no less than to invite the reader to reflect on what it takes to resolve disputes in a fair, timely and cost-effective manner.

Mediation is now being widely marketed as the fashionable way of resolving disputes.

It is true that mediation enjoys many advantages over arbitration. Mediation is more flexible. It is more informal, less structured. It is capable of resolving a dispute more quickly and thus more cheaply.

But mediation also has distinct disadvantages in comparison to arbitration. For one, it may not truly satisfy an innate need in human beings to be vindicated by the law, even despite the cost and effort involved. We crave for a definitive pronouncement of right from the Court. We seek justice. Arbitration (I suggest) can cater for that profound human need. That is why, provided that there exist good and competent arbitrators of the sort that I have described, I believe that arbitration has a rosy future as a means of dispute resolution.

There is much potential in arbitration that remains to be unlocked. The Ordinance was an important step. But it is only the start.

---

1   I follow here the description of mediation in Chapter 6 of my *Reflections on Civil Procedure under Civil Justice Reform*. But I have updated that account with references to case law.

2. A stay will not automatically be granted pending the conduct of a mediation. In *Faithbright Development Ltd. v. Ng Kwok Yuen and others* HCA No.9058 of 1999, 20 September 2010, Master Lung observed that much will depend on the circumstances of a given case. For instance, if there has been long delay progressing an action, it is unlikely that a stay of Court proceedings will be granted.

3. HCA No.153 of 2008, 8 June 2011 (at para. 20). Lam J went on to observe that, in the construction field especially, "adjudication can provide a more efficient and effective mode of dispute resolution" than the Court. Thus, "as a matter of proper case management, this option should be considered by everyone involved in construction disputes". Disputes may arise in construction projects which have to be resolved quickly if the works are not to be unduly delayed with possibly serious consequences in costs and liquidated damages. Adjudication provides a means of obtaining a quick decision on the merits of a dispute to enable a project to move forward. The parties agree to be bound by the adjudicator's decision for the time being and to get on with

a project until completion. Thereafter, if still unhappy, a party may take the dispute to the Court which can re-open the adjudicator's decision.

4. In *Incorporated Owners of Shatin New Town v. Yeung Kui* CACV No.45 of 2009, 5 February 2010, Cheung JA (with whom Stone and Lunn JJ agreed) thought (at para. 8) that litigation involving the correct interpretation of a Deed of Mutual Covenant (DMC) was a situation where the Incorporated Owners were entitled to refuse to go to mediation. That was because the case involved a decision of law concerning the proper construction of a DMC and the Incorporated Owners had the responsibility of applying the DMC correctly not just in relation to the respondent, but also in respect of all unit-holders.

5. This principle has been affirmed by the Court of Final Appeal in *Champion Concord Ltd. v. Craigside Investments Ltd. and others* FACV Nos.16 and 17 of 2010, 27 May 2011. There Ribeiro PJ speaking for the Appeal Committee stated (at para.17): "The fundamental importance of confidentiality in mediation is universally acknowledged and it can only be in highly exceptional circumstances that evidence which invades such confidentiality will be permitted to be adduced." An early articulation of the Court's approach to the confidentiality of mediations may be found in *Wu Wei v. Liu Yi Ping* HCA No.1452 of 2004, 30 January 2009, at paras. 69-77 (Deputy High Court Judge Lisa Wong SC). But that case must now be read in light of the recently promulgated Mediation Ordinance discussed below.

6. HCA No.198 of 2010, 16 July 2010 (at paras. 13-15).

7. HCA No.1915 of 2009, 5 August 2010. In *Resource Development Ltd. v. Swanbridge Ltd.* HCA No.1873 of 2009, 31 May 2010, Registrar Lung indicated (at para. 6): "Everything being equal, the discrepancy in the costs between the mediators becomes the most significant factor for the choice of the mediator."

8. *Golden Eagle International (Group) ltd. v. GR Investment Holdings Ltd.* HCA No.2032 of 2007, 25 June 2010 (Lam J).

9. MO s.4(1).

10. MO s.5(1)

11. MO s.5(2).

12. MO s.6.

13. MO s.10(3)(e).

Ackonwledgments

This book is based on 5 lectures which I delivered under the auspices of the HKMLA and the Law Faculty of Hong Kong University in January and February 2012. I am grateful to both institutions for their support and encouragement. I am especially grateful to the HKMLA for helping with the publication of this book. I would particularly like to thank Steven Wise and Peter Mills (the present and immediate past secretaries of the HKMLA) for their help in organising the lecture series. I would also like to acknowledge the generosity of Samuel Wong in making available copies of his commentary on the new Ordinance free of charge to everyone attending the lectures.

Chapter 1 is a revised version of a presentation which I gave at a 2011 conference of Asia-Pacific judges in Sydney. The conference was sponsored by the New South Wales (NSW), Hong Kong and Singapore Judiciaries. I benefitted greatly from the event which provided an occasion to study and compare aspects of arbitration in Hong Kong, NSW, the Australian Commonwealth, Singapore and elsewhere.

Chapter 2.B incorporates a talk on "Interim Measures" delivered at a conference on *International Arbitration in Hong Kong: Some Issues and Recent Developments* in May 2012. The conference was sponsored by the Hong Kong Institute of Arbitrators and the Hong Kong Academy of Law. I thank both establishments for inviting me to give the presentation.

Chapter 4.B incorporates a talk on "Judicial Support of Arbitration" delivered at the Inauguration Ceremony of the CIETAC Hong Kong Arbitration Centre and Conference on Arbitration in September 2012. I thank the Department of Justice and the CIETAC Hong Kong Arbitration Centre for inviting me to give the talk. During the conference, I learned much from the presentation by Judge Yang Honglei of the Beijing Supreme People's Court on the "Enforcement of Foreign Arbitral Awards in the Mainland".

Sunny Chan has kindly agreed to translate this book into Chinese. It is anticipated that the Chinese version will be published by Joint Publishing (HK) Co Ltd. later this year.

There are other individuals and institutions who have contributed to the reflections in this book. They are too numerous to list. I thank them all. But I alone am responsible for infelicities that remain in the text.

I would like to single out 3 persons for mention. They are Michael Delaney, Robin Peard and Philip Yang. Michael Delaney, then a solicitor, now a barrister, believed in me sufficiently after I had just completed pupillage to instruct me to appear as counsel in my first arbitration trial. Robin Peard first introduced me to the concept of arbitration when I was his summer student in August 1981. Philip Yang has kindly invited me over the years to give talks to his arbitration students on topics of my choice. Those talks and ensuing discussions with him, his students and his colleagues have been invaluable in clarifying my thinking about arbitration.

I hope that the 3 individuals just named will not mind if I dedicate this book to them in appreciation.

Anselmo Reyes
Hong Kong
15 October 2012

淺談香港
仲裁法

HOW TO BE AN ARBITRATOR:
A PERSONAL VIEW

作者
芮安牟　ANSELMO REYES

翻譯
陳星楠　SUNNY CHAN

責任編輯　　任秀雯
封面設計　　嚴惠珊
書籍設計　　黃沛盈

出版　　　　三聯書店（香港）有限公司
　　　　　　香港北角英皇道 499 號北角工業大廈 20 樓
發行　　　　香港聯合書刊物流有限公司
　　　　　　香港新界大埔汀麗路 36 號 3 字樓
印刷　　　　陽光印刷製本廠
　　　　　　香港柴灣安業街 3 號 6 字樓
版次　　　　2013 年 6 月香港第一版第一次印刷
規格　　　　大 32 開（140mm×210mm）416 面
國際書號　　ISBN 978-962-04-3381-8

Editor　　　Daisy Yam
Cover design　Alice Yim
Book design　Kacey Wong

Published by
Joint Publishing (Hong Kong) Co., Ltd.
20/F., North Point Industrial Building, 499 King's Road, North Point, Hong Kong

Distributed in Hong Kong by
SUP Publishing Logistics (Hong Kong) Ltd.
3/F., 36 Ting Lai Road, Tai Po, N.T., Hong Kong